# *Testimonials*

**This is a phenomenal book.** However, I do not recommend **An An**
Wiccans, or those who practice Ceremonial Magic. It lacks the conc
writing in this genre today. **This author writes with clarity, the style is ɪʟᴜɪᴅ, ᴀɴᴅ ᴛɦᴇ ᴄᴀᴜᴛɪᴏɴꜱ ᴀʀᴇ ᴘ**
**in a simply stated manner**. This book reflects the author's roots in European, African, and Folk magic.

This new edition includes how to make magical candles and tallow candles, (glass encased, moulded, and double action). Also, a chapter on Ceromancy has been added and new spells have been added throughout the collection of spells, which are beautifully cataloged. There are also recipes for how to make and use oils, incenses, spiritual baths (banos), floor washes, and other infusions.

I also appreciate the author's **Occult Mémoires** where she shares a glimpse into her experiences on her occult journey and how she managed challenging occurrences. This in turn could help others when meeting with similar circumstances and how to handle matters. **This would be a great addition to any occult library**.
*J. Hildebrand -- Kansas City, Missouri*

\* \* \* \* \* \* \* \* \*

**I like this book because it helps you help yourself**. I like this author because she does not patronize nor make herself out to be the only one who has the answers and is sharing her knowledge benevolently and if you contact her she will respond. **The types of spells within this book are the type of spells that are highly sought after, proven and true**. How many of us have spent hundreds of dollars on books, psychics, which proved to be useless, quacks or worse when all we need to know is how to help ourselves. This book is worth every penny. *B. Yates -- Overland Park, Kansas*

\* \* \* \* \* \* \* \* \*

I embrace my dark passenger and with this being said I appreciate this author's understanding that nature is both kind and cruel, that there is negative and positive in all things for one does not exist without the other. **This book is for real witches**, not fairie chasers -- over half of the spells are benevolent in nature, but the rest is not for the weak minded and the faint of heart. **Working true magic requires focus and effort to move energy**. You don't just blink your eyes, wiggle your nose, or say Abracadabra. **The formulas in this book are real recipes passed down through the ages --- spells that have meat, substance. It is my opinion that the information in this book is a great investment!** *P. Schilling -- Lincoln, Nebraska*

\* \* \* \* \* \* \* \* \*

**Alex G. has produced an excellent resource. She has provided to the point information relevant to your chosen task. Information is precise concerning the oils, elements, measurement, timing, tools etc. Adapting the use of this knowledge will allow you to work with or upon certain energies, good or not so good, in your life. This book puts Universal Knowledge at your fingertips.** *A. Livingston*

\* \* \* \* \* \* \* \* \*

This book is not bad at all! I do disagree with some reviews I have read that do not recommend this book for newbies. **I feel this book is perfect for beginners for it is meticulously and accurately written**. A newbie would not be mislead and could reap the benefits of beautiful magick from the get go. However it is a non-Wiccan book, with more knowledge dedicated to European, Hoodoo, Brujeria, and Voodoo magical traditions. **I am an experienced witch and it is my opinion that this book is some of the best money spent.**
*A. Justice -- Orlando, Florida*

\* \* \* \* \* \* \* \* \*

This publication is designed to provide accurate and authoritative information in regard to the subject matter covered. It is published with the understanding that the publisher and author are not engaged in rendering legal accounting or other professional service. If legal advice or other professional advice, including financial, is required, the services of a competent professional person should be sought--- From a Declaration of Principles, jointly adopted by a Committee of the American Bar Association and a Committee of Publishers.

First Edition Published in the United States of America by Jade Emperor Publishing, LLC, P.O. Box 51541, Jacksonville Beach, FL 32240-1541. Email: jade_emperor2000@yahoo.com

Library of Congress Cataloging-in-Publication Data:
Bennington, Alex G.
An American Witch's Book of Spells:
Nine Generations of Formulas that Work / by Alex G. Bennington

1. Spell Books – United States – Handbooks, manuals, etc. 2. Witches, American – United States – Handbooks, manuals, etc. 3. Spells. 4. Magic Formulas. 5. Earth Magic. 6. Magical Spells. 7. Witchcraft - Spells. 8. Occult Stories. 9. Witches Hereditary Spells. 10. Kabbalah. 11. Spells - Herbal. 12. Metaphysics. 13. Occult Experiences. 14. Psychic Protection. I. Bennington, Alex G. II. Title.
ISBN-13: 978-1477410400. ISBN-10: 1477410406.
Author and Cover Design: Alex G. Bennington.
Artwork: Elisabeth Benton.
Editor: Paul G. Ellsworth

# An American Witch's Book of Spells

## Nine Generations of Formulas that Work

By

Alex G. Bennington

# Disclaimer

Due to the legalities of this society, this disclaimer is necessary. This book presents information and techniques that have been in use for many years. These practices, strategies and metaphysical ideas utilize concepts within the natural and occult world. However, there are no claims to effectiveness. The information offered is valid to the authors' best knowledge and experiences. This information is to be used by the reader(s) at their own discretion and liability. You need to accept legal and moral responsibility for doing a thing you do not thoroughly understand. Because people's lives have different conditions and different stages of growth, no rigid or strict practice can be applied universally. The adoption and application of the material offered in this book is totally your own responsibility.

This book contains the author's opinions. Some material in this book may be affected by changes in the quality of materials used in recipes by the reader. Hence, the accuracy and completeness of the information contained in this book cannot be guaranteed. Neither the author nor the publisher is engaged in rendering investment, legal, tax, accounting, or other similar professional services. If these services are required, the reader should obtain them from a competent professional.

The author and publisher of this material are not responsible in any manner for any loss, or injury, real or perceived or otherwise, which may occur through reading or following the instructions in this material. Although we make no supernatural claims, effects or power from these formulas, the strategies, occult based activities and suggestions described in this material may be too risky for some people, and the reader should consider the risks before applying any strategies put forth in this book. The reader may need to consult with a spiritual advisor for any implications due to the practice of any occult or ritual based activity.

**From the Author**

I do not dispense medical advice or prescribe the use of any technique as a form of treatment for physical or medical problems without the advice of a physician, either directly or indirectly. The intent of the author is only to offer information of a general nature to help you in your quest for emotional and spiritual wellbeing. In the event you use any of the information in this book for yourself, which is your constitutional right, the author and the publisher assume no responsibility for your actions.

Although many believe that they are the almighty wizard, in reality each of us are powerful and less powerful during certain seasons. Each of us is subject to our own DNA, karma, gifts, zodiac blueprint, etcetera. It is my recommendation that anyone desiring to work magic consult with a competent astrologer and have a solar return chart calculated each year in addition to an interpretation by the Astrologer. This will provide you with a blueprint necessary for planning your magical projects. Often you can perform your spells as a solitary witch, but there may be times when you may need to call in reinforcements, for the assistance of 1 or more could provide more satisfactory results. Although, I do acknowledge that there are forces on this Earth that can over-ride astrology -- astrology is what it is, an investment in success.

"Astrologers are not magicians and gods ... they are only interpreters of destiny."
--------- (*Professor Nikola Stojanovic*)

# Acknowledgements

I need to begin by thanking my ancestors all the way back to the beginning for sharing this knowledge and trusting me to do them justice in cataloging it.

I thank all those who contributed to this text, intentionally and unintentionally.
I especially thank those who challenged me most, for without all of you I would not have grown spiritually.

I thank my family for their patience and support. Especially my grandchildren for the love they share unconditionally.

I pay homage to my paternal grandmother who was the kindest woman I came to know.

I thank my spiritual sista Millie my comrade in arms, with whom I went to war with when we literally fought for our lives against   the forces of darkness.

I thank my best friend Alice for her continued love, wisdom, and support.

A special mention to Rev Elizabeth Mayo. One of the greatest Astrologers that I have come to know on my journey.

I thank Rev's Harold and Ethel Tunks, Founders of the C.C.O.T for their guidance, and direction, and for making my Ordination a reality.

A special thanks to Royal Starr for his assistance and for showing me my strength.

I thank the late Donald B. for all of his generosity and assistance during the Battle of the Botanicas.

I thank Dikki Jo for her inspiration.

I thank my publisher for his continued encouragement.

# An American Witch's Book of Spells
## Table of Contents

# Section I
# Nine Generations of Formulas that Work

# Section II
# Occult Mémoires

# Foreword

It is with great pleasure that I write this Foreword for Alex G. Bennington.

Alex has skills & abilities beyond one's years. Dr. Bennington comes from a long line of Irish, Welsh, French, African-American, and Hispanic witches (brujas) & mentors. Additionally, practitioners of Voodoo and Hoodoo have served as advisors and have made contributions to this collection as well. Alex has studied many of the unlimited facets to arcane wisdom knowledge & arts. This book has been long overdue.

Alex G. has a unique perspective on numerous ancient, wisdom arts based topics. Alex G. is a treasured rarity, in that, Alex G. is an experienced life coach and counselor in all matters, covering such areas as spiritual, personal, business, love, romance, soul-mates, & finances. Besides this endeavor, I consider myself fortunate to know Alex G. as a friend.

As we had spoken about this topic and the formation of it, as a written published work, I felt that Alex G. needed to seek further distribution as the advice and knowledge on this sometimes misunderstood topic matter is greatly needed. This is a rare treasure that hopefully others will enjoy & use wisely. I firmly believe that few individuals have such a complete understanding of these topics, or can better advise how to use these recipes, spells or formulas to make things happen. As in many instances, success depends not only on the formulas themselves, but on how, and when, to apply them. Personally, I put considerable trust in an individual's own track record. Alex G. has had Nine Generations of success. We strongly recommend that you keep track of your experiences through a journal or results record, your own Book of Shadows as well. Past performance is an excellent indicator of how you are doing…

Wishing you the best of success in all of your endeavors, & hoping that, perhaps, this material will assist you in attaining heightened magical skills and strategic techniques, specifically with regards to arcane knowledge & arts. Use wisely.

Kind regards,

*Paul G. Ellsworth*
CEO, Jade Emperor Publishing, LLC

# About this Book

## AN INTRODUCTION

"**An American Witch's Book of Spells**" is a serious collection of formulas that I and others have utilized successfully and have mutually agreed to share. This volume of information has been meticulously cataloged and composed by myself and others.

We are in a time at present where a number of people are involved in New Age and Alternative Religious practices with more interest evolving each day. Unfortunately many, just as many in organized traditional religions, do not responsibly practice their theories and due to such negligence and manipulations a tremendous amount of negativity is literally dumped within our world of physicality. My goal with this written text is to "Create Awareness for Informed Choices." Of course, I had considered the subtitle "Covering your ass with more than a loin cloth", and naturally I am being facetious.

Although there may be many spell books on the market my text will distinguish itself from the others due to its poignant content and a variety of proven techniques. I wish to provide others with the information necessary to stand on their own legs and hone their will. At a time during my wanton youth I was physically and mentally taken hostage by a cult and the fact that I am still alive enjoying the freedom to share this experience is a testament to perfecting the Will. The experiences of the past were indeed a great teacher and I will be sharing some crucial information without embellishing that energy, but surviving such a challenge is an experience in soul evolution to be appreciated. However, I have learned as they say "the hard way." After wrestling with my demons, I came to realize that I do not personally need to experience particularly dangerous or questionable challenges in order to understand or appreciate the lessons offered. The demons of self- justification are something we all can identify with and we all have satanic impulses, however we truly can come to understand these matters through the shared experiences of others. I am wise enough to understand that each of us will do what we must and for those who choose to investigate the dark side may the information within these pages assist them in staying one step ahead.

This book of spells includes a number of different formulas or techniques which can be adapted and employed by any human on this Earth. I am providing a variety for choice, so that the one in need can choose that which is in agreement with their comfort zone and conforms to their beliefs. Also each of us are at different levels of soul evolution so by merely sharing the methods that only I or others in my soul family would be comfortable with could be compared to expecting a grade school student to accept measures and perform on the same level as a high school senior. Additionally, I personally believe that each of us rightfully choose our path due to the freewill granted to us by the Creator, so with this in mind I do not wish to pigeon hole people into feeling that there is only one method of practicing the Craft when indeed there are many.  Also I have included some dark spells for at times in order to fight evil, it requires another form of evil or as the saying goes you have to fight fire with fire.  I have called up the Kraken on occasion when someone dear to me has been threatened with physical harm or death.  We are expected to protect ourselves for this is survival thus the Universe concedes with acts of protection as being justified.

It is my intention to provide information geared toward affording the opportunity to make educated choices.  I sincerely wish to impart knowledge to help perfect the Will so as to cultivate wisdom which would enable one to stand on his or her, own legs.  I consider myself an angel form working under the radar to assist in elevating the vibrations of our beautiful planet Earth, which is the place our Creator affords us the opportunity to cultivate soul evolution.

**To New Heights,**
**Alex G. Bennington**

# SECTION I

# Nine Generations of Formulas that Work

## CHAPTER ONE

### PROTECTION AND SECURITY

**The Herbs** -- each plant is covered by a brief description and specific use relating to protection, banishing, or defense. The common name is listed first, secondly the scientific name, thirdly the gender (G), then the ruling planet (P), and the element (E).

### THWART THE POWERS OF A NEMESIS
Unicorn Root    *Aletris farinosa*

Ingredients:
Ague Root also called Unicorn Root, 4 ounces (115 grams) cut in small pieces
Patchouli Leaves, crushed, 4 ounces (115 grams)
Myrrh, small pieces, 4 ounces (115 grams)
Olibanum Tears, 4 ounces (115 grams)
Wood Betony, 4 ounces (115 grams)
Saltpeter, 1 ounce (30 grams)

Combine and thoroughly mix; use as an incense burning on self-igniting charcoals.  As the incense is burning use an appropriate prayer if spiritually inclined or your own words of power.

### PROTECTION FOR CHILDREN

**ALTHEA**    *Althea officinalis*    G -- Feminine    E -- Water
Ingredients:
Althea, 1 oz., (30 grams)
Water, 1 Gallon (4 liters)

Prepare as a cold infusion.  Soak Althea in Water for nine days in a dark place.
Strain after nine days.
Add 1 cup (230 cc) to a child's daily bath.
Althea is also referred to as Marshmallow and is used primarily as a protection for children.  *You can also grind a small amount of this herb and blend with protection incense, then burn a little in a child's bedroom daily.

**ANGELICA**  *Angelica Archangelica*    G -- Masculine    P -- Sun    E -- Fire
Angelica sprinkled in the corners of each room of a home will ward off any evil. Sprinkle all around the outside perimeter of your home to prevent the entry of malevolent spirits including but not limited to a nemesis.

**ASAFOETIDA**  *Ferula foetida*   G -- Masculine    P -- Mars    E -- Fire
Burn small amounts in exorcism and protection incenses; Destroys manifestations of spirits. Use sparingly for Asafetida is indeed powerful in vibration and odor, – it is very pungent.

**BAMBOO**  *Bambusa vulgaris*
Bamboo is used for protection and hex breaking. It is recommended that crushing Bamba wood provides the most desirable base powder for incenses.

## Thwart Evil

**BASIL**  *Ocimum basilicum*   G -- Masculine    P -- Mars    E -- Fire
Ingredients:
Water, 1 pint (230 cc)
Basil, 1 Tbsp. (15 cc)
Prepare as an infusion.  Add to the bath and/or sprinkle around the home.

## Remove Negative Energy

**BAY LEAVES**  *Laurus nobilis*   G -- Masculine    P -- Sun    E -- Fire
Bay leaves mixed with sandalwood can be burned to remove curses and negative spells. It is said that placing Bay leaves in the windows assists in protection against lightening and is hung up to discourage sixth class or noisy and boisterous spirits from acting out. Also Bay leaf may be carried in a small pouch in the pocket.

**BLACKBERRY**  *Rubus villosus*

Ingredients:
Black Human Figure Candle (Male for a man or Female for a woman)
Red Cloth
Blackberry Leaves, 9
Black Salt
Black Thread

Take the Black figure which represents your nemesis, holding the candle away from you (feet to head) write the name of your nemesis using a coffin nail.  Lay it on the red cloth with blackberry leaves and sprinkle it with black salt. Wrap it well and tie with black thread. Take a hammer and hit three times with a hammer calling out what you wish to return to the sender. At this point I ask the Universe in its infinite wisdom to determine a suitable punishment for the one who came up against me. Do this for seven days. Take to a graveyard, dig a hole and throw parcel in then cover. Leave 9 shiny pennies and ask the spirits of the dead to see that justice is done.

## BLUEBERRY  *Vaccinum frondosum*

Sprinkle a small amount of Blueberry herb or blueberries beneath your front doormat to discourage undesirables or negativity. It is advisable to ingest blueberries whole or in foods such as muffins, tarts, or pies if you believe that you are under psychic intrusion for this increase the herbs power. I have an acquaintance who rather than an apple a day claims that *"eating blueberries each day keeps the bad witches away"!* Some logic exists here for in the scientific word *Vaccinum is the Latin word* from which vaccinate is derived; a vaccination is a proven measure to prevent the onset of some virus, bacteria, or intrusion.

## CAMPHOR  *Camphora officinarum*
If you have allergies to incense camphor can be used successfully in cleansing and purifying a room. These can be purchased in packs of 4 squares. Place a square in each corner of the room. You can also place these under your car seats for protection and purification. You can also buy a bottle of camphor to use when you get a soreness in your left ear. Take a cotton swab and dip in the camphor and clean in and around your ear good. It is said this type of soreness is attributed to bad spirits trying to communicate or influence you. If the right ear gets too sore it can be used on this one as well, for too much information could be coming through the ear.

## CARAWAY  *Carum carvi*   G -- Masculine   P -- Mercury   E -- Air
It is believed that a bit of Caraway placed in a red bag and sewed shut with white cotton thread then placed in a child's bed protects them from illness, harm, and particularly from *Lilith*; who represents the Angel of Death for children seven years and under.

## CARNATION  *Dianthus carophyllus*   G -- Masculine   P -- Sun   E – Fire
Carnations when prepared as an infusion for a bath provide a protective and healing vibration. This bath thoroughly cleanses the aura and washes away negativity. Take 7 White Carnations, soak in 1 quart (1 liter) of water for 7 days; strain and add to bath. You may also simply take the Carnations and directly place them in the bath. I recommend taking this bath on a Sunday during the waxing moon (new moon to full moon).

**CINQUEFOIL**  *Potentilla Canadensis*  G -- Masculine  P -- Jupiter  E -- Fire
Also called Five Finger Grass, Cinquefoil is used to wash away negativity. To make an infusion add 1 Tbsp. (15 cc) Of Cinquefoil to 1 gallon (4 liters) of water, boil for 5 minutes; strain and divide into 9 portions. Add to the bath for 9 consecutive nights before retiring.

## THWART GOSSIP

**CLOVES**  *Syzygium aromaticum*  G -- Masculine  P -- Jupiter  E -- Fire
Cloves burned as incense dispel negative forces, purify, and stop others from gossiping about you. As a formula to stop gossip; add 1 tsp. (9 grams) of Cloves Powder to 8 oz. (225 grams) Of Tiphareth incense, burn once in the morning and once in the evening. On a piece of parchment in red ink write the name of the one slandering you, 9 times, then burn to ashes and bury in your back yard or somewhere North of your residence. Read Psalm 48 and perform this ritual for 10 consecutive days.

**CUMIN**  *Cumimum cyminum*  G -- Masculine  P -- Mars  E -- Fire
Cumin is burned with frankincense for protection and scattered on the floor to dispel low vibrational energies. To create peace and harmony (bless) a home; prepare a cold infusion of 1 tsp. ( 9 gr) Of Cumin in 8 oz. (225 cc) Of Holy Water for 3 days; strain and sprinkle a few drops in every corner of every room. Burn a preparation of 4 parts benzoin to 6 parts frankincense on self-igniting charcoal.

**DRAGON'S BLOOD**  *Daemonorops drac; Draconena, spp.*
G -- Masculine  P -- Mars  E -- Fire

Dragon's Blood resin is used for protection and to exorcise negative energies. This powerful cleansing smoke will bring balance and clarity wherever it is used. When melted on hot charcoals it enhances spiritual work creating a calm sacred atmosphere. It is a deep powerfully spicy resin that resembles benzoin and cinnamon mixed together. It is mixed with Frankincense to intensify the vibrations in addition to its disinfectant properties. It is a strong antiseptic and bactericide so is useful in cleansing physically as well as spiritually. It is additionally a great insecticide. In ancient China it was carried by warriors to relieve pain and coagulate blood from wounds in addition to using it as ink which is still a popular practice. I do not recommend using this resin on Mondays or Saturdays; for further explanation refer to Dragon's Blood Oil.

**EUCALYPTUS**  *Eucalyptus spp.*  G -- Feminine  P -- Moon  E -- Water
Eucalyptus is an excellent protection from illness particularly colds.  It is also said to keep backstabbers and snitches away.

**FEVERFEW**  *Chrysanthemum parthenium*
G -- Masculine    P -- Venus    E -- Water

Feverfew is considered an effective measure of protection against accidents and illness. Prepare an infusion of 1 tsp. (9 g) Feverfew in 8 oz. (230 cc) of water, strain and ingest as a tea once a week for health benefits.

**FRANKINCENSE**  *Boswellia carterii*
G -- Masculine    P -- Sun    E -- Fire

When burned Frankincense releases powerful vibrations which not only purify and uplift an area but also drive out all negativity.

**HYSSOP**  *Hyssopus officinalis*   G -- Masculine    P -- Jupiter    E -- Fire
Hyssop is a purification herb and is used to purge negativity. Prepare an infusion of 1 part Hyssop to 8 parts water; strain, add to bath water, ingest as tea, or sprinkle on objects. I recommend consuming Hyssop tea with lemon if you believe that you are experiencing psychic intrusion of any type.

**LEMON**  *Citrus limone*
G -- Feminine    P -- Moon    E -- Water

Lemon is used for purification and washing away negative vibrations. Add fresh lemon to hot and cold beverages for detoxification and spiritual cleansing. Some choose to add Lemons to their bath during the Full Moon for its purificatory benefits.

**LILAC**  *Syringa vulgaris*   G -- Feminine    P -- Venus    E -- Water

Lilac drives away negative vibrations where it is planted or strewn. When I was a young person in New England Lilacs were near my bedroom window and I always felt so comforted particularly during the Spring and Summer months when they were in bloom. To this very day I know when Angelic beings are near and reassuring me for I will smell the fabulous aroma of Lilac.

**MYRRH**  *Commiphora myrrha*   G -- Feminine    P -- Moon    E -- Water

Myrrh burned as incense purifies, lifts the vibrations, creates peace, and increases the power of any incense or oil to which it is added.  One part Myrrh is usually burned in conjunction with three parts Frankincense or other resins such as Benzoin or Copal.

**PASSION FLOWER**  *Passiflora incarnata*

G -- Feminine    P -- Venus    E -- Water

Passion Flower, contrary to what its' name suggests, is used to diffuse anger and create a calming atmosphere. The following incense blend is very effective in diffusing anger: 1 oz. (30 g) Passion Flower, 2 oz. (60 g) Orris, ½ oz. (15 g) Rosemary, ½ oz. (15 g) Saffron, 1 oz. (30 g) Thyme, 2 oz.(60 g)  Violet, and 1 oz.(30)  Indian Hemp. Be certain that these ingredients are thoroughly mixed and ground as fine as possible with a mortar and pestle.

**ROSE**  *Rosa spp.*    G -- Feminine    P -- Venus    E -- Water

Roses provide a loving, calming vibration wherever they are present.
Prepare a cold infusion using the Petals and Buds of 6 Roses soaking in one quart of water for 7 days; strain and add to a bath. Knowledge of the energy associated with the color of the Rose used can be significant. Red – Passionate Love * Pink – Universal, Unconditional Love, "True Love" * Yellow – Friendship, Platonic Love * Peach – Sweet, Gentle Love * White or Lavender – Emits the Highest Vibrations, Pure Love * Fire & Ice – Pure Passion and Pure Love (*Mars and Venus)*.

**ROSEMARY**  *Rosemarinus officinalis*

G -- Masculine    P -- Sun    E -- Fire

The vibrations of Rosemary are very powerful and when burned it thoroughly cleanses negativity. Prepare 1 part Rosemary to 8 parts water as an infusion; strain and consume as tea, add to a bath, or sprinkle around the home. Cooking with Rosemary and ingesting it provides potent protection and detoxification. Additionally Rosemary can be used as a substitute for Frankincense.

**RUE**  *Ruta graveolens*    G -- Masculine    P -- Mars    E -- Fire

Prepare an infusion of 1 part Rue to 8 parts water; add to the bath or use as a floor wash for cleansing away low level negative vibrations and if another has come up against you the energy will be returned to sender.  This *Herb of Grace* is particularly advisable when experiencing headaches or confusion for its properties do appear to provide clarity and alleviate pain within the head. It can also be used as incense and added to others for reinforcement. Some believe that ingesting it as tea or in food offers protection from the evil eye, shape shifters and even poison.

**SAGE** *Salvia officinalis*
G -- Masculine    P -- Jupiter    E -- Air
Sage is popular incense used by many during the Full Moon. It is considered the herb of longevity and immortality; it is said that this is done by consuming daily particularly in the month of May. A dear friend of mine who is a beautiful child of nature advises not to plant sage in your own garden, employ another to do this, and that a full bed of sage creates ill fortune. Also she says that toads are infatuated with this herb.

**SAGEBRUSH**   *Artemisia*
G -- Feminine    P --Venus    E -- Earth
Sagebrush has been burned in American Indian Ceremonies for centuries and many others use this herb in rites of exorcism and purification rituals. Self-fumigation is recommended during the Full Moon to purify you of your own misdeeds and negativity.

**SANDALWOOD**   *Santalum album*    G -- Feminine    P -- Moon    E -- Water
Sandalwood emits extremely high spiritual vibrations and is burned for protection, healing, and exorcism. Blended with Lavender as incense it attracts benevolent spirits. It can also be used as a base for incense formulations.

**SOLOMON'S SEAL**   *Polygonatum officinale or P. multiform*
G -- Feminine    P -- Saturn    E -- Water
Also called Saint Mary's Seal this root is used for protection and exorcism. It is believed that placing this root at the four corners of the house or property exerts a barrier or force field, guarding it from unwelcome energies. Prepare an infusion by soaking the roots in one quart of water for 7 days then sprinkle around the home or where needed. Solomon's Seal is popularly used as offertory incense and can be blended with other incenses.

**ST. JOHN'S WORT**   *Hypericum perforatum*
Poison.  G -- Masculine    P -- Sun    E -- Fire
St. John's Wort is popularly used as a naturopathic treatment for depression and melancholy. In ancient days it was said to gather it on Midsummer or on a Friday and worn it would keep mental illness away.

Prepare an infusion of 1 oz. St. John's Wort and 1 oz. Huckleberry Herb, simmer for 20 minutes in 1 quart of water; strain and use as a floor wash to create a peaceful atmosphere.

**THYME**   *Thymus vulgaris*
G -- Feminine    P -- Venus    E -- Water
Thyme is a purificatory and powerful healing herb. An incense mixture for good health is to blend and grind as fine as possible the following:

16 oz. (450 G) Winters bark, 8 oz. (225 G) Olibanum, 4 oz. Violet flowers, 2 oz. (60 G) Thyme, 1 oz. (30 G) Sage, 4 oz. (115 G) Cinnamon, 2 oz. (60 G ) Myrrh, 2 oz. (60 G) Eucalyptus leaves, 2 oz. (60 G) Orris, and ¼ oz. (7 G) Saltpeter.


**TONKA**   *Coumarouna odorata*
Poison.   G -- Feminine    P-- Venus    E -- Water
Tonka beans are added to incense mixtures for added potency.


**VIOLET**   *Viola odorata*
G --Feminine    P -- Venus    E -- Water

Violet flowers offer protection from earthbound entities, promote good fortune and create a calming atmosphere. A bath mixture offering the vibrations of purification and protection are as follows:
2 oz. Tonka beans, 1 oz. (30 G) Lavender, 1 oz. (30 G) Anise seeds, 2 oz. (60 G) Violet leaves, ½ oz. (15 G) Althea, 2 oz. (60 G) White or Lavender Rose petals or buds, 1 ¼ oz. (37 G) Verbena leaves; Mix thoroughly and place in a porous bag, drop in hot water and steep for 10 minutes, squeeze the bag and add infused water to the bath.

# CHAPTER TWO

# ABUNDANCE & PROSPERITY

Next to Love, in my opinion, Prosperity is equally if not more coveted. Money may be the root of all evil, but it is necessary in the world we live. Prosperity formulas should only be utilized during the waxing phase of the moon, which is from the New Moon to the Full Moon. Sunrise or High Noon on Sundays (Sun) and Tuesdays (Mars) are good days to initiate these formulas. If you have money in your bank account to expand on you can also initiate on Thursdays (Jupiter). Do not initiate any Prosperity formulas when the sun or moon is in Taurus particularly if you need money fast. Taurus energy is great for long term investments, not immediate gratification.

Be sensible with your requests for greed has a way of backfiring. Often what we believe we need and what we actually need are totally opposite.

## Prosperity Formula
**Basil Leaves**   *Ocimum basilicum*
Gender: Masculine   Planet: Mars   Element: Fire

Place 1 Tbsp. (15 ounces) of Basil into 1 Pint (230 cc)
Place in a dark space for 7 days.
Sprinkle in a place of business and/or your home to attract money and success and thwart evil. Give a Basil Plant as a house warming gift to ensure good fortune.
Plant in your garden for good fortune and protection.

## Money Amulet
Buckeye   Horse Chestnut (*Aesculus*)
Gender: Masculine   Planet: Jupiter   Element: Fire
Ingredients:
Buckeye, 1
Money Oil
Money Drawing Powder
Brown Jumbo Candles, 2
Dollar Bill, 1
Small Green Bag, 1

To charge your Buckeye anoint with Money Oil, sprinkle with Money Drawing powder, and place between the 2 brown jumbo candles. Light the candles from right to left. Meditate and visualize prosperity. Allow the candles to burn out. Throw any remains outside. Wrap the buckeye in the dollar bill, place in the small green bag, and carry in your right pocket or women in your purse.

## Prosperity Incense

Camphor   (*Cinnamomum Camphora*)
Gender: Feminine   Planet: Moon   Element: Water

Ingredients:
Camphor Powder, ½ oz. (15 grams)
Sandalwood Powder, 3 oz. (90 grams)
Myrrh Resin, 1 oz. (30 grams)
Patchouli Leaves, 1 oz. (30 grams)
Orris Powder, 1 oz. (30 grams)
Frankincense, 4 oz. (115 grams)
Saltpeter, 1 oz. (30 grams)

Grind the Patchouli Leaves with a mortar and pestle.  Combine and blend well with remaining ingredients.  Burn on self-igniting charcoal.

## Money Incense

Cinnamon   (*Cinnamomum zeylanicum)*
Gender: Masculine   Planet: Sun   Element: Fire

Ingredients:
Cinnamon Powder, ½ oz. (15 grams)
Shi Shi Powder Incense, 2 oz. (60 grams)
Frankincense, 1 oz. (30 grams)
Saltpeter, ½ oz.  (15 grams)

Mix thoroughly and burn on self-igniting charcoals at the appropriate time.

## Prosperity Wish Formula

Four Leaf Clover   (*Trifolium)*
Gender: Masculine   Planet: Mercury   Element: Air

Ingredients:
Four Leafed Clover, 1 oz. (30 grams)
Anise Seed, 2 oz. (60 grams)
Fast Luck Incense Powder, 8 oz. (230 grams)
Orange Seven Day Candle (Glass Encased)
Parchment Paper
Dove's Blood Ink
Bamba Wood Charcoal or self-igniting charcoal
 ***Blend Four Leafed Clovers, Anise Seed, and Fast Luck Incense Powder
together.  Do not grind the Four Leaf Clovers.  Write your wish using the Dove's Blood

Ink on the Parchment Paper. Light the Orange candle and place the parchment paper with your wish underneath. Allow candle to continue burning. Light charcoal and once hot place some of the incense mixture on it. Read Psalm 57. Meditate on your desire. Do this for nine consecutive nights. Start after the sun sets on a Saturday night, Monday night, or Wednesday night.

## High John the Conqueror Oil

Ingredients:
High John the Conqueror Root, 3 pieces
Vegetable, Olive or Mineral Oil, 1 bottle
Make a multitude of cuts into the 3 pieces of John the Conqueror root and place in Oil. Place in a dark place and allow to infuse from the start of a Full Moon through the New Moon returning to the Full Moon. This formula is for Money, Success, Happiness, and Love.

## Formula of Success for Artists

Lemon Verbena    (*Lippia citriodara*)
Gender: Masculine    Planet: Mercury    Element: Air
Ingredients:
Lemon Verbena, 1 Tbsp. (12 grams)
Linden Flowers, 1 Tbsp. (12 grams)
Saffron, 1 Tbsp. (12 grams)
Cinnamon Powder, 1 Tbsp. (12 grams)
Nutmeg Powder, 1 Tbsp. (12 grams)
Rose Powder, 1 Tbsp. (12 grams)
Saltpeter, 1/2 Tbsp. (7 grams)
Self-Igniting Charcoal
***Grind Lemon Verbena, Linden Flowers, and Saffron with mortar and pestle then blend thoroughly with remaining ingredients. Burn a little each evening before retiring. Upon rising each morning read Psalms 57.
This incense is designed for those interested in attaining success in the Arts, Music, Acting, Painting, Dancing, Writing, etc.

## Formula for those Seeking Employment
MEADOWSWEET   (*Spiraea filipendula*)

Ingredients:
Meadowsweet, 1 Tbsp. (12 grams)
Water, 1 Pint (120 cc)
Mix together and allow to infuse for 7 days in a dark place. Strain and add to your bath before going to an interview or filling out applications. This is to create an energy of favor regarding first impressions.

## Formula for Influencing People in a Positive Manner

Ingredients:
John the Conqueror Incense, 4 oz. (110 grams)
Senna Powder, 2 oz. (60 grams)
Special Favors Oil
Your Zodiac Oil
Attraction Powder
Self-Igniting Charcoal
Mix John the Conqueror Incense and Senna Powder thoroughly. Burn a little on self-igniting charcoals in your home or business each day. Put 10 drops of Special Favors Oil in your bath each day. Use Attraction Powder and your Zodiac oil on your body each day.

## Incense Formula for Prosperity and Success

Ingredients:
Sacred Bark, 8 oz. (220 grams)
Olibanum, 6 oz. (180 grams)
Myrrh, 4 oz. (110 grams)
Sandalwood, 4 oz. (110 grams)
Saltpeter, 1/2 oz. (15 grams)
Success Oil
Bamba Wood Charcoal or Self-Igniting Charcoal
Triple Power (Action) Candle

Grind Sacred Bark and Olibanum well, then, add Myrrh, Sandalwood, and Saltpeter. Anoint Triple Power Candle with Success Oil from bottom to top. Light Incense and then light candle. Read Psalm #4. Repeat daily until you have achieved your goal.

# Formula to Gain Good Fortune and Respect at Work

MASTER ROOT   *Imperatoria ostruthium*

Grow Master Root in your garden or yard. Collect rain water and sprinkle this on the plant each day before work and clean your hands in the water as it drips off the plant.

# Formula for Burning Red Onion Peelings for Good Fortune

Red Onion   *Allium cepa*

I use a lot of red onions in recipes. I take the red onion peelings and throw them onto a hot burner. They bring good fortune to your home or business and is said to keep the law away.

# Money Blessing Formula for the Home

Sarsaparilla   *Similax officinalis*

Burn 3 parts Sarsaparilla with 2 parts cinnamon chips, 2 parts sandlewood, 2 parts frankincense, and a little myrrh over self-igniting hot charcoals to bring money into the home.

# Formula for Changing your Luck

When moving to a new residence or location, take what is referred to as a leaving bath. Before dawn, bathe in plain water, immerse yourself nine times and if you are spiritually inclined say a prayer nine times, each time before you immerse yourself. Visualize all misfortune leaving you with the sun now shining on your face. After your bath, take a pan of the bath water and throw outside toward the rising sun in the East.

When you arrive at your new location, take a bath in 1 Tbsp. (15 g.) of each – saltpeter, alum, sugar, and bluing. Immerse yourself nine times visualizing all the new luck and love coming your way. After bathing take a pan of this water and throw out the front door. If you live in an enclosed apartment building throw outside the door coming into the area where you apartment is.

# Rose of Jericho   *Anastatica hierochuntica*

Also referred to as the Resurrection Plant, this desert flower is used in businesses and the home for prosperity and to draw money. Place in a shallow dish and replace the water every Tuesday, but do not go overboard with the watering. The plant should be sitting on top of the water and no water should be covering it. Place near the front door of your business, drop in five shiny pennies. Pour the old water over the doorstep and if you are spiritually inclined you can repeat Psalm 23 as you water the plant. In the home you can place near the front door or if you have a designated spiritual room you can place it there. In the home use the old water as a floor wash to welcome wealth and abundance.

# MAGIC MONEY JAR

A friend and magician shared this formula with me. He considered creating this financial aid to be of great significance. The following is his recipe.

***Begin with a jar or a can. I use a can, its opaque. A jar may be better, because glass is an insulator. Leyden jars are batteries you can make yourself, with tin foil and a jar, but that just illustrates a glass jar has a certain quality as an insulator. The jar should obviously be large enough to contain what must go inside it. It will contain several seeds and coins.

1. Prepare the jar inside with a couple of drops of money oil. Add to this some chips of cinnamon bark, or if you prefer, five small sticks of cinnamon.

2. I get my seeds together in a small dish. It's easier to count them. Some people say you can make a jar with one seed or one of each coin, but I heard 5 of each first, and it seems to work, so I use five of each. I don't think it makes much difference which seeds you use as long as they're in good condition and not cracked or rotten. Remember, the seeds will be banging against the coins as you shake the can in a ritual, so you want the seeds to be without splits or cracks. But important seeds to include are mustard and sesame seeds, five of each for they symbolize growth. I put a few kinds of progressively larger seeds, almonds, pecans, with hard whole shells. I try to make the five of each kind of seeds clean and as similar in size and color as possible.

3. Next, the coins. Five pennies, five silver dimes, five silver quarters is the traditional formula. An interesting fact about pennies, right now I use pennies from 1982 to the present, because they're 97.5 percent copper. From 1864 to 1982 they were only 95% copper. Going on the premise that purer makes the magic better, I'm ordering some pennies from 1795-1857. They were made with 100% pure copper then. As to the coins, you can buy silver dimes and quarters from a coin shop or order them on the internet. US dimes and quarters were silver until 1965. I use matching coins of each type whatever year I use. I also expand the list to include silver half dollars, and will put five silver dollars in the can as soon as I have a matching set. But quarters should work just fine, even one of each coin if you have enough faith.

4. When your money can is assembled, I believe it works as a kind of wish generator, attracting money. Intention is very important in any magic. According to some you should pronounce the 23rd psalm, blessing it to make it white. When you want to attract money, memorize this chant and say it three times: "Copper and silver, seeds and grain, I need to increase my money gain." However simple the words sound, take them seriously. Say them with intention.

That's all there is to making a money jar. I made three over the years, and my income increased dramatically each time I made a can. The first one was a jar. My current one is in a small can, the kind with a metal cap which covers the top. As a final note and speculation about making and using these money jars, can you possibly improve the design? Yes, one way would be to add a lodestone or five lodestones. To attract money the use of magnets or magnetic rocks is a popular idea in magic. Another thing with promise I already mentioned is adding five matched silver dollars. I also believe for silver older coins are better because they have history, they've been around longer, and they've exhibited staying power. Finally, and I believe this has considerable possibilities for study and experiment, the use of magic stones to decorate the jar. Records indicate the old Jewish priests of the pre-Christian temple decorated their magical items with precious stones in a certain way because they attributed different magical properties to specific gemstones. It's a tradition with them and others that emeralds and rubies attract money. Emeralds and rubies are costly of course, but you can get a bag of uncut, unpolished rubies or emeralds on the net, if you want to go that far and would like to experiment decorating your money jar. I epoxied evenly spaced emeralds around the rim of the can. It can't hurt. But you don't need to add them. That's all I have to say about money jars.

# CHAPTER THREE

## LOVE AND ATTRACTION

Love is Universal and available in various forms, however the most coveted is that of romantic love. Due to the power of this desire it is my advice to use these formulations with responsibility and the knowledge that whatever you send out will come back to you at least three fold.

Before beginning, cleanse yourself physically and mentally. Meditate; be certain that the one you desire is truly the one for you. It is never advisable to use any formula in an experimental manner for tearing at another's heartstrings can bear serious consequences.

Once you begin your workshop, as I refer to it, you cannot just stand by and expect love to drop into your lap. It is wise to take opportunities to make yourself seen and heard by the one you desire. I strongly advise men to write love letters and/or poetry. Don't over kill for you may risk appearing to be perceived as a stalker. Be yourself. Don't pretend to be someone you are not, for people can only hide behind a mask for so long. If the person you have your heart set on is truly the one for you, the energy will work in your favor and you will be brought together without much difficulty. If not, accept accountability and examine your true intentions.

**_BE CAREFUL WHAT YOU WISH FOR_** because what you may believe you want may not be what you need nor last. Neurobiologists have found that there is a chemical released in the brain when a couple falls in love. This chemical is called phenylethylamine and it functions in the body much like an amphetamine thus explaining the superhuman feelings of a couple who is falling in love. But unfortunately, phenylethylamine highs cannot last. As with any chemical your body builds up a tolerance to it and the body requires more and more of the substance to acquire loves special spark. Neurobiologists say it takes about four years for the chemical to fade, to run its course. Once the chemical is gone, the couple is faced with the difficult challenge of doing love with their own basic brain chemistry. This can create quite a struggle for many couples for after the so called feeling of love is gone are you willing to put real effort into the relationship to make it last?

**ARCHANGEL HERB**   *Angelica archagelica*
Ingredients:
Archangel Herb, 1 oz. (30 grams)
Love Incense, 2 oz. (60 grams)
Dove's Blood Ink
Parchment Paper
Thoroughly mix and burn on self-igniting charcoal. While this is burning, write your loved ones name using the Dove's Blood Ink on the parchment paper. Burn the paper in

the incense. Once the paper has burned to ashes, throw a little of the ashes to the Watchtowers of East, North, West, and South while visualizing your loved one.

**BETH ROOT**   *Trillium spp.*   G: Feminine   P: Venus   E: Water
Women, grate some of this and add to your man's food to keep him hungry for only you. It is also common knowledge in root work that women use their vaginal secretions or menstrual blood and cook it into food they are preparing for a man they desire or want to keep faithful.

## Love Incense
Ingredients:
Black Musk Powder, 1 oz. (30 grams)
Sandalwood Powder, 1 oz. (30 grams)
Cassia Powder or Bark, 1/2 oz. (15 grams)
Myrrh, 1/2 oz. (15 grams)
Saltpeter, 1/16 oz.  (5 grams)

Mix thoroughly and burn on self-igniting charcoal.

## A Mamba's Love Spell

Ingredients:
Witch Grass
Luv Luv Oil
Love Powder
Red Seven Day Candle
Love Oil
Dove's Blood Ink
Parchment Paper

*Sprinkle the Witch Grass under mattress.
*Each morning upon rising, apply the Luv Luv Oil and the Love Powder.
*Anoint a red seven day candle with the love oil while visualizing your loved one.
*Using the Dove's Blood Ink write your loved ones name on the parchment paper 6 times.  Place under the red candle you anointed.
*I advise starting this on a Venus Day, which is Friday, at sunrise or high noon.  Each day upon rising and retiring meditate for at least a few minutes visualizing your intentions.

## Mama's Spell to Bring Back a Lost Love

Ingredients:
Compelling Oil
Come to Me Powder
Pink Votive Candles, 2 (2 x 21=42)
Coumarin Powder (Tonka), 1 tsp. (7 grams)
Damiana, 1 tsp. (7 grams)
Bottle of Wine, your choice
Bible

For 21 days apply 7 drops of compelling oil while saying the name of your loved one passionately.
Apply Come to Me powder daily.
Light 2 pink votive candles in your bedroom after sunset each night for 21 days while reading Psalms 45 & 46 aloud 3 times each.
Mix the coumarin and damiana in a glass of wine and allow to infuse for 3 hours.  Sprinkle outside your front door and your back door for 21 days.
Perform this faithfully for 21 days and it is said that your lover will return to you.

**DULSE**   *Rhodymenia Palmata*   G: Feminine   P: Moon   E: Water

I have known many occultists who add Dulse powder to party beverages to loosen people up so that they will have a good time.  It can act as an aphrodisiac when added to mulled wine or other beverages.  It is also referred to as an herbal rapier.

## Recipe for Attracting Friends
GENTIAN ROOT   *Gentiana Lutea*   G: Masculine   P: Mars   E: Fire

Ingredients:
Gentian Root, 1 tbsp. (12 grams)
Water, 1 Liter
Dragon blood Bath Crystals, 1 tsp. (7 grams)
Bible

*Make an infusion with the Gentian Root and the water by simmering for ten minutes and then strain.
*Add the Dragon's Blood Crystals and 1 Tbsp. of the Gentian Water to your bath daily.
*Read Psalm 72 daily.
*I recommend starting this on a Sunday with the moon in waxing.

## A Bruja's Love Binding Formula
HEART'S EASE...PANSY  *(Viola Tricolor)*
G: Feminine   P: Saturn   E: Water

Ingredients:
Pansy, 1 oz. (30 grams)
Lavender Flowers, 2 oz. (60 grams)
Spikenard, 1 oz.  (30 grams)
Frankincense, 1 oz. (30 grams)
Powdered Love Incense, 6 oz. (175 grams)
1 Red Male Image Candle
1 Red Female Image Candle

Mix the Pansy, Lavender Flowers, Spikenard, Frankincense, and Love Incense through.  Burn this on self-igniting charcoal.

For Men:  Write your name on the back of the male image candle with a clean sharp nail from feet to head.  Write your woman's name on the back of the female image candle from feet to head.  For Women:  vice versa.

With the incense mixture already burning, light the candle with your name first and then the other.  Visualize you and your love forever together.

While candles are burning chant:  "Oh, Flame of Love Blessed from Above...Incense Burn Her (His) Love for me, to me forever."

Allow the candles to burn for one hour each day, extinguish.  Repeat this ritual each day until the candles have completely burned out.

For Men:  Start this on a Venus Day, (Friday) or on a Moon Day (Monday) during a waxing moon.
For Women:  Start this on a Mars Day (Tuesday) it would be best to perform during a Full Moon.

## Love Tea
KAVA  *Piper Methysticum*
G: Feminine   P: Saturn   E: Water

*Make an infusion and allow to steep in the refrigerator overnight.
*Share as a tea with your loved one.

## A Bruja's Attraction Bath

Ingredients:
Khus Khus (Vetivert) 1 tbsp. (12 grams)
Passion Flower, 1 tbsp. (12 grams)
Water Enyngo, 1 tbsp. (12 grams)
Water, 1 Gallon (4 liter)

Mix together and allow to infuse in a dark place for 5 days. Add 1 cup to your daily bath to make you irresistible.

## A Celtic Witch Love Incense

Ingredients:
Linden Flowers, 5 oz. (140 grams)
Basil, 1 oz. (30 grams)
Bayberry, 1 oz. (30 grams)
Dittany of Crete, 2 oz. (60 grams)
Cloves Powder, 1/2 oz. (15 grams)
Saltpeter, 1/2 oz. (15 grams)

Blend & Grind thoroughly with a mortar and pestle.
Burn on self-igniting charcoal.

**MAGNOLIA** *Magnolia Grandofolia*
G: Feminine   P: Venus   E: Earth
It is said that keeping some of this plant near the bed and/or under the bed will make even the most prudent amorous.

## Formula to Win the Respect and Admiration of Others

Ingredients:
Marigold, 1 Tbsp. (12 grams)
Calamus, 1 Tbsp. (12 grams)
Hops, 1 Tbsp. (12 grams)
Lemon Verbena, 1 Tbsp. (12 grams)
Mace, 1 Tbsp. (12 grams)
Water, 1 gallon (4 Liters)

Mix together and place in a dark place for 9 days to infuse. Strain and add 1 cup to your bath daily.

## An American Witch Love Formula

Ingredients:
Orris Root Powder, 1 oz. (30 grams)
Anise Seed, 1 oz. (30 grams)
Lavender, 1 oz. (30 grams)
Vanillin, 1 oz. (30 grams)
Dittany of Crete, 1 oz. (30 grams)
Bayberry, 1/2 oz. (15 grams)
Rose Powder, 5 oz. (140 grams)
Saltpeter, 1/2 oz. (15 grams)
Pink Seven Day Candle
Parchment Paper
Doves Blood Ink
Bamba Wood Charcoal
Luv Luv Luv Oil

Mix and Grind with a mortar and pestle, the Orris root, Anise seed, Lavender, Vanillin, Dittany of Crete, Bayberry, Rose Powder, and Salt Peter thoroughly.
Heat up the Bamba Wood charcoal and begin adding the incense mixture to it a little at a time. If you cannot find Bamba Wood incense use self-igniting charcoal. On the inside of the Pink glass encased seven day candle with a sharp clean nail write your name at the top of the candle and your loved one's under yours. Light the candle. On the parchment paper, with the Dove's Blood Ink write the name of your loved one's 5 times. Place this under the lighted candle. If you have a photo of your loved one, place this under the candle as well. Allow the candle to burn until it goes out on its own. Wear a little of the Luv Luv Luv oil daily on your pulse areas.

Every evening before you retire, burn some of the incense and meditate on your desire. I recommend starting this in a waxing moon on a day and hour of Venus, Friday at Sunrise.

## Passion Incense

Ingredients:
*Satyrion* (Orchid), 10 oz. (285 grams)
Olibanum Powder, 4 oz. (115 grams)
Dittany of Crete, 2 oz. (60 grams)
Myrrh, 1 oz. (30 grams)
Orris Powder, 1 oz. (30 grams)
Saltpeter, 1 oz. (30 grams)
Cloves, 1 oz. (30 grams)

Cinnamon Powder, 1/2 oz. (15 grams)
Pimento Powder, 1/2 oz. (15 grams)
Bamba Wood Charcoal

Grind and Blend the Orchid thoroughly with a mortar and pestle. Combine and blend thoroughly with the remaining ingredients. Burn this before you expect a visit from your love or even during their visit. Some choose to burn this before entertaining to make their guests more uninhibited thus more fun to be around.

## Love Binding Formula
SPIKENARD  *Inula conyza*  G: Feminine  P: Venus  E: Water

Ingredients:
Spikenard
Photo of your loved one
Luv Luv Luv Oil
Attraction Oil
Piece of Brown Paper

Anoint the photo of your loved one with the Luv Luv Luv Oil and Attraction Oil. Place face up on the brown paper. Sprinkle 1/2 oz. (15 grams) of the Spikenard on the photo and wrap the photo in the brown paper. Bury the photo in the brown paper close to your home. Sprinkle the earth which covers the photo with 1/2 oz. (15 grams) of Spikenard. Every three weeks sprinkle with 1 Tbsp. of Spikenard and 10 drops of Attraction Oil. I recommend starting this in a waxing moon on a day of Venus, Friday at Sunrise or on a Sunday. Women: Start on a Full Moon or a Mars Day, Tuesday at Sunrise in a waxing moon.

## An American Witch Formula to Attract a Soulmate

Ingredients:
Sweet Bugle, 1 oz. (30 grams)
Cinnamon Powder, 2 oz. (60 grams)
Sandalwood Powder, 16 oz. (450 grams)
Anise Seed, 4 oz. (115 grams)
Saltpeter, 1/4 oz. (7 grams)
Attraction Oil
White Sabbath Candles, 2
Self-Igniting Charcoal

Mix the Sweet Bugle, Cinnamon Powder, Sandalwood Powder, Anise Seed, and Saltpeter thoroughly. Burn over self-igniting charcoal. Clean yourself thoroughly and dress well, just as if you would for an engagement ceremony. Anoint your 2 white candles with attraction oil starting from the bottom to the top.

Make a tea from some of the Sweet Bugle, don't boil, steep in boiling water for 15 minutes to make a tea.

This ritual is to be performed on Friday after the sun rises or before the sun sets for men and on Tuesday for women. Men should use Venus energy and women should take advantage of Mars energy. It should be started during a waxing moon. If a woman desires a good provider perform your ritual on a Mars / Jupiter cusp. Men if you want to speed up the process you can use a Venus / Sun cusp or if you would prefer a woman with an Intelligence, you can use a Mars / Mercury cusp. If you need help with these configurations please refer to my Planetary Tables page. If you are homosexual, gay men should use the Mars energy and gay women should use the Venus energy. Also you can go a step further. Men you could start your ritual in Libra during the waxing phase which usually is successful for life partners and marriage. Women you could start your ritual in Aries or Scorpio during the waxing phase. Also you may want for example your partner to be a Taurus or a Leo, etc…, so you would start your ritual during the waxing phase of these months. Also, **DO NOT** start this ritual during a Mercury, Mars, or Venus retrograde.

Start the incense, light the candles, the right one first and then the left. Use the Pink Cloud Meditation to call your soul mate. You may drink some of the tea during the ritual and share with your soul mate within the Pink Cloud. Allow the candles to burn out. Bury the remains in a beautiful park or near a place you feel a strong connection to. Each Friday (for men) or Tuesday (for women) until your soul mate arrives, repeat the ritual. Drink the Sweet Bugle tea each night before retiring and keep putting your intention out there.

This is my favorite formula for you are calling for the right person to come to you and not affecting the will of someone you have chosen.


## THE PINK CLOUD MEDITATION

Sit or lie in a comfortable position. Visualize a beautiful soft pink cloud above you. Call the soul of the person to whom you wish to communicate with to the pink cloud. Usually no soul declines this invitation for the pink cloud is a safe place of Universal love and protection. Communicate with the soul you have invited and once you are both satisfied with the session, thank and dismiss the invited soul. Thank the Universe and then return to your being. Some actually create a pink cloud from fabric and place it above their bed. Others have created a photo which they say they have used until they perfect the meditation.

# A Bruja's Power of Love Attraction Formula

Ingredients:
Sandalwood Powder, 20 oz. (570 grams)
Frankincense Powder, 8 oz. (225 grams)
Wood Betony, 4 oz. (115 grams)
Vanillin Powder, 4 oz. (115 grams)
Orris Root Powder, 2 oz. (60 grams)
Saltpeter, 1/2 oz. (7 grams)
Seven Power Candle
Bend Over Oil
Luv Luv Luv Oil
Your Zodiac Oil
Self-Igniting Charcoal

Grind the Wood Betony into a powder using a mortar and pestle. Combine and blend thoroughly with Sandalwood, Frankincense, Vanillin, Orris, and Saltpeter. Anoint the candle with the Bend over Oil.

Start this in a waxing moon on a day of Venus, Friday at sunrise, high noon, or before the sun sets. You may also start on a Sunday at Sunrise or high noon during a waxing moon.

Begin with burning some of the incense on the self-igniting charcoals. Anoint yourself (daily) with the Luv Luv Luv Oil and your personal Zodiac Oil.
Light the Seven Power Candle. Meditate on bringing the one who is meant for you into your life. Allow the candle to burn out on its own.
This is another favorite of mine for again, this is formulated to attract the right person into your life and not someone you have chosen.

## An Attraction of Love Incense

Ingredients:
Bayberry Herb, 32 oz. (900 grams)
Gilead Buds, 16 oz. (450 grams)
Sandalwood Powder, 8 oz. (225 grams)
Indian Hemp (Dogbane), 2 oz. (60 grams)
Cubeb Berries, 2 oz. (60 grams)
Lavender Flowers, 8 oz. (225 grams)
Violet Powder, 4 oz. (115 grams)
Paradise Grains
Cinnamon Powder, 4 oz. (115 grams)

Saltpeter, 1/2 oz. (15 grams)

Grind Bayberry, Gilead Buds, Indian Hemp, Cubeb Berries, and Lavender Flowers well with a mortar and pestle. Combine with other ingredients and blend well. Burn a little 3 times daily, on self-igniting charcoals to attract real love.

*Start during a waxing moon in Venus (Friday) or on a Sunday. Burn at sunrise, high noon, and before the sun sets.

## Formula to Remove the JuJu of a Sexual Nature

Calamus   *Acorus calamus*

Take a good size piece of Calamus root, add one quart (950 ml) of whiskey. Cook until mixture is reduced to a pint (475 ml). Strain and add a fresh pint (475 ml) of whiskey. Take a dose daily medicinally until remedied.

## Formula to Attract a Man

Catnip   *Nepeta cataria*

Ingredients:

Catnip, 3 oz. (84 g.)

3 Red Knob Candles

Whiskey, 1 quart (950 ml) of Whiskey

Soak the Catnip in Whiskey for seven days. Sprinkle the mixture on your doorstep for 21 consecutive days. Carve the name of your desired clockwise on each knob of the red candles. Burn one knob each day for 21 consecutive days.

## Formula to Bind a Lover

Knot Weed   *Polygonum arenastrum*

Ingredients:

Recent Photo of yourself

Recent Photo of you lover

Red Cloth

Knot Weed, 2 parts

Periwinkle, 1 part

Red Rose Buds, 2 parts

Love Me Powder

Love Me Oil

1 Shoelace from each person

Place half of the Knot Weed, Periwinkle, Red Rose Buds, sprinkle half of the Love Me Powder on the red cloth. Now take the photos, face to face and place on red cloth. Put the remaining mixture on the photos in the red cloth. Fold the cloth into a neat package and tie with the 2 shoestrings. Dress with the Love Me oil and place and keep under your bed.

# Love Potion #9

Ingredients:
Equal parts of the following: (1 or 2 oz. - 28 or 56 g.)

| | |
|---|---|
| Red Rose Petals | *Rosa* |
| Red Clover | *Trifolium pratense* |
| Catnip | *Nepeta cataria* |
| Lavender | *Lavandula officianlis* |
| Damiana | *Tutnera aphrodisiaca* |
| Cubebs | *Piper cubea* |
| Juniper Berries | *Juniperis communis* |
| Gentian Root | *Gentiana lutea* |
| Deer's Tongue | *Trilisa odorata* |
| Muslin Bags 9 | |

Grind the herbs with a mortar and pestle, except for the red rose petals. Divide into portions of 9, place into muslin bags. You can take one bag per day, steep to make tea for nine minutes and meditate on your goal during this time and when drinking the tea. Also you can take the steeped herbs and place in a bowel or pan. For nine consecutive days before dawn breaks, use a clean white handkerchief and wash your face, breasts, and genitals while meditating on your purpose. To strengthen this ritual dress a red taper candle with come to me oil holding the candle from the base with the tip towards you because you want to draw this person to you. Place a recent photo of your desired under the candle and burn while you are washing yourself. Take the wash water to a crossroads (a four way stop, where two roads cross). Call the name of your beloved while throwing your wash water over your left shoulder toward the rising sun in the East. This mixture can also be used as an incense for attracting love and romance (burn on self-igniting charcoal). Either gender can utilize these formulas. You can make your own oil using these ingredients and following the directions for making oils in Chapter 13. Use the oil to anoint candles and wear on your pulse areas.

# Formula to Attract a Woman
Sampson Snake Root    *Orbexilum pedunculatum*

Ingredients:
Sampson Snake Root
Parchment Paper, 2" x 4"
Red Ink Pen (Exclusively used for magical purposes)
Magnetic Sand
Lodestones, 2
Attraction Oil
Red Flannel Bag
Hair from desired woman, 1
Hair from yourself, 1

Take the parchment paper with your red pen and write the woman's full name and then cross her name with your full name.  Fold the hair into the parchment paper.  Place this in the red flannel bag along with Sampson Snake Root and the two lodestones that have been rolled in the magnetic sand.  Dress the red bag with attraction oil Wear in the front pocket near your penis, on the your attracting or receiving side.  Your attraction side is the side of the hand that you don't write with, your projection hand is the hand that you write with.  Most people's attraction side is the left side.

# Floor Wash for Love
Ingredients:
Lavender
Red Rose Buds or Petals
Rosemary
Linen Bag

Place the Lavender and Rosemary in the Linen Bag.  In a large pot of boiling hot water add the ingredients in the linen bag and the rose petals or buds.  Steep for 6 minutes while visualizing you and your husband or lover being very much in love.  Strain the mixture and use as a floor wash throughout your home, especially the bedroom.  You can use the remaining water to clean window sills, doors, and doorways to invite more love into your home.  You can additionally make up enough ingredients and place in between or under your mattress as an energy booster.

# CHAPTER FOUR

## HEALING, BLESSINGS, & WISHES

## Formula for Healing Another

Ingredients:
Capsicum Powder
Rosemary Oil, 1tsp. (1dram)
Violet Oil, 1 tsp. (1 dram)
Witches Formula, 1 tsp. (1 dram)
Voodoo Doll (Poppet)
Blessing Oil
Special Oil #20
Piece of Red Cloth

At Dawn mix a portion of the Capsicum Powder with the Rosemary Oil, Violet Oil, and Witches Formula creating a smooth paste. Take the Voodoo Doll (Poppet) and dip your right forefinger into the Blessing Oil, place a small dab on the forehead of the Voodoo Doll (Poppet). Place a dab on the throat and the heart area as well. Put some Special Oil # 20 in your hands and rub your palms together. Hold your palms over the Voodoo Doll (Poppet) and say,
"I name thee, (name of the person who is ill).

While covering the Doll thoroughly with paste say, "Be thou (name of person who is ill) healed. Be thou, (the name of the person who is ill) healed". Repeat this for a third time. Wrap the Voodoo Doll (Poppet) in a piece of clean red cloth and put it in a safe place where no one can see or touch it.

The next morning at dawn, while covering the doll with paste repeat, "Be thou (name of person who is ill) healed", three times. Place back in the red cloth and return to a safe place. On the dawn of the third day repeat the ritual, with the exception that when you place the doll back in a safe place it will remain there for three days untouched.

On the seventh day at sunrise take the doll and burn it saying, "Purge Oh Mighty Flame the body of (name of the person who is ill). Purify, Oh God of Fire, the body of (name of the person who is ill). Oh Lord of the Flames, burn out all that is evil and alien to the body of (name of the person who is ill)". When the doll is completely burned scatter the ashes to the North.

*The Doll can be made from the sick person's clothes. I would add some of the person's

DNA such as hair or nail clippings and sew these up inside the doll. You can find a recipe for Blessing Oil and Special #20 Oil in Chapter 13. While performing this ritual or any ritual give it your all.

## Secret Wish Formula

Ingredients:
Sandalwood Powder, 3 oz. (85 grams)
Myrrh Grains, 1oz. (30 grams)
Patchouli Leaves, 1 oz. (30 grams)
Orris Powder, 1 oz. (30 grams)
Frankincense, 4 oz. (120 grams)
Saltpeter, 1 oz. (30 grams)
Camphor Powder, 1 oz. (30 grams)
Self-igniting Charcoal

Mix all ingredients thoroughly with a mortar and pestle. In the morning, upon rising, and in the evening, before retiring: Focus on your secret wish, and while lighting the incense say: "Adonai, Elohim, Eliohim, Adonai!" It would behoove you to meditate at least 5 to 15 minutes while visualizing your desire into fruition.

## Formula to Bless Another

ELDER FLOWERS  *Sambucus Canadensis*
Gender: Female    Planet: Venus    Element: Water

*Facing the East scatter some Elder Flowers and say, "Powers of the Watchtowers of the East Bless (name of the person you want blessed)".
*Facing the South scatter some Elder Flowers and say, "Powers of the Watchtowers of the South Bless (name of the person you want blessed)."
*Facing the West scatter some Elder Flowers and say, "Powers of the Watchtowers of the West Bless (name of the person you want blessed)."
*Facing the North scatter some Elder Flowers and say, "Powers of the Watchtowers of the North Bless (name of the person you want blessed)."
*Face the East and with Elder Flowers in both hands throw the flowers upward and forward while saying, "In the name of Yod He Vau He, the Blessing is now done."
*Vibrate the Yod He Vau He when saying it.

# Four Leaf Clover Wish Formula

Four Leafed Clover    (*Trifolium*)
Gender: Masculine   Planet: Mercury   Element: Air

Ingredients:
Four Leafed Clover, 1 oz. (30 grams)
Anise Star, 2 oz. (60 grams)
Fast Luck Incense, 8 oz. (225 grams)
Parchment Paper
Dove's Blood Ink
Orange Seven Day Candle
Self-Igniting Charcoal

Mix the Four Leafed Clover, Anise Star, and Fast Luck Incense together thoroughly. Write your wish with the Dove's Blood Ink on the Parchment paper. Light the Orange seven day candle and place the paper with your wish under the candle. Burn some incense while reading Psalm #57. Repeat this ritual for nine consecutive nights after sundown. Start this ritual in a waxing moon.

# Make a Wish Formula

Ingredients:
Ague Root (*Aletris farinose)* 2 oz. (60 grams)
Saltpeter, 2 oz. (30 grams)
Orris Root, 4 oz. (120 grams)
Cinnamon, 2 oz. (60 grams)
Vanillin Powder, 2 oz. (60 grams)
Myrrh, 4 oz. (120 grams)
Olibanum, 8 oz. (225 grams)
Sandalwood, 16 oz. (450 grams)
Special Favors Oil
Self-igniting Charcoal

Grind and Blend well, using a mortar and pestle. Burn once in the morning and once in the evening. Meditate on your desire for five through fifteen minutes. Anoint yourself with Special Favors Oil daily. Recipe for Special Favors Oil can be found in Chapter 13.

# Formula to Maintain Health to all residing in the Home

Ingredients:
Winters Bark, 32 oz. (900 grams)
Olibanum, 16 oz. (450 grams)
Violet Flowers, 8 oz. (225 grams)
Thyme Leaves, 2 oz. (60 grams)
Cinnamon, 8 oz. (225 grams)
Myrrh, 4 oz. (120 grams)
Sage, 2 oz. (60 grams)
Eucalyptus Leaves, 2 oz. (60 grams)
Orris Root, 4 oz. (120 grams)
Saltpeter, ½ oz. (15 grams)
Self-Igniting Charcoal

Crush, Grind, and Blend as fine as possible with a mortar and pestle the Thyme, Eucalyptus, Orris Root, and Winters Bark. Add then add and crush the remaining ingredients. Burn once daily.

# CHAPTER FIVE

## BUSINESS, SUCCESS, & LEGAL MATTERS

All entrepreneurs desire a successful business. Most clients who have approached me or other advisers usually are small business owners. Energy work is definitely a plus, however traditional methods must be employed as well. An example is advertising, great customer service, quality merchandise, a sound business plan, organizational skills...in a nutshell is just good business acumen.

During the years that I served as an advisor to those who were seeking energy workshops to promote business success, there were also those who wanted me to aid in destroying their competition. I refused the latter for I believe healthy competition is good and that a business owner should focus on increasing their own success rather than destroy that of another

Timing is critical regarding energy work. Work done during Cosmic Danger Zones (Tebeth, Tammuz, and Av) will yield no fruit. Also, Mondays and Wednesdays are considered days of negativity, but there are exceptions. If your business needs expedited help, it is wise to start energy work on a Sunday at sunrise or high noon. Never start work during the Sun or Moon in Taurus. Taurus provides long term assistance and if you are at this place of stability then the energy is good for maintaining or stabilizing capital and is great for Protection work. Most of the recipes for incenses and oils can be found in Chapter 13.

Learn to use energy from the formulas within these pages to cleanse, protect, attract, expand, and of course, don't forget traditional business acumen.

### A Bruja's Business Formula
ECHINACEA   (*Echinacea augustifolia*)
Ingredients:
Echinacea, 1 oz. (30 grams)
Cubeb Berries, 1 oz. (30 grams)
Shi Shi Incense, 8 oz. (220 grams)
2 Seven Day Candles, Green
Success Oil
Powerful Hand Charm

Grind the Echinacea and Cubeb Berries well, and then combine with the Shi Shi Incense. Burn some Incense before your doors open for business and after you close for the day. Anoint the Candle with the Success Oil from bottom to top. Allow the candle to burn out and you must start another one before this one completely extinguishes for the force behind the fire of the candle must burn for 9 days.  Read Psalm #4 daily in the morning and carry the Powerful Hand Charm in your right pocket.

## Formula to Increase Business
Golden Seal   (*Hydrastis canadensis*)
Gender: Masculine   Planet: Sun   Element: Fire

Ingredients:
Golden Seal, 1 oz. (30 grams)
Money Crystal, 1 (Ex: Marcasite, Yellow Sapphire, Green Tourmaline)
Money Oil
Brown Candles, 3
High John the Conqueror Incense
Self-Igniting Charcoals
Start this on a Sunday or a Tuesday.

Take a little of the Goldenseal and sprinkle in each of the four corners of your place of business.  Anoint the Money Crystal with Money Oil and place in your cash register or the place you keep your money.  Burn a little of the High John the Conqueror incense each morning before you start your day and meditate for a moment visualizing a busy day producing many sales.  Before leaving at night burn the 3 brown candles lighting from right to left & meditate for 5-15 minutes. Each night before retiring read Psalms 8.

Often the candles are not burnt out before you leave for home so to prevent possible fires, if you have a sink in your business place them there, if not take a large pan, fill partially with water and set the candles in candle holders in this pan.  Take any remains of wax bury or throw outside.

## Formula to Increase Business II
High John the Conqueror   (*Ipomoea Purga*)
Gender: Masculine   Planet: Mars   Element: Mars
Ingredients:
High John the Conqueror, 1 piece
Dollar Bill
Money Drawing Gold Dust
Money Oil

Wrap your piece of High John the Conqueror in the Dollar Bill and then apply Money Oil.  Place in the back of your cash drawer.  Sprinkle with Money Drawing Gold Dust.  Every 7 days repeat by reapplying the Money Oil on the High John the Conqueror root wrapped in the Dollar Bill and sprinkling with the Money Drawing Gold Dust.

# High John the Conqueror Oil

Ingredients:
High John the Conqueror Root, 3
Vegetable or Mineral Oil, 1 bottle

Make a multitude of cuts into the 3 pieces of John the Conqueror root and place in Oil. Place in a dark place and allow to infuse from the start of a Full Moon through the New Moon returning to the Full Moon. This formula is for Money, Success, Happiness, and Love.

# A Mamba's Formula for Expanding a Minister's Congregation

Ingredients:
Kelp, 1 Tbsp. (12 grams)
Nutmeg, 1 Tbsp. (12 grams)
Orris Powder, 1 tsp., (7 grams)
Water, 1 Gallon (4 Liters)

Mix thoroughly and allow it soak for 7 days in a dark area. Once infused, use as a floor wash in the main area of the church or meeting room.

# Formula of Success Incense for Artists
Lemon Verbena    (*Lippia citriodara*)
Gender: Masculine    Planet: Mercury    Element: Air

Ingredients:
Lemon Verbena, 1 Tbsp. (12 grams)
Linden Flowers, 1 Tbsp. (12 grams)
Saffron, 1 Tbsp. (12 grams)
Cinnamon Powder, 1 Tbsp. (12 grams)
Nutmeg Powder, 1 Tbsp. (12 grams)
Rose Powder, 1 Tbsp. (12 grams)
Saltpeter, 1/2 Tbsp. (7 grams)
Self-Igniting Charcoal

Grind Lemon Verbena, Linden Flowers, and Saffron with mortar and postal then blend thoroughly with remaining ingredients. Burn a little each evening before retiring. Upon rising each morning read Psalms 57.

This incense is designed for those interested in attaining success in the Arts such as Music, Acting, Painting, Dancing, Writing, etc.

## Formula for a Landlord to Attract a Tenant

Ingredients:
Nutmeg Powder, 1 oz. (30 grams)
House Blessing Incense, 4 oz. (115 grams)
Fast Luck Incense, 3 oz. (75 grams)
Chinese Wash
Success Floor Wash
Peace Water
Blue Votive Candles, 1 for each room

Mix the Nutmeg, House Blessing Incense, and Fast Luck Incense thoroughly.

To your mop water add 4 Tbsp. (60 cc) of Chinese Wash and 4 Tbsp. of Success Floor Wash. Clean each room with this mixture.

In the corners of each room sprinkle some Peace Water. In each room burn a blue votive candle.

On a large metal plate or I use a large metal skillet with a handle (and I only use this for energy work), create a circle of nine piles of this incense mixture on top of 9 self-igniting charcoals. Light the charcoals first and then place the incense mix on top. Thoroughly incense each room and pause in each room and visualize the removal of all negativity and attracting the right tenant with all who dwell in your rental home peace and prosperity.

Return to the room where you started. The incense and the candles must burn out on their own. Once they have extinguished throw or bury remains outside.

## Formula for Those Seeking Employment
MEADOWSWEET   (*Spiraea filipendula*)

Ingredients:
Meadowsweet, 1 Tbsp. (12 grams)
Water, 1 Pint (120 cc)
Mix together and allow to infuse for 7 days in a dark place. Strain and add to your bath before going to an interview or filling out applications. This is to create an energy of favor regarding first impressions.

## Incense Formula for Success

Ingredients:
Sacred Bark, 8 oz. (220 grams)
Olibanum, 6 oz. (180 grams)
Myrrh, 4 oz. (110 grams)
Sandalwood, 4 oz. (110 grams)
Saltpeter, 1/2 oz. (15 grams)
Success Oil
Bamba Wood Charcoal or Self Igniting Charcoal
Triple Power Candle

Grind Sacred Bark and Olibanum well, and then add Myrrh, Sandalwood, and Saltpeter. Anoint Triple Power Candle with Success Oil from bottom to top. Light Incense and then light candle. Read Psalm #4. Repeat daily until you have achieved your goal.

## Formula for Influencing Others in a Positive Manner

Ingredients:
John the Conqueror Incense, 4 oz. (110 grams)
Senna Powder, 2 oz. (60 grams)
Special Favors Oil
Your Zodiac Oil
Attraction Powder
Self-Igniting Charcoal

Mix John the Conqueror Incense and Senna Powder thoroughly. Burn a little on self-igniting charcoals in your home or business each day. Put 10 drops of Special Favors Oil in your bath each day. Use Attraction Powder and your Zodiac oil on your body each day.

## Formula for Landlord to Keep Property Rented

Ingredients:
Spearmint, 2 oz. (60 grams)
Sandalwood Powder, 4 oz. (110 grams)
House Blessing Powder, 4 oz. (110 grams)
Van Van Floor Wash
Spring Mint Oil
Success Oil
Self-Igniting Charcoal

Grind the Spearmint with a mortar and pestle and blend with the Sandalwood and House Blessing Powder.

Wash all floors with the Van Van Floor Wash (Mix bottle into mop water). Incense each room thoroughly. Anoint door knobs with Spring Mint Oil and apply the Success Oil on yourself.

## Formula to Rescue a Failing Business

Ingredients:
Squill Root, 1 Tbsp. (12 grams)
Sea Salt or Kosher Salt, 1 Tbsp. (12 grams)
Water, 1 Pint (120 cc)
John the Conqueror Root, 1 piece
Red Bag, one that will accommodate the piece of John the Conqueror root.
Red Clover, 1 tsp. (7 grams)
Broom Top, 1 tsp. (7 grams)
White Thread
Money Oil
Money Drawing Incense
Double Strength John the Conqueror Incense
Cubeb Berries
Self-Igniting Incense

*Mix the Squill Root, salt, and water. Place in a dark place for 7 days. Strain and sprinkle the isles and corners of your business each day before opening. *Place the John the Conqueror Root with the Red Clover and the Broom Top herb in the Red Bag. *Sew shut with the white thread. Sprinkle the bag with 7 drops of Money Oil every 7 days. *Mix the John the Conqueror incense, Money Drawing Incense, and Cubeb Berries together. Burn a little each morning before opening for business. Read Psalm 114 daily.

# Floor Wash for Business Success

DOCK    *(Anethum graveolens)*
Gender: Masculine    Planet: Mercury    Element: Fire

Ingredients:
Dock, 1 oz. (30 grams)
Water, 1 Quart (950 cc)

Mix and bring to a boil.  Remove from heat and steep for 15 minutes.  Strain and use to clean all doorknobs in a business or home and add to mop water to clean floors.  This formula is considered a money drawing blend.

# Formula to Influence a Trial Verdict

Ingredients:
Cascara Sagrada    (Sacred Bark, *Rhamnus Purshiana*)
Black Arts Oil
Clean Piece of White Cloth
John the Conqueror Incense
Self-Igniting Charcoal
Success Candle
Calendula Flowers

Take a tsp. (dram) of Cascara Sagrada and sprinkle it with ten drops of Black Arts Oil.  Mix thoroughly and place on a piece of clean white cloth.  Fold the cloth in a square and place under your mattress for nine consecutive nights before your Trial.  On the morning of the Trial, light some John the Conqueror Incense with a little Cascara Sagrada added.  Light a Success candle and read Psalm #7 aloud.  Take the white cloth from under your mattress and burn it.  Before leaving for Court place some Calendula Flowers in your pocket.

You can find the recipes for the Oils and Incense in Chapter 13.  Prior to the date of your Trial you additionally could burn some Success incense daily, meditate for fifteen minutes visualizing a favorable verdict.

The perfect time for spells of liberation are with a Moon in a Fire Sign exactly on a Mars-Sun cusp.  I know that often this is not possible, but if so there is a much better chance for success.

If you cannot find a Success candle you can use a small brown candle daily or a seven day glass encased brown novena candle. You could also make your own Success Candle following the directions in Chapter 14. Recipes for oils and incenses can be found in Chapter 13. Make sure your candles are clean physically and then visualize them energetically clean. On small candles anoint from top to center with Success Oil, then from bottom to center. On glass encased seven day candles anoint in a clockwise motion. You can burn a little John the Conqueror incense while performing the ritual. Take the remains of your candle drippings and bury in the Earth dropping a penny in before covering the remains.

## Formula for Success in Court
Ingredients:
Galangal Root    (*Alpina Officinalis*)
Gender: Masculine     Planet: Mars      Element: Fire

1 Piece of Galangal Root
1 part Olibanum Incense
1 Part Mystic Incense
Orange Cross Candle
Success Oil
Self-Igniting Charcoal

Cut the Galangal Root into small pieces. Mix equal parts of both incenses together and each night before your case goes to Court, burn some of this incense mix with a piece of the Galangal Root. Anoint the Orange Cross candle with the Success Oil from top to center and bottom to center. Light the Candle while reading Psalm #20. Repeat this ritual every night at sundown until the day you must appear in Court. Place a piece of the Galangal Root in your pocket before leaving for Court.

The perfect time for spells of liberation is with a Moon in a Fire Sign exactly on a Mars-Sun cusp. I know that often this is not possible, but if so, there is a much better chance for success.

# Formula for Helping Someone released from Prison

Ingredients:
Hydrangea Root    (*Hydrangea arborescens*) (Seven Barks)
Hydrangea Root, 1 oz. (30 grams)
Mystic Incense, 6 oz. (180 grams):  See Chapter 13 for recipe.
Frankincense Powder, 2 oz. (60 grams)
Salt Peter, ½ oz. (15 grams)
Parchment Paper
Dove's Blood Ink
Orange Seven Day Candle
Large Metal Pan (ex:  a medium size pizza pan)

Mix and grind well with a mortar and pestle the Hydrangea Root, Mystic Rites Incense, Frankincense powder, and Salt Peter.  Place a mound of mixture in the center of the metal pan and then make six small mounds around the large mound in the center.  Light the center mound first and then the six other mounds.

On the parchment paper write the name of the person you want released from jail or prison with the Dove's Blood ink.  Light the Orange Seven Day Candle and place the parchment paper under the candle.  Read Psalms #26 three times.  Allow the candle to burn out.  Repeat the ritual daily after sunset until the person you want is released.  If the Orange candle goes out, light another.

**\*Please bear in mind with these types of spells it will depend on the person's Karma and on the type and degree of the crime committed.**

# CHAPTER SIX

## BANISHING AND UNCROSSING FORMULAS

Banishing and Uncrossing formulas are used for those who are believed to be enchanted or cursed. These rituals should be used during the waning of the Moon, from Full Moon to New Moon. Do not perform on a sunset Friday to sunset on Saturday, this energy should only be used to thwart. The exception is when using a 7, 14, or 21 day spell. If the one cursing you is a woman do not perform on a Tuesday or in any Mars energy (sunset Monday to sunset Tuesday). The exception is a gay woman for in Kabbalah we believe that lesbians are male souls in a female vessel. Additionally, an effeminate gay man would, within my belief system, would be a female soul in a male vessel, so the Mars energy should not be used on these. However, the Mars energy could be used on a very masculine gay man. Again, this is the specs according to my belief system. Unless you are a Scorpio or have many Scorpio aspects in your natal chart, DO NOT go after anyone in a Scorpio sun or moon, for often it will backfire. During this time it is best to let sleeping dogs lie.

## Uncrossing Incense
BAYBERRY   (*Myrica cerifra*)

Ingredients:
Bayberry Herb, 4 oz. (115 grams)
Uncrossing Incense, 4 oz. (115 grams)
Dragons Blood Oil
Self-igniting charcoal

Grind the Bayberry with a mortar and pestle. Blend well with the Uncrossing Incense. Drop 7 drops of Dragon's Blood Oil on the hot charcoal then add the Bayberry blend as needed. It is recommended once in the morning and once in the evening with the exception of Saturdays and after vespers on Friday. Perform this during the waning of the moon from the Full Moon to the New Moon.

## Floor Wash to Thwart Poltergeists
BISTORT   (*Polygonum bistorta*)
Gender: Feminine   Planet: Saturn   Element: Earth
Ingredients:
Bistort, 1 oz. (30 grams)
Water, 1 quart
Add Bistort to boiling water and steep for 15 minutes. Strain and add to mop water.

## Banish an Enemy from your Space

**Ingredients for Banishing Incense:**
Patchouly Leaves, 3 oz. (90 grams)
Lavender, 12 oz.
Frankincense, 8 oz.
Sandalwood, 12 oz.
Myrrh, 4oz.
Orris Powder, 8 oz.
Black Hawk Bark, 2 oz.
Winters Bark, 2 oz.
Saltpeter, 1 oz.

Grind and mix all ingredients thoroughly.

**Ingredients for Ritual:**
Dragon's Blood Powder
Dove's Blood Ink
Parchment Paper
Lodestone
Self-igniting charcoal

This ritual is to be performed at Midnight for seven consecutive nights. Ignite your charcoal 10 minutes before midnight so it is hot. At Midnight start adding a little incense and while the incense is burning on a small piece of parchment paper write the name of the one coming up against you in Dove's Blood Ink. Lay it on the Burning Incense and using all that is within you, say the name of that one 3 times. Now make of circle around the incense burner using the Dragon's Blood powder. Place the Lodestone in front of the incense burner and go to bed. In the morning clear everything away and repeat until you reach a total of seven nights.

## Uncrossing Formula
**Blood Root**   (*Sanguinaria canadensis L*)
Gender: Masculine   Planet: Mars   Element: Fire

Ingredients:
Blood Root, 4 oz. (115 grams)
Uncrossing Powder, 8 oz.
Self-Igniting Charcoal
*Grind Blood Root with a Mortar and Pestle then blend well with Uncrossing Incense. Burn for seven consecutive nights to remove Ju Ju from a residence. Sprinkle outside around the residence.

*Pieces of Blood Root can be thrown on the doorstep of the person coming up against you and it is said that the negative energy they are sending you will be returned to them three to tenfold.

## Spell Breaking Formula
Boneset   (*Eurpatorium perfoliatum*)
Gender: Feminine    Planet: Saturn    Element: Water

Ingredients:
Boneset Herb, enough to stuff doll
Material to make a doll to stuff
Thread and Needle to sew Doll
Red Embroidery Thread and Needle
Ju Ju Oil
Small Hammer or Mallet
Goofer Dust
Balmony Herb
Small piece of a brown paper bag
Red Ink Pen

Make a doll with the fabric and sew leaving an opening.  Stuff the doll with the Boneset Herb.  Write the person's name on the brown paper 9 times with red ink.  Place this inside the doll before sewing it up.

Embroider the eyes, nose, and mouth with the red thread.  With the Ju Ju Oil while anointing the doll say: With this oil I do officially name you (name of the one coming up against you).  Lay the enemy on his back and hit the leg with the hammer while saying:  With this hammer I break your (if it is a man the right leg, if it is a woman the left leg) ____ leg (enemies' name).

Exactly at Midnight during a waning moon sprinkle the doll with Goofer Dust and bury.  As you are covering the doll representing your enemy, say:  "In the Dark of the Night by the waning of the Moon I bury (offender's name) All is Done, All is Done, All is Done to seal his (or her) Doom.  What you have sent to me and mine will be returned to you three to tenfold.  As I say it so it shall be done!"

Sprinkle the Grave with Balmony Herb.  Turn, walk away and <u>DO NOT LOOK BACK,</u> otherwise your spell will be broken and the Ju Ju will be brought upon your own head.

## Brimstone Fumigation

Brimstone (Sulphur) is a mineral and is used to thwart evil.
Place on self-igniting incense.

If you are going to fumigate your home, make certain that no one is in the home including pets.
At Midnight during a waning moon burn a little outside your front and back door.

## Formula for Creating a Shield of Protection around your Home
Ingredients:
Sulphur, 4 oz. (115 grams)
Bone Meal, 4 oz. (115 grams)
Egg, 4
Small Plastic Bags, 4 (sandwich size)

You can purchase the Sulphur and Bone Meal at a hardware store. Evenly distribute the Sulphur, Bone Meal, and Eggs in the 4 plastic bags. On a Saturday at Midnight during a waning Moon bury one bag at each of the four corners of your home while visualizing a force field around your home. Start at the front right corner then to the left right corner. In the back, first right and then left corner.

## The Equalizer Reversible Formula
*Please note this formula is very powerful despite the appearance of so called light ingredients. Only use this if you know who is coming up against you and the harm they directed your way must be of a serious nature not petty. This is not a toy to target just anyone randomly.

Ingredients:
White Shabbat Candle, 1
Small White Plate, 1
Clear Glass, 1-8oz
Kosher or Sea Salt
Small Piece of Brown Paper, no larger than 2" x 3"
Red Pen
Knives, 2 small
Poster Putty, white
Self-Igniting Charcoal
Power Incense

<u>Preparation</u>: An hour before Midnight during a waning moon, gather your materials and start burning some Reversible Incense. On The brown paper with the red pen write the name of the one coming up against you 9 times. If there is more than one person on another piece of brown paper write their name 9 times. <u>Do not reverse to more than 3 people at one time</u>. While you are working inject your energy.

Take the white Shabbat candle and cut the top off to form a flat surface. On what would have been the bottom, take a lighter and burn off enough until you have enough wick to light. If you only have tea candles, remove from metal, take the wick out and place in the other end and return to metal holder. Add 9 drops of Reversible Oil on the candle. Wearing plastic gloves at the middle of the candle in a counter clockwise manner stroke the oil out to the top and repeat from the middle to the bottom of the candle.

Take the knives and form an X. If the knives will not stay together use a little of the poster putty. Fill the 8 oz. glass with water, place white plate on top of glass. Take this where you will be performing ritual. I recommend the back door. Turnover and set on floor. Sprinkle a generous amount of salt around the glass. Place the brown paper with names face down on top of glass. Place the X knives on top of papers. Place the white candle on top of the knives. If the candle will not hold, place a little poster putty on the bottom and then place on the knives.

At Midnight during a waning moon, light add more Reversible Incense, light the white candle, stand or sit in front of the candle and visualize all negative energy returning to those who have come up against you. Do not dictate your desired retribution for the Universe will determine this. Plead your case as though you were in a court of law. Meditate on this for at least 15 minutes. Turn and walk away and allow candle to burn out.

In the morning take remains out the back door, release the water with your projective hand (the one you do not write with). Burn the remaining paper and send the negative energy back in the wind Wear a pair of plastic gloves and rinse the plate, glass, and knives. Secure these and only use for ritual purposes. Usually within 3 days you will hear information which will confirm that your reversal has worked. The Universe tends to exact justice in a balanced manner.

# Uncrossing Bath
Ingredients:
White Clover, 1/2 oz. (15 grams)
Blue Vervain, 1/2 oz. (15 grams)
Broom tops, 1/2 oz. (15 grams)
Water, 1 gallon
Uncrossing Oil
Dragon Blood Bath Crystals

Mix White Clover, Blue Vervain, and Broom tops in the water. Store in a dark place for 3 days. On the fourth day strain and add 21 drops of uncrossing oil. Add 1 cup of this mixture and 1 Tbsp. of Dragon Blood Crystal to your bath each day or 10 consecutive days.

Burn Uncrossing Incense each day while taking your bath. Visualize the negative energy leaving you and your space.

## House Clearing Formula

This formula if performed properly will remove all unwanted spirits from a home.

Ingredients:
Red Clover, 1 oz. (30 grams)
White Vinegar, 1 pint (460 cc)
Qabal Incense
Self-Igniting Charcoals
Seven Day Trinity Candle

Add the Red Clover to the White Vinegar and soak in a dark area for 3 days. Strain and sprinkle this in each corner of every room each day for seven days. Burn Qabal incense each morning and each night for seven days. Place a Seven Day Trinity Candle in the appropriate room and allow to burn out. Use the Lord's Prayer or your favorite deliverance prayers while using this formula to banish the unwanted spirits.

After finishing this ritual always perform a House Blessing during the Waxing of the Moon.

## Anti-Gossiping Formula

This formula is used to stop others from slandering and/or gossiping about you.

Ingredients:
Cloves Powder, 2 oz. (60 grams)
Tiphreth Incense, 8 oz. (225 grams)
Self-Igniting Charcoal
Brown Paper, 2" x 3"
Red Pen

Blend the Cloves Powder and the Tiphreth Incense thoroughly. Once in the morning and again after sunset burn some of this incense while writing the name of the gossiper nine times on the brown paper with red ink. Carefully burn this paper to ashes as you visualize the tongue of the slanderer burning with all their words coming back on them. Bury the ashes in the North in your back yard or elsewhere as long as it is in the North. Read Psalm 48. Perform this ritual for ten consecutive days and nights.

## Uncrossing Bath

Cinquefoil   (*Potentilla canadensis*) also called Five Finger Grass
Gender: Masculine   Planet: Jupiter   Element: Fire
Ingredients:
Cinquefoil, 1/2 oz.  (15 grams)
Water, I Quart (1 Liter)
Boil the water and steep the Cinquefoil for 15 minutes and then strain.
Add 1/4 (60 cc) to running bath water. Soak for at least 15 minutes for nine consecutive nights.

## Reversible

Ingredients:
Nettle, 1 oz. (30 grams)
Goofer Dust
Graveyard Dust (actual dirt from a cemetery)
Double Action Jumbo Candle (Black & Red, glass encased can be used as well)
Obeah Oil
Coffin Nail
Black Cord
Brown Paper Bag

Thoroughly mix the Nettle, Goofer Dust, and Graveyard Dust.

Anoint the Candle with Obeah Oil. Lengthwise from top to bottom with the coffin nail engrave the name of the one coming up against you. If you do not know the name engrave, "The one who is coming up against me."

If you use a glass encased candle, engrave the name in the one coming up against you in the top of the candle. Anoint with the Obeah Oil. Take 9 Cloves and stick into the top of the candle. Add a little black pepper and 1 drop of Mercury as well.

Tie the black cord into 9 knots 1 inch apart. As you tie each knot say: "I bind you, (name of enemy), from doing harm to me and others. Again if you do not know the name, say "I bind you who are coming up against me."

Light the candle and say: May the evil that you (name of enemy) be reversed back to you tenfold. May the monster that you have created, now be your own and the harm fall upon your head. You may even spit as if you are spitting on your enemy.

Place the Nettle Mixture in the Brown Paper Bag including the black cord with the 9 knots.

Take the package to the nearest cemetery and throw the package on the first grave you see and **do not look back**. Leave 9 pennies or 9 purple flowers at the entrance of the cemetery.

Allow the candle to burn out. Take all the remains and discard far away from your home.

## Uncrossing Amulet

Ingredients and Supplies:
Chamois Bag, 2
Stone Root
Wolfbane
Tanna Berries (Devil's Pepper)
Goofer Dust
Unakite Stone
Black Thread and Needle
Uncrossing Oil
Uncrossing Incense
Self-Igniting charcoal

Add a little of the Stone Root, Wolfbane, Tanna Berries, Goofer Dust and the Unakite Stone into the Chamois bag and sew it shut. Anoint the bags with uncrossing oil. Carry one on your person and place the other under your pillow. Each day for 9 consecutive days burn a little of the uncrossing incense.

# Anti-Gossiping Ritual

Ingredients and Supplies:
Egyptian Kyphi
Controlling Incense
Self-Igniting Charcoal
Southern John the Conqueror Root
Slippery Elm Herb
Red Bag
Uncrossing Bath
Poppet (Voodoo Doll)
Long Stick Pin
Crossing Oil
Red Pen or Marker
Peace Water

Place a small piece of John the Conqueror Root in the small red bag and carry on your person.

Burn a little of the Egyptian Kyphi and Controlling Incense each day for nine consecutive days.

Add one 1 Tbsp. (15 cc) of Uncrossing Bath to your daily bath for nine consecutive days.

Anoint the Voodoo Doll with the Crossing Oil while officially giving the doll your enemy's name. With the red pin or marker write your enemy's name on the torso of the doll, lengthwise from the neck down. Sprinkle the doll, your enemy, heavily with the Slippery Elm herb. Place the Long Stick Pin all the way through the mouth through the back of the head. Bury far away from your home.

Sprinkle Peace Water in every corner of your home for ten consecutive days.

# CHAPTER SEVEN

# SPIRITUAL, PSYCHIC & CONJURING SPIRITS

## Spirit Vision
Ingredients:
Canadian Snake Root, 2 oz. (60 grams)
Tibet Powder Incense, 8 oz. (225 grams)
Self-Igniting Charcoal

Grind the Snake Root and mix thoroughly with the Tibet Powder Incense.  Use when scrying, performing readings, etc...

## Concentration Incense
Ingredients:
Celery Seed, 1 oz. (30 grams)
Nirvana Incense (grain and resin type, not sticks), 6 oz.  (180 grams)
Self-Igniting Charcoal

Use this for spiritual work that requires intense concentration.

## Spirit Vision Tea
Ingredients:
Dandelion, 1 oz. (30 grams)
Water, 1 Quart (950 cc)

Perform this procedure before retiring.  Boil Dandelion in Water for 7 minutes.  Drink one cup as tea.  Place the remaining in a bowl near your bedside.  Retire and you should receive visions within your dreams.

## Astral Travel Incense

Ingredients:
Dittany of Crete
Sandalwood
Benzoin
Vanillin Powder
Self-Igniting Charcoal

Mix in equal parts Dittany of Crete, Sandalwood, Benzoin, and Vanillin Powder. Burn this mixture when you plan Astral Travel.

## Prophetic Dreams Incense

Ingredients:
Dragon Blood Powder, 1/2 oz. (15 grams)
Aloes Powder, 1/2 oz. (15 grams)
Cinnamon Powder, 1 oz. (30 grams)
Tibet Incense Powder, 8 oz. (225 grams)
Self-Igniting Charcoal

Mix together well and use when retiring to encourage prophetic dreams.

## Prophetic Vision Incense

Ingredients:
Sandalwood Incense, 1 oz. (30 grams)
Hermes (Mercury) Incense, 1 oz. (30 grams)
Mystic Incense, 1 oz. (30 grams)
Meditation Incense, 2 oz. (60 grams)
Anise Seed, 1 oz. (30 grams)
Myrtle, 1 oz. (30 grams)
Gentian, 2 oz. (60 grams)
Saltpeter, 1/2 oz. (15 grams)
Self-Igniting Charcoal

Grind Myrtle, Gentian, and Anise Seed well with a mortar and pestle. Blend well with Incenses and Saltpeter. Burn a small amount of this mixture during meditation and/or before retiring. Recipes for the incenses can be found in Chapter 13.

## Past Lives Recall Ritual

Ingredients:
Periwinkle, 1 oz. (30 grams)
Mystic Incense, 2 oz. (60 grams)
Tiphareth Incense, 1 oz. (30 grams)
Frankincense, 1 oz. (30 grams)
Hermes (Mercury) Incense, 1 oz. (30 grams)
White Jumbo Candle
Purple Jumbo Candle
Master Oil
Large Mirror for scrying (Restrict the use of this mirror for spiritual work)

Crush and Grind the Periwinkle with a mortar and pestle. Blend into Incenses and mix all together thoroughly. Place white candle on a 3" stand in the middle of an altar or table. Place the purple candle directly in front of the white candle. Place a mirror behind the candles propped up or leaning against a wall. Light the white candle first and then the purple. To the right with hot charcoal in an incense holder add some of the incense mixture.

Anoint your temples and palms of your hands with Master Oil.

Sit in a comfortable chair and gaze, don't strain, at the candles. Usually the mirror will cloud up and you may see your face as it was in a prior incarnation. You may also see scenes of past incarnations as well. At times there may be several changes. If you tire within 30 minutes snuff the candles out, don't be discouraged, and try another day for the timing may not be right.

Recipe for oils and incenses can be found in Chapter 13.

## Prophetic Dreams Incense II

Ingredients:
Sea Spirit, 16 oz. (450 grams)
Gentian, 8 oz. (225 grams)
Sandalwood Powder, 6 oz. (180 grams)
Myrrh, 2 oz. (60 grams)
Dittany of Crete 3 oz. (85 grams)
Cinnamon Powder, 2 oz., (60 grams)
Spikenard, 3 oz. (85 grams)
Olibanum Tears, 3 oz. (85 grams)
Self-Igniting Charcoal

Crush and Grind with a mortar and pestle the Sea Spirit, Gentian, Dittany of Crete, and Spikenard as fine as possible. Blend well with the other powders. Burn a little each night before retiring or during meditation.

## Astral Travel & Prophetic Vision Formula

Ingredients:
Sandalwood Powder, 24 oz. (680 grams)
Lavender, 24 oz. (680 grams)
Bayberry Powder, 8 oz. (225 grams)
Capsicum Powder, 1 oz. (30 grams)

Cassia Powder, 1 oz. (30 grams)
Orris Root Powder, 8 oz. (225 grams)
Patchouli Leaves, 4 oz. (115 grams)
Gentian, 2 oz. (60 grams)
Winters Bark, 4 oz. (115 grams)
Elm bark, 1 oz. (30 grams)
Frankincense Powder, 16 oz. (450 grams)
Rose Petals & Hips, 8 oz. (225 grams)
Saltpeter, 2 oz. (60 grams)
Tannis Berries (Devils Pepper)
Tryst Oil (Recipe in Chapter 13)
Self-Igniting Charcoal or Bamba Wood Charcoal

Crush and Grind with a Mortar and Pestle the Lavender, Gentian, Winters Bark, Elm Bark, and Rose Petals and Hips as fine as possible. Blend thoroughly with the other powders and Saltpeter.

Before retiring or meditation burn a little of this mixture. Anoint your temples and palms in additions to your pillow with Tryst Oil.

## Scrying, Prophetic Dream, and Astral Travel Formula
Mugwort   (*Artemisia Vulgais*)
Gender: Feminine  Planet: Venus  Element: Earth

Ingredients:
1 part Mugwort
1 part Wolfbane
1 part Tanna Berries
1 part Mystic Incense
Self-Igniting Charcoal

Blend the Mugwort, Wolfbane, Tanna Berries, and Mystic incense well. Burn a little on self-igniting charcoal while crystal gazing or other forms of scrying. You can also make an oil from the ingredients by following the directions under OILS in Chapter 13. The recipe for Mystic incense can be found in Chapter 13 as well.

You can stuff a pillow with Mugwort which is said to attract prophetic dreams. It is also said you can soak a little Mugwort into some red wine and when taken exactly before bed time will aid in astral projection.

# Formula for Invoking the Angelic Forces

Ingredients:
1 part Pipsissewa
2 parts Rose Hips
1 part Violets
1 part Vanillin
1 part Salt Peter
Seven Color, (Seven Powers or Rainbow) Candle
Self-Igniting Charcoal

Grind and Blend the Pipsissewa, Rose Hips, Violets, and Vanillin. Add the saltpeter. During an hour of Venus at sundown light some of the incense. Light the Seven Power candle and read Psalm #61 aloud. Meditate for five to fifteen minutes. Petition the Angels regarding your desire or what troubles you. Repeat this ritual for seven days and the angels will come to your aid as long as it does not interfere with your karma. Allow the candle to burn out, do not extinguish it yourself.

The Angels must be called upon for assistance for they cannot interfere with our free will. Call upon **Archangel Michael** first for he and the Angels of Protection clear the path and remove obstacles. Call upon **Archangel Raphael** if you or someone you know needs healing. **Jophiel** can help with studying for tests, freedom from addictions, dissolution of arrogance and ignorance, clarity, and illumination. **Chamuel** for protection against slander and gossip, new friendships, repairing damaged relationships, finding a job, and finding lost objects, ( if you are looking for a lost item repeat the word "reach" over and over, if it is within your vicinity you will find it.). **Gabriel** for guidance, communication issues, home purchases, and your life mission. **Uriel** for peaceful resolution of issues, personal, social, or professional. Divine justice in matters in courtrooms and between nations. **Zadkiel** for tolerance, joy, and diplomacy. The angels of abundance and prosperity are **Archangel Raziel, Gadiel, Barakeil, Gamaliel,** and **Pathiel.** Call on them individually or as a team. Naturally your Guardian Angel is always with you, unless you have sold your soul to either Satan or another example would be those who have been initiated into Palo Mayombe for they now rely on other sources for protection.

**Formula to Request the Assistance from Elementals who Guard Earth Treasures**

Ingredients:
Pipsissewa, 1 oz. (30 grams)
Eucalyptus, ½ oz. (30 grams)
Acacia, 1 oz. (30 grams)
Bayberry Herb, 5 oz. (150 grams)
Juniper Berries, 1 oz. (30 grams)
Job's Tears, 1 oz. (30 grams)
Red Cinchona Bark, 1 oz. (30 grams)

Grind and Blend all ingredients in a mortar and pestle as fine as possible. Locate a clearing outdoors were it is permissible to make a small fire. Build a small fire and once it is burning well, face the West and sprinkle a handful of the herb mix into the flames and then say, "Hearken unto me, Guardians of the Earth yield to me thy goods of worth!"

Sprinkle another handful of herbs into the fire and repeat the command. Sprinkle another handful of herbs into the fire and repeat the command once more. Sit in quiet meditation for at least thirty minutes. After your meditation extinguish the fire. Repeat the ritual every seven days and it is said that the Gnomes will reveal to you in a dream the location of treasures.

## Formula for Invoking the Water Spirits

Ingredients:
Bladderwrack   (Seawrack, *Fucus visiculosus*)
Gender: Feminine   Planet: Moon   Element: Water

Bladderwrack, 8 oz. (225 grams)
Anise Seed, 4 oz. (120 grams)
Lavender, 12 oz. (450 grams)
Orris Root, 8 oz. (225 grams)
Witch's Grass, 3 oz. (85 grams)
Dittany of Crete, 4 oz. (120 grams)
Winters Bark, 2 oz. (60 grams)
Bayberry, 8 oz. (225 grams)
Caraway Seeds, 1 oz. (30 grams)

Grind and Blend ingredients well. Find an open clearing on a beach, near an ocean or river. Build a small fire. Sprinkle a handful of the herbs into the fire while facing the water and say, "Hearken unto me, Spirits of the Water and Sea, Hear my Voice, Leap,

Rejoice, Come now unto me." Repeat this two more times. Pause and while facing the Water make your request to the Water Spirits aloud. Pour the remaining herb mixture into the fire and meditate for at least thirty minutes. Carefully extinguish the fire. It is said that if this ritual is done once a week for nine weeks the Water and Sea will grant your wish.

## Formula for Calling the Spirits of the Dead

Ingredients:
Wood Betony, 16 oz. (450 grams)
Olibanum, 8 oz. (225 grams)
Wormwood, 2 oz. (60 grams)
Cubeb Berries, 2 oz. (60 grams)
Sandalwood, 6 oz. (180 grams)
Gentian, 1 oz. (30 grams)
Vetivert, 2 oz. (60 grams)
Musk Powder, 4 oz. (120 grams)
Saltpeter, ¼ oz. (7 grams)
Self-Igniting Charcoal

Grind and Blend as fine as possible the Wood betony, Wormwood, Cubeb Berries, Gentian, and Vetivert, then add the remaining ingredients. This is commonly used for séances.

It is recommended that you burn some of this incense at Midnight. Meditate and call the name(s) of those you wish to come forth. Bear in mind that on the person you wish to speak with may not be available for on the other side time is factored in for it is indigenous to this planet. Be tenacious, but if you do not receive any results the person you wish to contact more than likely has moved on and is on another plane.

# The Green Fairy
## Wormwood (Artemisia absinthium)

**Wormwood** is the common name for *Artemisia absinthium,* the plant whose aromatic oil is used to make absinthe. Although absinthe contains extracts from a whole variety of different plants, wormwood oil is *the* key ingredient of the famed green drink, and perhaps the reason why absinthe is quite unlike any other liquor ever produced. Wormwood is a wild plant of the daisy family. Native to Europe, it can now be found in many other parts of the world, especially North America.

But the otherwise ordinarily-looking wormwood plant holds a secret: its aromatic leaves and flowers are naturally rich in the terpene thujone an aromatic, bitter substance *believed to induce an inexplicable clarity of thought, increased sense of perception, enhanced creativity, inspiration and the ability to "see beyond"* --- as all the famous absinthe drinkers amongst nineteenth century poets, writers, painters and other artists discovered.

**The Green Fairy** is the English translation of ***La Fee Verte,*** the affectionate French nickname given to the celebrated absinthe drink in the nineteenth century. But Green Fairy isn't just another name for absinthe: she is a metaphorical concept of artistic enlightenment and exploration, of poetic inspiration, of a freer state of mind, of new ideas, of a changing social order. To the original bohemians of 1890s Paris, the Fairy was a welcomed symbol of transformation. She was the trusted guide en-route to artistic innovation.

Transformation has always been the fundamental essence of the Green Fairy, for transformation is what she provides on several parallels. During the magical ritual of la louche, the drink itself first transforms from the concentrated, alcohol-rich, deep emerald green liquor into an alluring opalescent, cloudy greenish-white mixture. This, of course, is symbolic of the subsequent transformation that shall take place in the drinker's mind. As the cool water liberates the power of wormwood oil and the other herbal ingredients from the green concentrate, so will new ideas, concepts and notions be set free in the mind of the drinker --- be he a poet, an artist, a scientist, or the common man on the street.

**The Absinthe Ritual of La Louche** (pronounced " LOOSH") When absinthe is louched, cold water is added to the beverage, triggering a reaction which causes the original emerald green drink to cloud and turn an opalescent shade of milky green. When louching is performed with a practiced hand, billows of milky color ripple through the glass, creating a luminescent glow which is quite distinctive. The ratio of water to absinthe varies, depending on the absinthe and personal taste, although a 1:3 ratio of absinthe to water is very common.

In some cases, louching is performed by dripping cold water through a sugar cube positioned on an absinthe spoon at the top of the glass. This form of louching sweetens the absinthe as well as clouding it, masking the bitter flavor of natural absinthe. The sugar cube also acts as a filter, slowing the flow rate of the water to ensure that it drips slowly into the glass, as dumping water into a glass of absinthe does not achieve the desired aesthetic effect. La Louche truly *is* a ritual -- a fairly elaborate one -- and an essential absinthe experience: practical, symbolic, aesthetic. To *louche* your absinthe means so much more than to water it down. The Louche ritual, we might say, expresses the very essence of the phenomenon that is absinthe.

**To invoke the magic of the Green Fairy in the traditional way, you will need:**

- A Bottle of Absinthe, high quality which will louche
- A jug of iced, still water -- quality spring water such as Evian
- Sugar cube
- Glass
- Absinthe spoon

**(1)** To begin with, pour a shot of genuine absinthe (4cl) into a glass. A traditional-style absinthe glass (or even an antique one) will add to the magic of the ritual, but do not worry too much if you haven't got one -- just use a standard wine glass instead.

**(2)** Next, rest a perforated absinthe spoon over the glass, and place a cube of white sugar onto the spoon.

**(3)** Finally, slowly pour iced water over until the sugar dissolves, while observing the beautiful play of color that takes place as a result of the *louche* process. The amount of water to add depends on your own preference. Depending on the strength desired, you should end up with a mixture of one part absinthe and two to four parts water.

# CHAPTER EIGHT

# MISCELLANEOUS

## Peace Formula for the Home

Ingredients:
Cumin Seed, 1 tsp. (5 ml.)
Peace Water, 8 oz. (225 grams)
Peace Incense
Seven Day Peace Candle
Bergamot Oil
Peace Powder
Jinx Removing Powder
Self-Igniting Charcoal

Soak Cumin Seed in Peace Water for three days. Strain and sprinkle a few drops in each corner of every room of the house. Every evening after sundown burn some Peace Incense. Light a Peace Candle and allow it to burn out. Upon rising anoint yourself with Bergamot Oil and sprinkle some Peace Powder on your chest. Sprinkle the Jinx Removing Powder all around the outside of the house.

You can find the recipes for most of the ingredients in Chapter 13.

## Formula to Neutralize the Anger of Another

Ingredients:
Passion Flower, 1 oz. (30 grams)
Orris Root, small piece
Rosemary, ½ oz. (15 grams)
Saffron, ½ oz. (15 grams)
Thyme, 1 oz. (30 grams)
Violets, 2 oz. (60 grams)
Gentian, 1 oz. (30 grams)
Red Rose Oil
Clean New Sharp Nail
White Image Candle
Self-Igniting Charcoal

Grind and Blend well with a mortar and pestle the Passion Flower, Orris Root, Rosemary, Saffron, Thyme, Violets, and Gentian. Take the nail and inscribe the name of the person of interest on the back of the Image candle. Female if person of interest is a female and Male if the person of interest is a male. Write from the feet to the head. Anoint with Rose Oil. Anoint from the waist out towards the head and then from the waist out towards the feet. Light some of the incense you have prepared and read Psalm #16. Light the candle in an area with no drafts. Meditate for five to fifteen minutes visualizing the person of interest becoming a calm person and allow the candle to burn for one hour. Repeat this ritual daily until completely burned down. Gather the drippings and bury as far away from your home as possible. This ritual is best performed from Full Moon to New Moon, a waning moon.

Rose Oil can be made using a cup of golden colored olive oil and the petals of several red roses. Place in a dry safe place and infuse for 28 days. Initiate this during a waxing moon. Refer to Chapter 13 under OILS.

## Formula to Maintain Peace in the Home

Ingredients:
St. Johns Wort (*Hypericum perforatum*)
Gender: Masculine    Planet: Sun    Element: Fire

St. Johns Wort, 1 oz. (30 grams)
Huckleberry Herb, 1 oz. (30 grams) (Also known as Bilberry)
*Simmer this mixture in 1 quart of spring water for 20 minutes. Strain and 1 cup (250 ml) to your floor wash. Sprinkle on window sills and doors while visualizing a peaceful energy to your home.

## Formula for Protection from Home Invasion

Ingredients:
Vetivert Leaves, 3 oz. (90 grams)
Lavender, 12 oz. (340 grams)
Winters Bark, 2 oz. (60 grams)
Cloves, 2 oz. (60 grams)
Cinnamon, 2 oz. (60 grams)
Sandalwood, 4 oz. (120 grams)
Myrrh, 4 oz. (120 grams)
Olibanum, 8 oz. (225 grams0
Saltpeter, ¼ oz. (7 grams)
Self-Igniting Charcoal

With a mortar and pestle crush and grind Vetivert and Winters Bark as fine as possible then add remaining ingredients. Burn a small amount of this incense blend before leaving your home.

## Formula for Getting Rid of Monsters Inside You

What I am referring to are actual living things, such as snakes, spiders, frog spawn, insects, – yes, people can actually put these creatures into your body. Do not accept food from people that you do not know or frenemies. Ice cream is commonly used to hide insect eggs. If you are at an outing, get your own food and that of your children. If someone you know have monsters inside as a result of jujube make an emetic of Poke Root, Olive Oil, and Saltpeter. Another emetic is boiling Black Root with some Alum, make a tea and after three doses this should cause vomiting. You could also purchase ipecac at a pharmacy. Hold a pan while they are vomiting for these monsters may still be alive.

## Formula for Avoiding Being Poisoned through the Feet

Ingredients:
Black Pepper
Fear Not to Walk over Evil Powder
1 Dime

Often if you have enemies who are into unconventional belief systems they will place poisonous powders in your path. Also they could have lifted your footprint. You can shield yourself from this by making a mixture of the black pepper and fear not to walk over evil powder. Sprinkle this in your shoes. If you are right handed place the dime in the left shoe face up and if you are left handed place the dime in the right shoe face up. If the dime turns black, your footprint has been lifted, or poisonous powders have been placed in your path. If you can't get the fear not to walk over evil powder, simply sprinkle black pepper in your shoes.

## Floor Wash to Sweep Out Evil

Lemon Grass   *Cymbopogon marginatus*

Ingredients:
Lemon Grass, 3 parts
Broom Straws from a new broom, ¼ of the straws from the broom
Rosemary, 1 part
Agrimony, 1 part
Bay, 1 part
Rue, 1 part
Linen Bag, large

Place all ingredients with exception of the broom straws into the linen bag. Steep the ingredients in the linen bag and the broom straws in a large pot of boiling hot water for 9 to 15 minutes. Strain and add this to your mop water. Take the new broom. Dip into the floor wash and sweep out the house from the back to the front door and then out the front door and sweep down the sidewalk away from your home. You can use the remaining mixture to wash window sills, doors, and doorways. Take the broom and leave at a crossroads (where two main roads meet, cross) and do not look back.

## Formula to keep Dangerous People away from your Children

Ingredients:
Knotweed, ¼ oz. (7 g)
Goofer Dust, ¼ oz. (7 g)
Hot Foot Powder ¼ oz. (7 g)
Sulphur, 1 oz. (28 g)
Rue, 1 oz.     (28 g)
Brown Paper, 2" x 4"
Red Pen
Black Thread
Black Baby Doll
Lighter Fluid

Blend the Knotweed, Goofer Dust, and Hot Foot Powder together. Write the name of the person trying to negatively influence or possibly molest or assault your children – with a red ink pen 9 times. This red ink pen is to be used for curses, crossings, or spells of this nature. Place the mixture into this piece of paper, while folding away from you – with each fold firmly say, "May (the name of the person) be binded and kept away from my children." Tie with the black thread, the brown paper with the ingredients inside and pin it to the baby doll. Away from your home in a banishing or new moon dig a grave, line it with sulphur, place the doll in the grave and at midnight set it on fire with some lighter fluid. When it burns out, sprinkle with Rue, cover back up with the dirt and walk away backwards. If you plan doing this at a cemetery be sure to leave 9 shiny pennies at the entrance before walking or driving in.

# Formula to Assist Children with Learning

Ingredients:
King Solomon Wisdom Oil
Vervain, 1 part
Sage, 1 part
Peach Tree Leaves
Linen Bag

Place vervain and sage in linen bag, then place this along with the peach tree leaves into a pot of boiling hot water to steep for 7 minutes. Strain the mixture and place in children's bath water. Do not towel dry, allow the water to air dry. Anoint their heads with King Solomon Wisdom Oil each morning before leaving for school.

# Formula to Keep Johnny Law Away

Ingredients:
Oregano
Fennel
Eucalyptus

Take equal parts of the ingredients and place in a pot of boiling hot water to steep for 9 minutes. Strain and sprinkle in your yard. You can also take equal parts of these herbs and sprinkle in your yard without making an infusion.

# Formula to Resolve Harassment

Ingredients:
Red Pepper
Devil's Shoe Strings
Soil from the yard of your nemesis

Mix equal parts of Red Pepper and Devil's Shoe Strings with 3 parts soil.
Sprinkle this in your nemesis' yard while cursing them by name. This will reverse the energy they have sent your way.

# Formula for Exorcism of the Possessed
Wahoo Bark    (*Euonymus atropurpureus*)

Add 1 oz. (30 grams) of Wahoo Bark to 1 gallon (4 L) of spring water and boil for 20 minutes and then strain.  This can be used to sponge down someone being exorcised. (see Chapter Ten.)

### *Hoodoo Exorcism using a Wahoo Wash*
*Ask the person possessed to stand and cross their arms across their chest
*Use a clean white handkerchief while washing their head loudly say "Wahoo" seven times in conjunction with making seven x passes with your hand.
*Take the wash water and discard it to the East at a crossroads or at the trunk of a tree.
*The person in need can take home seven parks of Wahoo bark and make their own wash.  To continue the healing the client can sponge themselves from the neck down seven times while making the sign of the Cross seven times saying, "Wahoo."  This would be done for seven days consecutively.

## The Ancient Art of Limpia, Spiritual Cleansing using an Egg

La Limpia swiftly cleanses a person's aura.  The egg cleansing clears the client's energy field leaving them feeling lighter, blissful, and balanced.  Limpia's are used to clear Malochia (evil eye), blockages, bad luck, generational curses, bad karma, and spiritual illness.  It is a powerful technique for removing negative energy, however it is not a substitute for a doctor's care.  Physicians were blessed with the ability to heal under the divine energy of the Archangel Raphael and at times we must surrender ourselves to their care.

### Ingredients:
2 eggs
Holy Water
Holy Oil
Glass/Water, 2
White Plate, 2
Rue
Copal Resin Incense
Self-Igniting Charcoal

Designate one plate and glass of water for the left side and the other for the right side. Clean the eggs with Holy Water and let them dry.  Heat of the Charcoal and begin burning the Copal Incense.  Clean your area first and then place at the feet of the person receiving the healing.  Anoint the eggs with the Holy Oil.  If the client is right handed, the first egg will be used to clean the left side, if left handed – the right side.  Let's say the client is right handed, – Take one egg and make a cross on top of the head, then roll the egg clockwise around the head, face, neck, left shoulder and arm, around torso, around pelvic area, then down around the right leg and be sure to clean the soles of the feet. Break the egg into the glass of water on the plate for the left side. Sprinkle Rue around the glass of water for the left side. Now repeat the same method on the right side. Place plates with water/egg under the bed for seven days, making sure the left is on the left and the right is on the right. Some healers choose to pour the egg from the glass into the toilet, at the crossroads, or under a tree in the direction of the East.

It is suggested that a prayer be said during the egg cleansing. The Apostles Creed is suitable, one of the Psalms, or the Lord's Prayer. If you are not religiously inclined, you can use spring water to cleanse the egg, use your own type of oil, use a symbol affiliated with your beliefs on the head rather than the cross, and you can use your own words of wisdom or protection while performing the egg cleansing.
When you break the egg in the water and there is blood or the distinctive formation of an eye – you will need to perform another cleansing the following week. Continue to do so until the condition is cleared.

# CHAPTER NINE

## SPELLS FROM THE DARK SIDE

Before undertaking any of the formulas in this category, please refer to our Disclaimer in the front of the book, page 4. Formulas of these type are intriguing and usually do produce satisfactory results, however they come with a big price. Be certain that the contracts you make are thoroughly thought out, for the one or ones you are negotiating with are more manipulative than any human and work insidiously. All of the spells in the book are for the serious minded, not dabblers. Again the price for spells such as these is high, often a portion of your katra (soul) if not in its entirety. All ingredients listed must be used and directions must be followed exactly as listed, no shortcuts or the end result could be disastrous. Many of the recipes for the Oils and Incense listed can be found in Chapter 13.

## Formula to Curse a Nemesis

Ingredients and Supplies:
Black Arts Oil
Ju Ju Oil
Asafoetida, (Devil's Dung), 1/2 oz. (15 grams)
Crossing Incense
Obeah Oil
Latex or Food Service Gloves
Brown Paper, 2" x 3"
Red Marker
DNA of nemesis, (EX: Hair, Nail Clippings, piece of clothing, or recent photo.)
Self-Igniting Charcoal
Incense Burner
Small Spoon (To place incense on hot charcoal)

*Focus on your intention.
*Mix Asafoetida with seven drops of Black Arts Oil. Add three drops of Ju Ju Oil and 1/2 oz. (15 grams) of Crossing Incense. Mix together wearing latex gloves.
*Anoint brown paper with Obeah Oil and allow to dry.
*When dry, write the name of your nemesis nine times with the red marker. Five times forward and four times backwards.
*Place this paper in the bottom of the incense burner.
*Light the self-igniting charcoal on a plate or pan.
*Place half of the mixture on top of the paper in the incense burner.
*Add some of you nemesis' hair or other DNA item (if available), if not use recent

photo. If you are using a photo place the photo on top of the paper and then add half the mixture. If you are using a photo you must use your powers of visualization to see your nemesis clearly.

*Now place the hot charcoal on top of the mixture in the incense burner and little, by little add the rest of the mixture as you say nine times while visualizing your nemesis:

"By the fire, by this smoke, By this flame, Do I forever and eternally curse (name of nemesis). I (your name) put the curse of Samael, Ashtaroth, Bael, and Adrammelech, and Nahema upon thee."

*When all is completely burned, scatter the ashes to the four winds and wash your hands thoroughly in salt water.

*Prepare your incense and paper on a night hour of Saturn. Perform the ritual at Midnight or during the Devil's Hour or Dead Time. (3:00 a.m.) during the waning moon.

## Controlling Formula

Ingredients and Supplies:
Calamus Root, 1 oz. (30 ounces)
Graveyard Dust, 1 oz. (30 grams)
Mercury, 1 drop
Brown Paper, 2' x 3"
Red Marker
DNA of person (EX: Hair, nail clippings, piece of worn clothing) or recent photo
Incense Burner or metal dish
Self-Igniting Charcoal
Small Spoon (To place incense on hot charcoal)
*Focus on your intention.
*Grind the Calamus Root well and blend thoroughly with the Graveyard Dust.
*Write the name of the one to be controlled on the brown paper nine times with the red pen.
*Start this ritual during a Full Moon at Midnight or during Dead Time. (3:00 A.M.)
* Place paper and photo or DNA of nemesis in incense burner and ignite and while burning say:

"As this burns, so will the will of<br>
(name of one to be controlled)<br>
be burned away and<br>
(name of the one to be controlled)<br>
is mine to control."

*While doing this you must concentrate and visualize your outcome.
*Now while mixing ashes of paper with Calamus and Graveyard Dust mixture, 1 drop of Mercury, focus on your intent.
*Divide this into seven equal parts. If you are using DNA, such as hair or nail clippings, mix in with Calamus and Graveyard Dust.
*Bury one portion into the earth and then bury one part each night for seven consecutive nights in its own grave.
* I would perform this during Dead Time (3:00 A.M.) for it is best to perform such rituals during the time the person would be sleeping so that a seed can be planted subliminally.
* When burying each portion say:

"Now it is done
(name of one to be controlled)
will be mine, all mine."


*It is important to focus and pull up all the passion even emotions of anger from within your being to ensure success.

## Tool for Crossing a Nemesis

Ingredients:
Cramp Bark, 1/2 oz. (15 grams)
Dragons Blood Powder, 1/2 oz. (15 grams)
*Grind Cramp Bark with mortar and pestle and blend thoroughly with Dragons Blood. While you are preparing mixture focus on your intention.
*This is to be sprinkled before the door of you nemesis. Walk away and **do not look back**.
*This should be done during the Full Moon at Midnight or during Dead Time. (The Devil's Hour 3:00 a.m.)

## Confusion Formula
Ingredients:
Devil's Shoe String (*Viburnum alnifolium*)
Grind well with mortar and pestle

*Focus on your intention.
*Sprinkle this in the path of your nemesis or in front of their home. **Do not look back**.
*Wash your hands in salt water.

## Formula to Drive Away a Nemesis

Ingredients and Supplies:
Black Image Candle (Male if nemesis is a man and Female if nemesis is a woman.)
Rusty Nail
Ju Ju Oil
Gall of Earth Powder
Jalop Powder
Patchouli Leaves or Powder
Secret Wish Stone
War Water
Brown Paper Bag
Self-Igniting Incense
Incense Burner
Small Spoon (To place incense on hot charcoal)

*Focus on your intent.
*Perform this during a waning Moon phase at Midnight or Dead Time.  Starting during the Full Moon would be best.  Mondays or Wednesdays would be desirable.
*On the back of the image candle, inscribe lengthwise with the rusty nail for head to toe the name of your nemesis.  Anoint from top to bottom with Ju Ju Oil.
*Mix equal portions of Gall of Earth Powder, Patchouli Powder (if you use leaves, grind well), and Jalop Powder.
*Light the image candle.
*Start burning the incense.
*Speak the following:

"In the name of Azazel
I command that (name of nemesis) leave my environment
compel (name of nemesis) to leave
and that I see him/her no more."

*Burn image candle for one hour.  Meditate and repeat the above like a mantra for fifteen minutes or longer, visualizing your nemesis moving away.
*Sprinkle War Water on the burning incense after the hour is up.
*Place the wishing stone under your pillow and keep it there as you sleep.
*Repeat this for nine consecutive nights.

*On the tenth night, place all the remains in a brown paper bag along with the wishing stone and bury as far away from your home as possible.
Turn and DO NOT LOOK BACK.

## Formula for Vengeance

Ingredients and Supplies:
Small Box
Knot Grass
Black Jumbo Candle
Brown Paper, 2" x 3"
Red Marker or Pen
Aluminum Foil
Tanna Bark (Devils Pepper), 1 oz. (30 grams)
Prince's Pine Herb, 1 oz. (30 grams)
Red Candle

*Perform this during a Full Moon at Midnight or during Dead Time
(The Devils Hour, 3:00 a.m.)
*Make a bed of Knot Grass in the small box
*Cover your table or altar with aluminum foil.
*Melt the Black Jumbo Candle down and it must burn all the way through.
*On the brown paper with the red pen write the name of your nemesis nine times.
*As the wax is cooling push the piece of paper into the melted wax.  Roll into a ball and allow to harden.  If you have any items containing the DNA of your nemesis you may push these into the wax as well.  A recent photo can work as well.
*Place into box with Knot Grass.  Sprinkle the Tanna Bark and Prince's Pine Herb on the wax ball unit it is totally covered.
*Close the box and seal with red candle wax.
*Place the box in running water such as a river, brook, creek, or ocean.
Turn away and <u>DO NOT LOOK BACK</u>.

## Formula for Controlling Another

Ingredients and Supplies:
Mace Powder, 1/2 oz. (15 grams)
Compelling Oil, 1 Tbsp. (15 cc)
Red Image Candle, (Male for Man, Female for Woman)
Clean Sharp Nail
Brown Paper, 2" x 3"
Red Marker or Pen
Large Metal Plate
Compelling Incense, Cones or Powdered Compelling Incense
    and Self-Igniting Charcoals.
Small Spoon (To place incense on hot charcoal)

*Focus on your intention.

*Start this during a waxing Moon, a few days after the New Moon at Midnight or during Dead Time (3:00 A.M.).

*Mix the Mace Powder and Compelling Oil together thoroughly.

*Write the name of the one you want to control lengthwise from the feet to the head on the back with the clean sharp nail.

*Cover the image candle with the Mace mixture from toe to top.  Place on metal plate.

*Write the name of the one you wish to control on the brown paper with the red pen nine times. Place under the image candle face up.  If you have a recent photo, you can place this under the image candle face up as well.

*Place nine compelling incense cones around the image candle.  You can also use nine self-igniting charcoals, light, and add compelling incense powder to each one.

*Light the image candle and then the incense cones and as you light the incense cones say:

"(Name of Person you wish to control)
You are mine, all mine
I control you now
You will do all that I wish."

Repeat words nine times. While candle is burning meditate on your desire.

*Burn the image candle for half an hour, then extinguish.

*Do this each day until the image candle has burnt completely through and down.

*Take the remains and bury far away from your home.  **Do not look back**.

## Formula to Destroy the Harm of a Nemesis

Ingredients and Supplies:

Double Action Jumbo Candle (Special candle, red inside & black outside)

Black Arts Oil

Witches Formula Oil

Powdered Mullein Leaves

Latex Gloves or Food Service Gloves

Brown Paper, 2" x 3"

Red Marker or Pen

*Perform this in a waning Moon phase at Midnight or during Dead Time. (3:00 A.M.)

*Focus on your intention.

*Burn the Double Action Jumbo Candle for one hour.

*Extinguish Candle and melt the balance down.

*To melted wax add nine drops of Black Arts Oil, 9 drops of Witches Formula Oil, along with 1 Tbsp. (7 grams) of Powdered Mullein Leaves. Wear latex gloves to knead this together.

*With a red pen write the name of your nemesis nine times on the brown paper backwards.

*Push paper into wax and knead into a ball. If you have any DNA items, such as hair or fingernails you may add this to the wax as well. Also a recent photo is good.
*Take solidified ball and throw under the house of your nemesis. If you cannot get it under the house throw it as close as possible so it cannot be seen. Then say:

"You who would harm me
will bring your own evil on yourself."

*Say this nine times and turn and walk away, **do not look back**.

## Formula to Remove a Nemesis from your Space
Ingredients and Supplies:
Brown Jumbo Candle
Witches Formula Oil
Black Arts Oil
Nerve Root
Latex Gloves or Food Service Gloves
Brown Paper, 2" x 3"
Red Marker or Pen
*Perform this in a waning Moon phase at Midnight or during Dead Time.
*Focus on your intent.
*Burn the Brown Jumbo Candle for one hour.
*Extinguish Candle and melt the balance down.
*To melted wax add nine drops of Black Arts Oil, 9 drops of Witches Formula Oil, along with 1 Tbsp. (7 grams) of ground Nerve Root. Wear latex gloves to knead this in.
*With a red pen write the name of your nemesis nine times on the brown paper backwards.
*Push paper into wax and knead into a ball. If you have any of your nemesis' DNA items, such as hair or fingernails you may add this to the wax as well. Also a recent photo is good.

*Take the solidified ball to a river, creek, brook, or ocean. Throw it into the water as far as possible saying:

"(Name of your nemesis)
you want and will move away
(Name of your nemesis)
you who would bedevil me
(Name of your nemesis)
you who would cause me trouble
(Name of your nemesis)
now move and leave me be
as I say it so it shall be."

*Say this nine times and turn and walk away, **do not look back**.

---

## Formula to Curse a Nemesis

Ingredients and Supplies:
Patchouli Powder, 2 oz. (60 grams)
Gentian, 1 oz. (30 grams)
Black Arts Incense, 8 oz. (225 grams)
Prickly Ash Berries, 1 oz. (30 grams)
Yohimbe Bark, 1 oz. (30 grams)
Saltpeter, 1/2 oz. (15 grams)
Poppet (Voodoo Doll) with a feather.
Black Cloth (Large enough to wrap poppet in)
Stick Pins
Latex Gloves or Food Service Gloves
Brown Paper, 2" x 3"
Red Pen
Voodoo Oil
Black Votive Candle, 7
War Water
Self-Igniting Incense
Small Spoon (To place incense on hot charcoal)

*Perform this outside during a waning Moon at Midnight or during the Devil's hour.
(3:00 A.M.)
*Focus on your intention.
*Grind the Indian Hemp and the Yohimbe Bark well and blend well with Patchouli
Powder, Prickly Ash Berries, Saltpeter, and Black Arts Incense.
*On Brown Paper with Red Pen write the name of your nemesis nine times.
*Put on latex gloves and anoint the feather of the poppet with Black Arts Oil.
*Anoint body of the poppet with Obeah Oil
*Attach the brown paper with stick pins to the bottom of the poppet.
*Anoint the black votive candle with Voodoo Oil and light.
*Place some incense mixture on self-ignited charcoal in incense burner.
*Hold both hands, palms down, over the smoking incense and say:

"By the Power of Thebot
Ywote
Mephistophiles
Beelzebub
Arbu
(Name of your nemesis)
No Peace
No Joy
**No Love**
Will you know."

*Say nine times.
*Sprinkle War Water on Poppet.  Wrap in Black Cloth and hide where no one will find or see it.
*Repeat this ritual once every seven days.

## Formula to Separate Two People

Ingredients and Supplies:
Patchouli Leaves, 1 oz. (30 grams)
Black Arts Incense, 2 Oz (60 grams)
Saltpeter, 1/2 oz. (15 grams)
Black Image Candles, (Male for Men, Female for Women)
Voodoo Oil
Aluminum Foil
Nerve Root
Rue
Witch's Grass
DNA items for each person. (Examples: Hair, Nail Clippings) Recent Photo
Rusty Nail
Self-Igniting Incense
Incense Burner
Small Spoon (To place incense on hot charcoal)

*Focus on your intention.
*Perform this outside during a waning Moon at Midnight or at Dead Time. (3:00 A.M.)  If you perform inside, open the windows for Black Arts Incense is very intense.
*Cover your table or altar with aluminum foil.
*Take one of the image candles and write lengthwise from foot to head on the backside the name of one of the persons with the nail.
*Take the other image candle and write lengthwise from foot to head on the backside the name of the other person.
*Anoint each image with Voodoo Oil thoroughly.
*Stand the image candles back to back.
*Light both candles from left to right.
*Start burning some of the incense.
*When incense is smoking well throw hair, nails, or photo of each person you wish to separate.
*Allow the image candles to burn for half an hour, and then extinguish.
*Mix 1 Tbsp. (7 grams) of Nerve Root, 1 Tbsp. (7 grams) of Rue, and 2 Tbsp.'s (15 grams) of Witch's Grass.  Blend thoroughly and divide into two equal portions.
*Throw one in front of each of the person's doorway.  Throw in front of the male's first.  If it is 2 males or 2 females, the one who represents the male in the relationship.

*If the two are living in the same household, throw the entire portion in front of their doorway and **DO NOT LOOK BACK**.

*Repeat candle ritual every night until the image candles are completely burnt down. Take the wax drippings and incense ashes, divide.

 *Again, throw one in front of each of the person's doorway. Throw in front of the male's first. If it is 2 males or 2 females, the one who represents the male in the relations hip.

*If the two are living in the same household, throw the entire portion in front of their doorway, turn and **DO NOT LOOK BACK**.

## Formula for Vengeance

Ingredients and Supplies:
Red Cinchona Bark, 1 oz. (30 grams)
Black Art Incense, 2 oz. (60 grams)
Crossing Incense, 2 oz. (60 grams)
Devil's Shoestring, 7 pieces
Witch's Grass, 1 oz. (30 grams)
Mace Powder, 1 oz. (30 grams)
Pimento Powder, 1 oz. (30 grams)
Brimstone, 1 oz. (30 grams)
Calamus Root, 1 oz. (30 grams)
Vetivert, 1 oz. (30 grams)
Brown Paper, 2" x 3"
Red Pen
Four Thieves Vinegar, 1 bottle
Empty Glass bottle or Mason jar
Small Spoon (To place incense on hot charcoal)
Self-Igniting Charcoal
Incense Burner

*Focus on your intention.
*Perform this outdoors in an open space during the Full Moon at Midnight or the Devil's Hour. (3:00 A.M.)
*Grind the Herbs and mix thoroughly with other powders and incense.
*Light the charcoal in the incense burner.
*Add incense little by little and when smoking well say:

"(Name of Nemesis)<br>
Burn and Squirm<br>
Burn and Squirm<br>
Burn and Squirm<br>
A critical lesson you must now learn

> The Harm you sent
> Evil learned
> Now to you (name of nemesis)
> It is returned to you
> (name of nemesis)
> Burn, Burn, Twist and Turn
> Burn and Squirm."

*Repeat Three Times.
*Wait for incense to completely burn out
*While waiting, write the name of your nemesis on the brown paper with the red pen, five times forward and four times backward.
*Take the Four Thieves Vinegar and pour half the bottle into the other empty bottle.
*Take the incense ashes and the paper with your nemesis' name and place into the original bottle with the Four Thieves Vinegar.
*Place cap on and seal with Red Candle Wax.
*Throw into an ocean or a river. **Do not look back**.
*Do this every 7 days until you are satisfied.

## Invoking a Female Astral Dream Lover

Ingredients and Supplies:
Patchouli Powder, 16 oz. (450 grams)
Sage, 4 oz. (115 grams)
Orris Powder, 8 oz. (225 grams)
Wood Betony, 16 oz. (450 grams)
Winters Bark, 16 oz. (450 grams)
Saltpeter, 2 oz. (60 grams)
Absinthe, 8 oz. (225 grams)
Cubeb Berries, 8 oz. (225 grams)
Satyrion, 8 oz. (225 grams)
Saffron, 2 oz. (60 grams)
Pimento Powder, 2 oz. (60 grams)
Ju Ju Oil
Obeah Oil
Self-Igniting Charcoal
Incense Burner
Small Spoon (To place incense on hot charcoal)

*Focus on your intention. Create her visually, draw or paint a picture of her if you desire to do so.
*Grind with a mortar and pestle the herbs as fine as possible. Blend thoroughly with other powders.

*Cleanse and bathe yourself and wear some sexy boxers, etc... Also make sure the sheets on your bed are clean and appealing.

*Play some appropriate music. You could even have a single red rose to present her. I knew when a late friend of mine was calling up his astral lover for he would always play "Dream Lover" by Bobby Darin and the music would change once his astral lover arrived. On several occasions I am quite sure he called up a dominatrix for Billy Idol's "Flesh for Fantasy" became the song of choice, in addition to all the special sound effects coming from his room.

*Warlocks (and Witches) tell me they prefer starting this ritual in a waxing moon.

*Anoint your head with Ju Ju Oil. Anoint your body and palms with Obeah Oil

*Before going to bed, light the self-igniting charcoal and place in incense burner. Once hot, put a little of the incense mixture on the hot charcoal.

*Be tenacious! Some say they receive immediate results and others say it takes six weeks or more before she makes her appearance, but all say the wait was well worth it.

*Most women enjoy being pursued or chased by a man, an astral dream lover is no different.

*With certainty make sure that you maintain the upper hand with your astral dream lover or she may start coming to you at inopportune times. (ex: when you are with another woman!)

## Formula to Cross a Nemesis

Ingredients and Supplies:
Double Action Reversible Candle
Empty Jar with lid
Four Thieves Vinegar
Skunk Cabbage Root
Double Cross Powder
Good Luck Spiritual Incense
Dragon Blood Powder
War Water
Self-Igniting Charcoal
Incense Burner
Small Spoon (To place incense on hot charcoal)
Aluminum Foil
Brown Paper, 2" x 3" and Red Pen

*Focus on your intention.
*Start during a waning Moon at Midnight or Dead Time. (3:00 A.M.)
*Place Foil on your table or altar.
*Write the name of your nemesis backwards nine times with red ink.
*Light the Double Action Reversible Candle and allow to burn completely down.
*Burn the paper with nemesis' name in the wax drippings.
*Pour half of the Four Thieves Vinegar in a jar.
*Take the wax drippings with the ashes of the paper and place in either bottle or jar of Four Thieves Vinegar.
*Sprinkle in front of your nemesis" door, turn and  **Do not look back**.
*Each day burn a little Good Luck Spiritual Incense in your home starting at the front door, through the house, to the back door.
*Each day Sprinkle Dragon Blood Powder around the outside of your house starting at front right corner, to left front, to left back, right back, ending at front right.
*Three nights after you sprinkled the Four Thieves Vinegar with the candle drippings and the ashes in front of the door of your nemesis.  Grind and mix 1/2 oz. of Skunk Cabbage Root and a pinch of Double Cross Powder to some War Water.
*Throw this mixture in front of your nemesis' house, turn and **Do not look back**.
*Repeat this every 17 days if you want to keep your nemesis in a crossed condition.

## Formula to Render a Nemesis Vulnerable

Ingredients and Supplies:
Poppet with Feather (Voodoo Doll)
Recent Photo or Other DNA objects (Examples: Hair, Nail Clippings, worn clothing. You can actually make a poppet from a nemesis worn clothing and stuff with remaining cloth. Blow up the photo, cut out the face and use stick pins to attach to the face of the poppet. Before you finish sewing up the poppet in the back, insert some of nemesis' hair or nail clippings if you have these.)
Black Arts Oil
Voodoo Oil
Cardboard Box
Black Cloth
Obeah Oil
Vetivert Leaves, 1oz (30 grams)
Skullcap, 1 oz. (30 grams)
Elm Bark, 1 oz. (30 grams)
Brimstone, 8 oz. (225 grams)
Graveyard Dirt, 8 oz. (225 grams)
Latex or Food Service Gloves
Red Cord

*Focus on your intention.
*Grind with mortar and pestle then blend well the Vetivert Leaves, Skullcap, and Elm Bark.
*Anoint Feather of the Poppet with Black Arts Oil wearing latex gloves.
*Anoint the body of the Poppet with Voodoo Oil.
*Line the cardboard box with the black cloth.
*Drop seven drops of Obeah Oil on the Poppet and say:
                    "I name you
                  (name of nemesis)"
Repeat nine times.
*Sprinkle with Herb Mixture while saying:
              "I bind you (name of nemesis)
                  to your own evil
            Upon your head (name of nemesis)
                  your evil will be."
Repeat nine times.
*Cover the Box. Tie with the Red Cord making nine knots.
*Take far from your home to bury. Once buried, sprinkle with Brimstone and Graveyard Dirt, turn and **Do not look back**.
*If you take to a cemetery to bury, leave nine pennies or nine purple flowers at the

entrance before starting.  When you leave **do not look back**.
*Cleanse yourself in a salt bath when you return home.


## Formula to Get Someone to Move Away

Ingredients and Supplies:
Yohimbe (Pausinystalia Yohimbe)
Yohimbe, 1/4 oz. (7 gr)
Brown Jumbo Candle
Piece of Brown Paper, 2" X 3"
Red Ink Pen
Black Arts Oil
Aluminum Foil
Food Service Gloves
*Focus on your intention.
*Perform this during a waning moon phase.
*Place aluminum foil on the area where you intend to burn the candle.
*Burn the Brown Jumbo Candle for one hour and then melt down the remainder.
*On the brown paper with the red ink pen write the name of your nemesis five times forward and four times backward.
*Add the Yohimbe and the brown paper with the name to the candle wax.
*Add seven drops of Black Arts Oil.
*Put on a pair of food service gloves.
*As the wax cools, knead and roll with all items added into a ball.
*Once it is hardened, roll under or against the house of your nemesis.  Walk away and **DO NOT LOOK BACK**.

## Formula for Women to Attract Financial Benefits

Ingredients and Supplies:
Jezebel Root also called Dixie Iris (*Iris Hexagona*)
Jumbo Green Candle
Small Red Bag
Orris Root, small piece
1 part Dried Rose Buds
1 part Sweet Flag
½ part Catnip
Adam & Eve Root, small piece

Melt down the Green Candle. When it starts to cool and begins to firm, push a piece of Jezebel Root into the Green Wax and roll into a ball. Focus on your intent. When it is solidified take to a cemetery and bury. As you bury it say, "Jezebel, Jezebel send me a plenty! Let (name of a person you want money from) me spend his money." Say this three times. Perform this during a waxing moon during a moon in Leo. Also spells for control and domination can be done during a moon in Cancer. Repeat the ritual as needed.

Blend well the Dried Rose Buds, Sweet Flag, and Catnip. Add a piece of Jezebel Root, Orris Root, and Adam & Eve Root. Place in the red bag and carry on your person. For added power you can translate these ingredients into an oil, incense, and a bath by following the directions in Chapter 13 for OILS and INFUSIONS. For incense you would grind and blend the ingredients well with a mortar and pestle, then burn on self-igniting charcoal.

Jezebel Root also referred to as African Queen, is a woman's root. This root belongs to several varieties of Louisiana Irises, *Iris Hexagona, Iris Fulva, & Iris Foliosa*.

## Formula for Crossing a Nemesis

Ingredients:
Dogbane
Bittersweet
Black Salt
Crossing Powder

Using a mortar and pestle grind equal parts of the dogbane and bittersweet, then combine with equal parts of the black salt and crossing powder. I recommend using latex or food service gloves when handling this mixture. You can also crush up insects, such as scorpions, wasps, spiders...to the mixture. Throw across the area(s) where your nemesis walks with frequency.

# CHAPTER TEN

## EXORCISM FORMULAS FOR DELIVERANCE

Exorcism (from Greek *exorkizein*): an adjuration addressed to malevolent spirits to command them to abandon an object, place, or person; technically a ceremony employed in Jewish, Christian, and other traditions to banish low vibrational energies from those who have fallen victim to their influences. Deliverance or exorcism is the most dangerous ministry I know -- not only for those performing the exorcism -- but for the victim as well. However refusing to help such victims by restricting or even forbidding exorcism is far worse than mistakes that can be made due to inexperience or ignorance for it abandons these victims to a life time of oppression and worse -- probable suicide.

I do recommend that the situation must be evaluated carefully and is best managed by individuals in this aspect of believing, religious rites and rituals. This is not an area for play or experimentation for it can endanger all involved. These rituals may elicit psychosis and life-threatening situations for some individuals and this is a danger ministers must keep in mind and be prepared to act upon instantly. Fear is a powerful emotion and not in the control of reason in some situations which accompany the exorcism ritual. There can be instances where the remedy can be of equal or create greater harm than the malevolent energies themselves.

The first and most common way we find out that a person needs deliverance is that *they tell us.* Those who are affected know that for a certainty *"that something just isn't right",* and they know that it possibly could be caused by pernicious energies. Asking certain questions in a skilled manner can determine fraud or the need for traditional psychiatric care. It is my experience that it is extremely difficult for those who are truly victims of malevolent energies to bear their souls for first they feel they will not be believed and that they will receive a reputation of being mentally unstable. Additionally the evil surrounding them will create tremendous chaos making it as oppressive as possible in order to discourage the victim from seeking assistance.

Each experiences these pernicious energies in different ways. Some hear voices instructing them to expedite intemperate stygian acts such as suicide, homicide, hate crimes, and any relating to the destructive, reactive side of this world. Others are tormented relentlessly with nightmares and visions that are perceived so real that even the ordinary human senses are involved. Still others begin acting out in a manner contrary to their normal character.

The most convincing signs are bodily contortions, inflections, and changes in facial expression. Sometimes when the tone, pitch, and/or volume of the victim's voice changes - for example a woman will speak as a man or the content of speech changes and the victim may start speaking in plural *"we'd* rather than *"I"*. Usually the content will become vile, laced with colorful metaphors and innuendos.

***The eyes are the windows to the soul*** is especially meaningful for these victims eyes become filled with hate, mockery, pride, or whatever the nature of that particular spirit is. Many times the eyes roll upwards this being the entities way of avoiding looking at you in an effort to keep the victim from making contact with you and getting help. When the victims face changes you are not looking at the same person you began prayers with for usually the particular spirit is superimposed.

Other signs indicating the presence of malevolent energies are foul odors characterized by the smell of decomposing flesh. The odors come and go but during manifestation there is no doubt as to what it is and whether a person is sensitive or not they can smell this stench. Above all when low vibrational energies are present it is *"cold"* and the hair on the back of your neck stands up whereas with the *Holy Spirit* or high vibrational energies it is *"heat"* we experience. In fact when performing a healing or deliverance I usually have to remove my sweater or jacket. Another indication of the presence of unseen forces is if the *upper portion of the left ear* insistently itches or tingles. Also the accent upon vibration in the left ear is also a warning of negation telepathies or as my friend Millie and I always say so simply, *"that something just isn't right."*

A **Special Caution** and area of concern is Multiple Personality Disorder (MPD, also known as DID, Dissociative Identity Disorder). Since the external symptoms of the need for exorcism are ambiguous, we must ask what is causing the symptoms, a psychiatric disorder or a pernicious spirit. If we are not sure we must proceed with caution.

The worst thing you can do if the person does have MPD is to try to cast these personalities out, for this particular person has created these personalities as a survival measure due to severe trauma inflicted, generally during childhood.

Clearly, whenever possible you should get to know the person you are going to pray with and really listen to what they are saying. *Do not force them to subscribe to your interpretation of their experience.* If you are not certain what you are dealing with this gentle approach bypasses the problem of becoming involved too quickly in a direct confrontation.

Once again I reintegrate that exorcisms or deliverance are not to be taken lightly. Besides the tools of the exorcist one must consider the spiritual readiness of the deliverer and their team. The team must be responsible and ever vigilant for exorcism is tough spiritual warfare with challenging energies. I implore any who believe they are in need or someone they love requires this measure to seek out a genuine servant of the *Most*

*High God.* I myself am an intrepid id Spiritual Warrior however the ego must be restrained therefore I personally never go into this type of battle solo or blindfolded for the victims very being is at risk. If I cannot form a team it is wise to enlist at least one other person who is familiar with spiritual warfare and personally I choose a male soul, an alter ego, whose energy appears to provide a balance insuring success.

The Catholic Church in 1614 AD published the handbook "**Rituale Romanum**" that describes exorcism in the chapter "**De Exorcismis**". The ways of exorcism are manifold. It can consist of oral rituals, equipment like holy water, cruxes, salt, blessed artifacts, saint's relics, wine to symbolize Christ's blood, occult drawings or even summoning of benevolent spirits to overcome their evil counterparts. I am not going to share the English/Latin Catholic Prayer of Exorcism. However, I will share a couple of simple exorcisms for priests or laity for I do realize there are emergencies and extenuating circumstances. Also please recapitulate the information in *Methods of Defense* for there are many methods shared that can be used and in combination to secure a banishing of low vibrational influences.

Preparation for deliverance can be critical and hopefully there is an opportunity to form a team and interview the victim. It helps to have knowledge of the victim and learning as much as possible about how and why the entities gained entrance and their identity. We call on the authority of the Most High God and the Christ Light to guide us; to fill the room with His power and love, and work through us to cast out the entities. We call on the *Holy Spirit* to anoint us with Power and Love to Heal and Free the victim. The holy angels are called upon, especially Michael, to minister to us. Surround us with their protection and do battle for us, while the "communion of saints" who are in heaven, "the great cloud of witnesses" (*Hebrew 12:1)* intercede for us. Lastly we forbid in the name of God and the Christ any communication in the realm of evil spirits as it might affect those that are troubling the victim and we forbid these spirits to draw energy from any spirits outside the person. Now the team may proceed with the deliverance itself.

**The following are helpful suggestions which can insure success:**

- **Exercise Compassion** -- *Compassion is more powerful than anger,* -- we are not angry with the victim and by using angry tones we could further wound them by increasing the shame and self-loathing they already feel.

- **Speak in a Calm Voice** -- directing spirits in many ways is like communicating with children, they appear to respond better if the team is in control and maintains a calm demeanor. Please bear in mind they can sense insecurity as well and this is why it is recommended that persons familiar with spiritual warfare perform exorcisms.

- **Look the Person in the Eye** -- Looking into the person's eyes seems to confront the evil spirits directly and helps in casting them out. I have found that the spirits, even if they seem defiant, are afraid to look us in the eye and will do whatever they can to avoid it. Sometimes the eyeballs roll upward, leaving you looking at nothing but the whites of the eyes. Usually I ask the person to look at me. If they still have command of their body they will but if the spirit is strong, they will force the person to turn away. If this happens you may say to the spirit, "In the name of Jehovah God and Jesus Christ I command you to look at me" -- and keep doing it calmly until it releases its grip and the person does look at you.

- **Decide whether to touch the Person** -- There are two schools of thought here; some hold that you should not touch the person if you do not have to, that it is contaminating and possibly dangerous. My own experience, on the other hand, is that the power of the *Holy Spirit* flows out from us to the victim. If the malevolent spirit seems lodged in the victim's throat, I will place my hand lightly on the throat. These spirits cannot stand being close to the team and the laying on of hands in a loving manner increases the pressure on them to release the victim. By touching their host you increase the spirit's discomfort and hasten their departure. However if one chooses not to touch the victim this is all right for it is not essential.

## Prayer to St. Michael the Archangel

In the Name of the Father, and of the Son, and of the Holy Ghost. Amen.
Most glorious Prince of the Heavenly Armies, Saint Michael the Archangel, defend us in "our battle against principalities and powers, against rulers of this world of darkness, against spirits of wickedness in the high places" (*Eph. 6:12)*. Come to the assistance of men whom God has created to His likeness and whom He has redeemed at a great price from the tyranny of the devil. Holy Church venerates thee as her guardian and protector; to thee, the Lord has entrusted the souls of the redeemed to be led into heaven. Pray therefore the god of Peace, to crush Satan beneath our feet, that he may no longer retain men captive and do injury to the Church. Offer our prayers to the Most High, that without delay they may draw His mercy down upon us; take hold of "the dragon, the old serpent, which is the devil and Satan", bind him and cast him into the bottomless pit…" that he may no longer seduce the nations" (*Apoc.20:2-3)*

I. EXORCISM
In the Name of Jesus Christ, our god and Lord, strengthened by the intercession of the Immaculate Virgin Mary, Mother of god, of Blessed Michael the Archangel, of the Blessed Apostles Peter and Paul and all the Saints (and powerful in the holy authority of our ministry)*, we confidently undertake to repulse the attacks and deceits of the Satan.
*Lay people omit the parenthesis above*.

## Psalm 68: 1 & 2

God arises; His enemies are scattered and those who hate Him flee before Him. As smoke is driven away, so are they driven; as wax melts before the fire, so the wicked perish at the presence of God.
V. Behold the Cross of the Lord, flee bands of enemies.
R. The Lion of the tribe of Judah, the offspring of David, hath conquered.
V. May thy mercy, Lord, descend upon us.
R. As great as our hope in Thee.

*(The crosses below indicate a blessing to be given if a Priest or anointed minister of the Most High God recites the Exorcism; if a lay person recites it, they indicate the Sign of the Cross to be made silently by that person.)*

We drive you from us, whoever you may be (if you know the name say it here), unclean spirits, all satanic powers, all infernal invaders, all wicked legions, assemblies and sects. In the Name and by the power of Our Lord Jesus Christ, + may you be snatched away and driven from the Church of god and from the souls made to the image and likeness of God and redeemed by the Precious Blood of the Divine Lamb.+

Most cunning serpent, you shall no more dare to deceive the human race, persecute the Church, torment God's elect and sift them as wheat. + The Most High God commands you, + He with whom, in your great insolence, you still claim to be equal. "God who wants all men to be saved, and to come to the knowledge of the truth" *(1Timothy 2:4).* God the Father commands you. + God the Son commands you. + God the Holy Ghost commands you. + Christ, God's word made flesh, commands you; + He who to save our race outdone through your envy, "humbled Himself, becoming obedient even unto death" *(Phil. 2:8);* He who has built His Church on the firm rock and declared that the gates of hell shall not prevail against Her, because he will dwell with Her "all days even to the end of the world" *(Matthew 28:20).* The sacred Sign of the Cross commands you, + as does also the power of the mysteries of the Christian Faith. + The glorious Mother of Christ, Mary Queen of Angels commands you; + she who by her humility and from the first moment of her Immaculate Conception crushed your proud head. The faith of the holy apostles Peter and Paul, and of the other Apostles commands you. + The blood of the Martyrs and the pious intercession of all the Saints command you. +

Thus, 20cursed dragon, and you, diabolical legions, we adjure you by the living God, + by the true God, + by the holy God, + by the God "who so loved the world that He gave up His only Son, that every soul believing in Him might not perish but have life everlasting" *(John 3:16);* stop deceiving human creatures and pouring out to them the poison of eternal damnation; stop harming the Church and hindering her liberty. Be gone, Satan, inventor and master of all deceit, enemy of man's salvation. Give place to Christ in whom you have found none of your works; give place to the one holy church acquired by Christ at the price of His Blood. Stoop beneath the all-powerful hand of God; tremble and flee when we invoke the

Holy and terrible Name of Jehovah God and Jesus Christ which causes hell to tremble, this names to which the Virtues, powers and Dominations of heaven are humbly submissive, these names which the Cherubim and Seraphim praise unceasingly repeating: "Holy, Holy is the Lord, the God of Hosts".

V. O Lord, hear my prayer
R. And let my cry come unto Thee.
V. May the Lord be with Thee.
R. And with thy Spirit.

## LET US PRAY:

*"God of Heaven, God of Earth, God of Angels, God of Archangels, God of Patriarchs, God of Matriarchs, God of Prophets, God of Apostles, God of Martyrs, God of Confessors,=20 God of Virgins, God who has the power to give life after death and rest after work; because there is no other god than Thee and there can be no other, for Thou art the Creator of all things, visible and invisible, of whose reign there shall be no end, we humbly prostrate ourselves before Thy glorious Majesty and we beseech thee to deliver us by Thy power from all the tyranny of the infernal spirits, from their snares, their lies and their furious wickedness. Deign, O Lord, to grant us thy powerful protection and to keep us safe and sound.  We beseech thee through Jesus Christ Our Lord. Amen."*

V. From the snares of the Satan
R. Deliver us, O Lord
V. That thy Church may serve thee in peace and liberty
R. We beseech thee to hear us
V. That thou may crush down all enemies of thy Church
R. We beseech thee to hear us.
*(Holy water is sprinkled in the place where we may be)*

## A Revised Hail Mary

A revised Hail Mary refers to us as *"sons and daughters of God"* rather than as *"sinners."* Hail Mary is meant to revere not only the mother of Jesus but also *God as Mother*. Thus anyone who gives the Hail Mary is accessing the energy and power of *God as Mother*, and millions of angels answer when you give the Hail Mary.

Give it three times or more following your heartfelt prayers or for whatever spiritual or physical gifts you require.
*"Hail, Mary, full of grace.*
*The Lord is with thee.*
*Blessed art thou among women*
*And blessed is the fruit of thy womb, Jesus.*
*Holy Mary, Mother of God,*
*Pray for us, sons and daughters of God,*
*Now and at the hour of our victory*
*Over sin, disease, and death.*
*Amen."*

# II. THE ACTUAL PRAYER FOR DELIVERANCE

*"In the Name of Jesus Christ..."*
We cast these spirits out not by our own authority, but by the power of the name of Jesus Christ.
*"...I command you..."*

It is no polite request we make of the malevolent spirits; we in a controlled manner use the authority vested in us. If there is any lack of certainty in your voice, these spirits will perceive this as fear and begin intimidation strategies.

*"...you spirit of _____..."*
If possible, identify the spirit by name ( for example, *spirit of fear, hate , lust or simply say whoever you might be)*
*"...to depart..."*
*"...without doing harm to _____(name of the person by first name or entire name) or anyone else in this house, or in _____(person's name), and without making any noise or disturbance..."*
At times others present have been attacked or even entered by the spirits as they leave. Many times pets in the house have been invaded and behave strangely afterwards. This can be avoided by correct preparation and praying for protection before and during the deliverance.

Malevolent spirits thrive on chaos and creating turmoil with the intention of frightening you with their ugly and sickening performances. In a controlled manner with certainty command them to be quiet and stop the theatrics. This should cut down on the disturbance and violent displays.
*"...and I command you to go straight to Jesus Christ to dispose of you as He will. Furthermore, I command you never again to return."*
Some exorcists command the spirits to go to hell or return to the abyss but it appears to be more effective to send them into the Christ Light or to Jesus Christ and let Him do that with them that He wishes. A human failing is for us to become infected by what we fight, and it is an occupational hazard for an exorcist to become a harsh and judgmental.

## Other Tools

Certainty and the Power of the Spoken Word are the most powerful tools to insure success in spiritual warfare, however if a person so chooses there are other tools that can be utilized in conjunction with prayer. Having team member pray in the background using the appropriate Psalms or other prayers; chanting the appropriate names of God designed to free the person and create terror within such entities; playing spiritual music; asking someone to read pertinent Scripture passages, especially any sayings of Christ that run counter to the nature of the spirit that may be resisting you, all of these mentioned will torment malevolent spirits.

One may wish to employ the use of consecrated oil, water, and salt. The water is used to sprinkle the room or the victim; the salt is sprinkled in the room before prayer begins, and/or the victim may eat a bit of it. The oil is used for anointing the victim. Some exorcists choose to have the victim hold on to a crucifix or a Bible. I realize that according to each person's belief system some of these aids may be acceptable and others not, if they are not simply leave them aside; none is essential.

If at all possible encourage the victim to take part in their own deliverance for if they do so the session will go more quickly.

## How to Tell When the Spirits Have Left

Deliverance or exorcism is exhausting but very rewarding and it is not all that complicated. Some spirits will depart instantly and others hang on for hours and even days. At times they will even pretend to leave hoping that you will grow weary and leave them alone.

I am one of the many who have been entrusted with the gift of discerning spirits and this is the easiest way to know whether the malevolent spirit has truly departed. If you don't have this gift it is wise to have someone on the team who does, in fact I prefer that most of the team share this gift for confirmation and total certainty.

Also many times the person afflicted will positively know when the spirit has departed for they will feel "lighter' and will express this verbally.
About ninety percent of the time there are more than one malevolent spirit present and the person can usually tell when the last one has gone.
Also being as the eyes are the window to the soul often looking into the persons eyes you can detect the change for rather than looking into the eyes of alien hate -- the eyes soften with light emanating from them and you are looking into the eyes of a human being.

More often than not these spirits come out with a struggle. If they come out through the mouth it is usually accompanied by coughing. If the person retches phlegm often comes up. Allow the person to cough while the team is praying and when it ceases ask, "Is it gone yet"? If the person says no -- continue. Always be prepared for this by having a plastic-lined wastebasket ready for this coughing phenomenon occurs at least over half the time during deliverance prayer.

Another phenomenon is screaming or shrieking during deliverance. We read about such occurrences in Jesus' ministry: *"Be quiet!" said Jesus sternly. "Come out of him!" the evil spirit shook the man violently and came out of him with a shriek. -- Mark 1:25-26.* Here Jesus would not enable to the spirit to postpone its exit for often these spirits wish to engage in lengthy argument; so when these manifestations occur with convulsions giving way to peace; shrieks giving way to silence; then one can discern that the spirit has probably departed.

<u>Filling the Void</u>
After these spirits have departed it is important to fill the spiritual vacuum with the appropriate energy and according to individual beliefs this will be unique to each case. It is my personal belief that each deliverance or exorcism must end on a positive, proactive God centered note by praying for an infilling of every strength and virtue that characterizes *"Love and Light; Christ, The Light-Force."*

### *A Special Caution*
I wish to reintegrate, once again, that Exorcism or Deliverance is **not** a game. It is tough Spiritual Warfare. It is best to seek out and employ those who are ordained or anointed of the Most High God and who are experienced in accordance with this aspect of believing, religious rites, and rituals.

# CHAPTER ELEVEN

# METAPHYSICAL

Metaphysics is the part of philosophy having to do with the ultimate causes and basic nature of matters. Just as physics deals with the laws that govern the physical world such as those of gravity or the properties of different types of particles, metaphysics describes what is beyond physics -- the nature and origin of reality itself, the immortal soul, and the existence of a supreme being. Opinions about these metaphysical topics vary widely, since what is being discussed cannot be observed or measured or even truly known to exist. So most metaphysical questions are still as far from a final answer as they were when Plato and Aristotle were questioning them. Regardless of appearances the majority of methodologies associated with metaphysics are a paradox.

## THE PROTECTIVE AURA

Teachers of Metaphysics instruct their pupils in regard to creating and maintaining the "Protective Aura", which is a shelter of soul, mind, and body against evil influences directed toward them consciously. This Protective Aura affords a simple but very effective armor against psychic influences, "malicious mental magnetism", black magic, etc., and is also an effective armor against psychic vampirism, or the draining of magnetic strength.

Forming the Protective Aura is very simple. I consists merely of the formation of a mental image (accompanied by the demand of Will) of yourself being surrounded by an aura of pure, clear, white, LIGHT -- the symbol and indication of SPIRIT. A little practice will enable you actually to feel the presence and power of this Protective Aura. The White LIGHT is the radiation of SPIRIT, and SPIRIT is master of all things. A teacher has said; "the highest and deepest occult teaching is that the white LIGHT must never be used for attack or personal gain, but that it may properly be employed by anyone, at any time, to protect himself or herself against adverse psychic influences, no matter by whom exerted. It is the armor of SPIRIT, and may well be employed in such a way whenever the need arises.

## THE TOWER OF LIGHT EXERCISE

The exercise is a form of passive psychic self-defense and involves active mediation using visualization. It is easy to do and should be done two or three times a day, at least in the early morning and before retiring. The exercise is quite safe and can be done as many times during the day as desired. With practice, the visualization is more easily performed and can be called upon at will. Each step of this exercise serves an important function and should not be omitted.

1. Stand erect, feet shoulder-width, arms at your sides, breathing
Evenly and deeply.

2. Progressively relax your entire body starting from the top of your
Head working slowly down to the bottoms of your feet.

3. Mentally visualize that you are surrounded by a long ellipsoid of
Intense blue light that extends 9 inches outwardly from every
Point on the surface of your body.

4. Continue to maintain this image and visualize a globe of brilliant
White light above (but not touching) your head.  The globe
Is inside of your bright blue aura.

5. Concentrate on this bright white globe so that it becomes
Brighter, glowing white like burning magnetism.

6. Keep both images of the bright blue aura and the brilliant white
Globe and mentally aspire to the highest standards of morality,
Good, and love that you can.

7. Next, feel the white globe showering you with glittering white light
Filled with silver sparkles.  This white light should permeate
Your entire being, coursing vibrantly through you.

8. The outer shell of your aura should be an intense bright blue
Filled with the vibrant, sparkling white light.  Concentrate on this
Complete image as long as you can, fully believing in its reality.
Feel your outer auric shell as a hard, sharply defined blue as you
Feel blissful and alert.

9. As you close, let the image fade slowly while believing that it is
Not fading from reality.

# THE PINK CLOUD MEDITATION

This technique was shared by one of my mentors Kaimora who is now in spirit.

Sit or lie in a comfortable position. Visualize a beautiful soft pink cloud above you. Call the soul of the person to whom you wish to communicate with to the pink cloud. Usually no soul declines this invitation for the pink cloud is a safe place of Universal love and protection. Communicate with the soul you have invited and once you are both satisfied with the session, thank and dismiss the invited soul. Thank the Universe and then return to your being.

Some actually create a pink cloud from fabric and place it above their bed. Others have created a photo which they say they have used until they perfect the meditation.

# CHAPTER TWELVE

## Herbal Solutions:
## How to make Incense, Oils, Potions, Specialty Baths, and where to Purchase Supplies.

Herbal Technology is simple for the powers, the vibrations, are in the herbs themselves. Outside forces need not be called into play for the power is resident within the organic matter.

Naturally herbs won't do much good once something has manifested -- protective herbs should be viewed as preventatives for they create a type of force field or shield surrounding our person and space.

Tools I recommend. The following items are for those who are desirous of herbal treatments and these are to be exclusively used for potion making.

· A mortar & pestle to grind herbs and seeds.
· A large wooden or ceramic bowl.
· A large glass or enameled pot (avoid metals, unless instructed) for brewing
   infusions or potions.
· Simple Sewing supplies (needles, pins, scissors, cotton thread, thimbles, assorted
   colors of cotton and wool cloth, yarn).
· Candles & Herbs
· Candleholders
· Incense burner & self-igniting incense charcoals
· Jars & bottles to store your herbs: amber & clear.
· Parchment Paper
· Quills or pens with assorted inks
· Lighters & matches
· Farmer's Almanac and an Ephemeris
· Comprehensive Hebrew Calendar (Astrological)

Supplies can be obtained from metaphysical, new age, religious, occult, or herb businesses. I *prefer* to purchase most plants & herbs fresh from nurseries. Many items can be purchased reasonably from grocery, craft, or fabric stores. Additionally items can be bought securely and discreetly through the Internet. Enter Keywords such as magic or magical supplies, occult supplies, herbs, metaphysical supplies, and the search should result in a number of contacts.

**Infusions** are simply a process of soaking or steeping herbs in hot or tepid water. Prepare them in a glass or enameled pot keeping the liquid covered and in the case of hot infusions so that minimal steam is lost. Energize herbs before infusion by projecting your intentions upon them with prayer, meditation or thought. Use one teaspoon dried herb to every cup of water. For cold infusions allow to steep for 7 to 9 days. For hot infusions, heat water until just boiling. Pour over herb and cover. Let steep 9 to 13 minutes. Strain and cool before using unless you are consuming it as a hot tea. Infusions are also added to baths, used as floor washes and to anoint the body.

**Baths or Banos** offer a simple method of covering the entire body with herbal vibrations. The best method is to prepare an infusion and add the strained liquid to the tub.

*It is important to understand how to properly take a *spiritual or ritual bath*. First take a shower or bath to remove daily dirt and grime. Clean out the tub and be certain that the entire bathroom is clean as well. Prepare the bath by filling the tub half full and add *prepare d herbal bath formula or other treatment* while drawing the bath. Enter the bathtub nude and immediately immerse yourself, head included. You may rinse your mouth with the water but do not swallow it. Remain in the bath for 8- 10 minutes and meditate with certainty on its purpose. When leaving the tub wrap your hair in a white towel but do not dry it, likewise put on a white bathrobe but do not towel dry for you need the body to air dry. If the area in which you live is warm you may remain nude until completely air dried. Do not wash hair or bathe for 24 hours following a spiritual or ritual bath.

**Oils** are made of a blend of 50% olive oil or light mineral oil with the remaining 50% of ingredients being herbs, coloring, crystals or minerals, or other oils.

**Incense** is any combination of herbs, flowers, perhaps essential oils and a base which are mixed together and burned on self-igniting charcoals. A base can be made with Bamba Wood which is crushed bamboo; its pleasantly scented wood base makes an excellent foundation to which oils may be added. You can crush the Bamba with a Mortar and Pestle. Some of my acquaintances use a food processor, exclusive to herbal formulation, to pulverize or chop plants.

Each incense or blend can be compared to a telephone number or email address which will be answered according to the intention perceived. Each odor appeals to a particular spiritual force and it is that force=20 that answers

Saltpeter, potassium nitrate, may be added to incense blends to facilitate burning. It is common knowledge that many institutions add Saltpeter to food to decrease sexual desire, however if the *will* or issue of the recipient is power and control rather than sex, this measure has proven to be ineffective.

Burning a gum incense on charcoal is the most pure way and is not difficult. Self-igniting charcoal and appropriate incense burners can be purchased from any religious, occult, or herb store. The charcoal rapidly ignites across the entire surface. Soon the charcoal will turn red with heat and the incense powder or gum can be added with a teaspoon. Add only a ¼ of a teaspoon at a time, allow it to burn completely before adding more. When you place the incense on the charcoal you may pray or meditate upon your desire. I have several incense burners and my favorite is a large iridescent shell which I fill with a small amount of colored sand to absorb the heat.

When spell casting, it is possible to transform your body into a magical vessel via your diet. What we eat can be taken into consideration because as it is said, "we are what we eat." I certainly am not implying that a person should become vegan or abstain from food for I am a carnivore myself. There are books and much information on the net regarding not only the nutritional properties of food, but the magical energies as well. Example: If you are planning a prosperity spell, a fresh Asian style stir fry with rice is great or even Italian cuisine. For Love and Protection a fruit salad of Pineapple, Cantaloupe, Grapes, Strawberries, and Honey Dew is deliciously effective or fresh berries of Strawberries, Raspberries, Blackberries, and Blueberries with a Zabaglione Cream is fabulous. On New Year's Day our dinner to ensure prosperity for the New Year consists of cooked Cabbage or Greens, Black-eyed peas or beans, Sweet Potatoes, Pork Roast, Pecan Pie, Jell-O with Peaches, Grapes, and Bananas, Iced Sassafras Tea or Root Beer. It is said that if you feel -- you require grounding, it is recommended consuming some meat. However, before considering any dietary change, please consult with your physician especially if you have existing health conditions. Remember balance and moderation is the key to success, not excesses. I always cleanse my food with prayer or meditation especially when eating out for I have knowledge that many commercial kitchens run on chaos or drama. Also, thanking the plant and animal kingdom for their contributions and sacrifices so that we may consume wonderful food can result in rewards regarding karma.

Timing can be important however there are unforeseen occurrences which require immediate attention and cannot wait for the moon to be in a specific sign or other aspects. I personally do prefer to prepare potions and perform rituals for banishing during the waning moon (full moon to new moon) and those for protection during the waxing moon (new moon to full moon). Some prefer to avoid using the new moon until 24 hours have passed and I avoid treatments when the moon is void of course. The only times of the year I am particularly cautious of are *Cosmic Danger Zones,* which are the existence of energies created before the Earth existed whose forces shape human condition and exert their control over our physical universe. (Chapter 17)

Again if faced with an emergency the Universe is aware of the need and will reciprocate; proceed with certainty and all will be well!

# CHAPTER THIRTEEN

## Recipes for Oils, Incense, Infusions, Floor Washes, and Specialty Baths

### SPECIALTY INCENSES

I am sharing these incense formulations; one, because I believe everyone on this planet rightfully deserves access to information and tools for protection and defense -- self-preservation -- survival. After all, there truly are no secrets for there is nothing new under the sun. Many of these incense blends are a key ingredient in some formulas already disclosed. Use a mortar and pestle to grind/blend your herbs. I use self-igniting charcoal for burning incense. Also, you can create oils and baths from these incense recipes simply by using the key ingredients and following the instructions under **OILS** and **INFUSIONS**.

Proper Cleansing of a House, Apartment, or Business is essential for a successful outcome. Before starting, open all windows; start the cleansing from the back proceeding to the front then out the front door. If this is the first cleansing remain outside for 30 minutes, after this time passes return indoors and close the windows. Regardless, always wait 30 minutes before closing the windows so that the negative energy may break free and exit. *Please remember to release your prayers and intentions to the Creator while performing the cleansing!*

I must mention that some people when cleansing with sage or herbs of this nature prefer to keep the windows closed until the fumigation is complete and then open the windows. It is believed that this somewhat suffocates the low vibrational beings creating fear so that they will depart readily and hesitate returning. Please remember that certain herbs and minerals are poisonous such as sulphur (sulfur) and to keep the windows closed in this case would suffocate you or any living being residing within the premises as well.

Self-Fumigation is recommended on a monthly basis and most prefer the Full Moon for this type of cleansing. Simply take a straight back chair, a flat white bed sheet, prepare your charcoal and incense formula, place the incense burner directly beneath the chair, sit on the chair nude or in your underwear, drape your body and the chair with the sheet leaving your head uncovered and be certain that the sheet is not touching the incense burner. It will appear as though you are in a sauna; fumigate for 15 - 20 minutes while meditating on the significance of the cleansing.

### ARCHANGEL INCENSE

1 part Lavender, 2 parts Sandalwood, 7 drops of Holy Water, 1 drop of blue food coloring; blend well and grind into a fine powder, allow to dry then burn to attract Angelic assistance.

## ASTRAL PROJECTION

Equal portions of Dittany of Crete (*Dictamus origanoides*), Sandalwood, Benzoin, and Vanilla. Blend and Grind well then burn as an aid in astral travel. If you are planning travel across large bodies of water it is recommended to add Dulse *(Rhodymenia palmate)* to the mixture for this placates the spirits of the sea and increases contact with wind spirits. For those that use Dulse it appears to place them on a higher astral level so as not to get caught in any *knots* or other astral baggage.

## BANISHING OR UNCROSSING

3 parts Bay leaves, 2 parts Cinnamon, 9 drops of Red Wine, Red Rose Petals, 1 part Myrrh, 1 part Salt. Blend and Grind well; allow to dry. Then burn to eliminate negative energies.

## CROWN OF SUCCESS

Equal parts of Orris, Frankincense, Vetivert, White Sandalwood, and Gold Glitter. Blend and grind herbs well then add glitter. Burn to assist you when others appear to be holding you down, and/or to thwart gossip or slander.

## DOVE'S HEART INCENSE

Equal parts Lavender, Rose, Wisteria, and Lilac. Blend and grind well, add to Sandalwood base and burn when your heart is feeling heavy for it appears to calm even the most restless soul.

## EGYPTIAN KYPHI INCENSE

½ part Myrrh, 1part Balm of Gilead, 1 part Frankincense, 1 part grated Orange peel, 1 part Lotus, and 1 part Sweet Flag. Mix thoroughly with mortar and pestle. Burn on self-igniting charcoal.

## FAST LUCK INCENSE

1 part Patchouli, 1 part Rose, 1 part Juniper Berries, 1 pulverized Dollar Bill. Grind all ingredients well with a mortar and pestle. Burn on self-igniting charcoal.

## FIERY WALL OF PROTECTION

1 part Dragon's Blood, 3 parts Frankincense, 1 part Myrrh, 1 part Salt. Blend well and burn on self-igniting charcoal.

## GOOFER DUST, GRAVEYARD DUST
1 part Patchouli Leaves, 1 part Mullen, 1 part Vetivert, and Dirt from a Graveyard. Grind and mix all ingredients well. If you have an aversion to cemeteries, you can eliminate the dirt from a graveyard. However if you do choose actual Graveyard dirt, you need to make payment for the Graveyard dirt. When entering a cemetery at midnight, leave 9 dimes at the left side of the entrance. At the grave leave a small shot glass of whiskey at the head (optional). Dig a hole at the heart or head area, gather the dirt and then bury the dime in the soil.

## GOOFER DUST II
Graveyard Dirt, 1 part Sulphur, 1/2 part Salt, 1/4 part Red Pepper, 1/4 part Black Pepper, 1 part Bone Powder, 1/2 part Powdered Insects, 1 part Powdered Mullein, 1/2 part Magnetic Sand.

## HERMES INCENSE
1 part Lavender, 1 part Mastic, and ¼ part cinnamon. Grind and blend well. Burn on self-igniting charcoals.

## JYOTI
Equal parts of Galangal, Nasturtium seeds, and Patchouli. Blend and Grind well, burn for protection and purification.

## KABBALAH INCENSE
Equal parts Myrtle, Cedar, and Frankincense. Blend well. Add 10 drops of Kabbalah water and enough blue and red food color to make purple. Allow to dry. Burn only in group sessions and it is recommended that it is best to use only white candles - if needed.

## KYPHI INCENSE
1 part Myrrh, 1 part Frankincense, 1 part Olibanum, 1 part Balm of Gilead, 1 part Cassia, and 1 part Lotus. Grind and Blend well. Used to banish negativity, evil spirits, or bad luck.

## MYSTIC INCENSE
1 part High John the Conqueror, 1 part Lo John the Conqueror, ½ part cinnamon, 1 part Squill. Grind well with a mortar and pestle. Burn on self-igniting charcoal.

## PEACE INCENSE
4 parts Lavender, 3 parts Thyme, 2 parts Vervain, 3 parts Basil, 1 part Frankincense, pinch of Rue, pinch of Benzoin, 1 part Jasmine, ¼ part Bergamot. Blend and Grind well. Burn on self-igniting charcoal.

## PRAYER INCENSE

Equal parts Frankincense, Sandalwood, and Vanilla. Blend and grind well, burn during meditation to banish negative vibrations and to invite only benevolent energies.

## QABAL

Equal parts Gum Mastic, Lavender, Violet, Gardenia, and Deer's Tongue. Blend herbs well then add Gum Mastic, burn to set up positive vibrations. Is also added to other incense blends to promote success.

## ROOT

Equal parts High John the Conqueror, Low John the Conqueror, and Adam & Eve root. Grind well into powder and burn to counteract negative or intrusive energy.

## SALT AND ALUM

This combination when burned has little odor and produces stable vibrations within one's environment. Burn 1 tsp. (5 ml) ground salt adding 1 tsp. (5 ml) of Alum, to cleanse with this formula during the daylight hours on a Sunday preferably before two o'clock in the afternoon and ideally during the waxing moon *(new moon to full moon)*.

## SEVEN ROOT

2 parts Nutmeg, 3 parts Vetivert, 2 parts Tonka beans, 3 parts Patchouli, 2 parts Adam and Eve root, 3 parts Beth Root, and 3 parts High John the Conqueror root. Blend and Grind as fine as possible, burn for protection from secret enemies and to remove a hexed condition.

## SATAN BE GONE

Equal parts Lavender, Salt, Hyssop, Bay, and Vervain. Blend and Grind well, burn to remove low level negative vibrations from yourself or another. *Use with caution, this is a very strong banishing formula with some probable interesting psychic effects; if this is experienced simply proceed with the cleansing.*

## SHI SHI

Equal portions of Clove, Bay, and Angelica. Also, use some Sandalwood or Bamba wood as a base. Blend and Grind well. Add a few drops of green food coloring, allow the mixture to dry. Burn this formula when you feel that your prosperity needs a boost. If you suspect interference regarding your finances stemming from a psychic attack, first use a banishing formula then use the Shi Shi formula.

## SPIRITUALISTS INCENSE

1 part Patchouli, 1 part Gum Mastic, ½ part Cinnamon, and 1 part Dittany of Crete. Grind and blend well with a mortar and pestle the Patchouli, Cinnamon, and Dittany of Crete. Cut the Gum Mastic into small pieces and add to mixture. Used for séances or scrying.

## SUCCESS INCENSE

2 parts Orris, 1 part Allspice, 2 parts Patchouli, 1 part Myrrh, ¼ part Frankincense, 2 parts White Sandalwood, 2 parts Rose petals, and a pinch of Benzoin Blend well. Assists in removing obstacles, defeating competition, and effective in legal matters.

## TEMPLE INCENSE

1 part Myrrh, 1 part Balm of Gilead, 1 part Frankincense, 1 part grated Orange rind, 1 part Lotus, and 1 part Sweet Flag. Grind and Blend as fine as possible with a mortar and pestle. Burn on self-igniting charcoal. Use to purify your sacred area.

## TIPHARETH INCENSE

2 parts Dittany of Crete, 2 parts Pine, 1 part Myrrh, 1 part Dragon's Blood, 2 parts Patchouli, 220 parts Balm of Peru. Blend well and use with caution for this formula can easily draw its potency from the Qlippoth.

# OILS

**To prepare** all-purpose anointing oil simply take the herbs needed, blend well and grind into small pieces. *When I make oils I usually make enough for a dozen small bottles. I use a large, wide, mouth mason jar for preparation and after the recommended time factor for infusing, I transfer to smaller bottles. *Add your prepared herbs in a base of olive, vegetable, or mineral oil. *Some formulas will require different oils, such as grape seed. There are actually many other cooking oils you can use, I experimented, and I prefer extra light olive oil. *When adding roots make small cuts into them with a sharp knife. *For resins such as Frankincense, cut into small pieces. If the recipe calls for adding color, use candle dye for food coloring contains water and water & oil do not mix. *Allow this mixture to soak for one moon (4 weeks or 28 days). *Initiate Oils for constructive purposes during a waxing moon and those for destructive during a waning moon. <u>Do not store your oils made during waxing with those made during a waning moon.</u> You may then dispense into smaller bottles with a glass dropper if you wish or just keep in the large preparation jar or bottle. *<u>Do not store in direct sunlight or excessive heat.</u> Bottles can be purchased from wholesale bottle manufacturers or from the sources mentioned under supplies. *Also you can take any of the recipes for oils and translate into incense or specialty baths. Simply use the key ingredients and follow the directions under **INFUSIONS** for baths and floor wash. For **INCENSES** simply grind and blend well with a mortar and pestle.

## ATTRACTION OIL
16 parts Wood Base, 2 parts Orris Root, 4 Cinnamon Sticks, 2 parts Myrrh, 4 parts Sandalwood, 8 parts Oilbanum. Follow directions for OILS.

## HIGH JOHN THE CONQUEROR OIL
2 parts of High John the Conqueror Root, 1 part Vetivert, and 1 part Bergamot. Follow directions under OILS.

## BEND OVER OIL
1 part Honeysuckle, 1 part Vetivert, 1 part Frankincense, 1 part Rose. Follow directions for OILS.

## BIBLE OIL (Blessing Oil)
Equal parts Hyssop and Frankincense. Use for prayer, meditation and anoint candles with the exception of black. Put a few drops on hot charcoals before adding incense. Follow directions for formulation under OILS.

## BLACK ARTS OIL
1 part Myrrh, 1 part Patchouli, 1 part Cinnamon, 1 part Gum Mastic, 1 Part Graveyard Dust, 1 part Vetivert, and 1 part Sage. For Black Magic only. Use to curse only those you despise. Follow the directions for formulation under OILS.

## COME TO ME
1 part Rose, 1 part Jasmine, 1 part Gardenia, 1 part grated rind of Lemon.
Follow directions for OILS.

## COMPELLING OIL
4 parts Patchouli, 4 parts Vetivert, 1 part grated rind of Lime, 1 part Bay leaf.
Follow directions under OILS for formulation.

## DRAGON'S BLOOD OIL
1 part Dragon's Blood, 15 parts Oil, 1 part Arabic. Use a few drops on hot charcoal
before adding the appropriate incense formula. Do not anoint candles with this oil.
To make Dragon's Blood Ink substitute 15 parts 90% alcohol rather than the oil.

It is not recommended that this formula be used on Mondays or Saturdays. According to
the Bible code the negative energy intelligence known as purgatory emerged on the
second day of creation. As the energy which brought Purgatory into existence was of a
negative quality, the second day of the week, Monday, is a day of intensified negative
activity. Described by the ancient texts as an embodiment of this negative energy, Mars,
the "Red Planet," is associated with the second day and is thus considered a negative
influence. Although Tuesday is officially a Mars day, the third day was forged from the
right and left column on the Tree of Life. Tuesday the third day was infused with the
cosmic power of restriction which is the central column. The central column energy
forges unification between the right and left columns. Although the left and the right,
the positive and the negative are at odds, the left and the right merge with the central
column creating purposeful light and brilliance. Tuesday is the best day for any new
venture.

Saturday, the seventh day of the week was the day in which the Angel of Death came
into being. Some consider it Satan's day, but regardless it is not an energy intelligence
to disrespect. I have witnessed unusual happenings especially when the energy is
perverted or misused during these time zones. When the houses of Mars, Saturn and the
Moon prevail it is not wise to venture into any new undertakings and this includes the
weekdays they influence as well. Humans, who were born on Monday or Saturday, *if
proactive in nature*, are the exception and can effectively use this resin successfully
without repercussions.

## GREEN FAIRY OIL

Green Fairy Oil is used to stimulate creativity. Make sure your herbs are fresh and green, though dried. This is extremely important regarding the quality of the final product.

**Herbs:**
Cardamom - 1 part
Lemon Balm (Melissa) - 1 part
Hyssop - 1 part
Common Wormwood (*Artemesia absinthium*) - 3 parts
Petite Absinthe (*Artemesia Pontica*) - 3 parts
Green or Spanish Anise, powdered - 2 parts
Whole and powdered Fennel - 1/4 part
Calamus, powdered 1/16 part
Peppermint - 1 part
Grape seed oil – Base

If you have gathered your own wormwood, strip the leaves from the stems and only use the leaves. Gently macerate the herbs together until they are well mixed. Add the Grape seed oil. Allow this mixture to set for one moon. Do not use this oil internally. I advise moderation when using this formula.

**This oil can be used for:**
Anointing candles or yourself
Making magical candles
Omit the Grape seed oil to use as incense
Omit the Grape seed oil place in a linen or cotton bag to place in bath water

## HOLY OIL (Blessing Oil)

Olive oil base, 1 part Lily Petals, 1 part White Rose Petals or buds, 1 Small Cross. Blend and grind the flowers into small pieces. If you are able to find miniature rose buds, these can be used whole. Add ingredients into a bottle and soak for 28 days. Some persons prefer to begin this formula on a Sunday, during a Sun hour while the moon is in waxing (new moon to full moon).

## KING SOLOMON OIL

1 part Solomon Seal, 1 part Hyssop, and 2 part Roses. Follow directions for formulation under OILS.

## LOVE OIL
1 part Palm Oil, ½ part Musk, 1 part Frangipani. Follow directions for formulation under OILS.

## MASTER OIL
1 part Deer's Tongue, 1 part Patchouli, and 1 part Brick dust. Grind and blend well. Commonly used by men for love, luck, or material power. Follow directions for formulation under OILS.

## MEDITATION OIL or INCENSE
1 part of Sandalwood, 1 part Orris, 1 part Mastic, and ¼ part Cinnamon. Grind and blend well. Burn on self-igniting charcoal. Great for Psychic endeavors for it creates a strong attraction for spirits. To create an oil refer to directions under OILS.

## MONEY OIL
2 parts Frankincense, ½ part grated Orange rind, ¼ part Bay leafs, 1 Cinnamon stick, ¼ part Cassia,1 part Tonka,1 part Heliotrope, 1 part Golden sand. Follow directions under OILS. Use golden colored Olive Oil for your base and initiate process during a waxing moon.

## SPECIAL OIL #20
Equal parts of Gardenia, Jasmine, Orris, and Muguet. You can add some red coloring is you like. I recommend candle dye, for food coloring contains water and oil & water do not mix. Use for courage and to uncross. Follow directions under OILS.

## SPECIAL FAVORS OIL
1 part grated rind of Lime, 1 part Carnation, 1 part Gardenia, 1 part Teaberry. Follow directions for formulation under OILS. Anoint yourself, your altar and your room to attract friendly elementals along with luck and success.

## STAY AT HOME OIL
1 part Bay, 1 part Frangipani, 1 part Lavender, ½ part cinnamon. Follow the directions under OILS for formulation. Mix some of the oil with some sugar and make sure the mixture is finely ground and dry. While your partner is sleeping take the mixture and lightly sprinkle on their undergarments. It is said to cure infidelity.

## SUCCESS OIL
2 parts Orris, 1 part Allspice, 2 parts Patchouli, 1 part Myrrh, ¼ part Frankincense, 2 parts White Sandalwood, 2 parts Rose petals, and a pinch of Benzoin. Follow directions under OILS.

## UNCROSSING OIL

1 Lemon, ¼ part Bay leaves, 1 Red Rose, 1 Lily, 1 Palm Cross, 1 piece of Vetivert root, and Olive oil base. Cut the Lemon and the Vetivert root with a sharp knife. Place all the ingredients into a bottle and soak for 28 days. Begin preparations during the waning moon (full moon to new moon), preferably when the moon is in a fire sign (Aries, Leo, or Sagittarius). Place a few drops on hot charcoals before adding incense formula and/or anoint candles with the oil.

## VOODOO OIL

1 part Myrrh, 1 part Graveyard Dirt, 1 part Patchouli, 1 part Mullen, 1 part Vetivert, 1 part Pine, 1 Part Clove, and 1 part grated Lime rind. Follow directions under OILS for formulation. You can transform this into incense or powder by grinding and blending well with a mortar and pestle.

# SPECIALTY BATHS

The following baths classified as non-herbal have proven to be effective when used properly. Baths or Banos are infusions. Before taking a spiritual bath, shower cleaning your body and your hair. Refer to Chapter 12.

## BEER BATH

The beer bath is used to treat *Malochia* or *"The Evil Eye"*. After proper preparations add one quart of beer to half a tub of water. Add 1 Tbsp. (20 ml) Salt, and stir clockwise until thoroughly mixed. Enter the tub and immerse yourself totally 3 times. Then sit in the tub and pour the water over yourself. Remain in the tub for 7 minutes. Wrap your hair in a white towel and put on a white robe, *do not towel dry*. Relax and meditate to release the condition. Some use the 23 Psalm, some the Lord's Prayer; use what is comfortable for you and connects you to benevolent energies.

## COFFEE

Coffee baths can assist those recovering from a physical illness by providing revitalization. It may be employed while the person is in a weakened state, but recovering. Add 8 cups (2L) of strong fresh brewed *(no instant)* coffee to a tub of water and soak in it for 10 -15 minutes. This can also be used by those who *work hard* and in this case it is to only be done on a Saturday morning.

## DRAGON'S BLOOD BATH CRYSTALS

1 cup (230 grams) of Rock Salt Base, ¼ tsp. (1ml) Dragon's Blood, ¼ tsp. (1 ml) ground Cinnamon stick, and ½ tsp.(2 ml) ground mint. Blend well and add a few drops of red food coloring. This is a protective formula and is added to other mixtures for this purpose. Again, I do not recommend this formula to be used on Mondays or Saturdays; refer to Dragon's Blood Oil for explanation.

## TENSION BATH

Mix 1 cup (250 ml) of Epsom salt, 1 cup (250 ml) of bicarbonate *(baking)* soda, and ¼ (50 ml) cup of table or sea salt. Soak for 10 -20 minutes. If you feel that you are being overwhelmed with negative influences, substitute 1 cup (250 ml) of cider vinegar for the baking soda.

## WALNUT BATH

The walnut bath is used to break the astral strings of a past relationship. When we engage in sexual relations with another person an astral tie is created and often in order to move on these strings need to be severed. However this can only be done once for each person, so be certain that you truly wish to sever the relationship.

In an iron pot, boil 6 whole walnuts (in their shells) if you are male, and 9 if you are female in 3 quarts of water for around 3 hours. Add water as needed. Set aside to cool. Add the black liquid to one half tub of water. Bathe for 8 minutes, immersing yourself 7 times while meditating on severing the relationship. Do not towel off, allow your body to air dry.

**INFUSIONS** are simply a process of soaking or steeping herbs in hot or tepid water. Prepare them in a glass or enameled pot keeping the liquid covered and in the case of hot infusions so that minimal steam is lost. Energize herbs before infusion by projecting your intentions upon them with prayer, meditation or thought.

Use one teaspoon dried herb to every cup of water and or alcohol. For cold infusions allow to steep for 7 to 9 days. For hot infusions, heat water until just boiling. Pour over herb and cover. Let steep 9 to 13 minutes. Strain and cool before using unless you are consuming it as a hot tea. I use cheesecloth for straining. Infusions are also added to baths, used as floor washes and to anoint the body.

## FOUR THIEVES VINEGAR

2 parts High John the Conqueror root, 1 part Vetivert, 1 part Adam and Eve Root, 1 part Lo-John, 1 part Lemongrass, 1 part Rue, 1 part Sage, ½ part garlic, and 2 pints (950 ml) Red Wine or Cider Vinegar. Initiate this on a Monday or during the Full Moon. Place in pot of boiling hot water and steep for 13 minutes. Store in a dark place and infuse for nine days. Strain and use as needed. Commonly used to drive enemies away.

## FLORIDA WATER

2 pints (1 L) of 90% Alcohol, 1 part grated Lemon rind, 1 part grated Lime rind, 1 part Portugal, 1 part Lavender, 1 part Cloves, 1 part Bergamot, 3 Cinnamon sticks and 2 pints (1 L) of Spring water. Begin infusion in a waxing moon. Store is a safe place out of the sunlight for 14 days. Strain and use as needed. Florida water is used to banish negativity. It can be sprinkled in your home, business, or your sacred space before a ritual.

## PEACE WATER

1 cup (250 ml.) Holy Water, 1 cup (250 ml.) Spring Water, 1 cup (250 ml.) Rain Water, 1 cup (250 ml.) Rose Water, and 3 oz. Lavender. Start this infusion during a Waxing Moon. Place in a clean safe place and infuse for 7 days. Strain and sprinkle throughout the home to create peace.

## WAR ( MARS ) WATER

**Part I:**
2 pints ( 1 L ) of 90% Alcohol, 1 part grated Lemon rind, 1 part grated Lime rind, 1 part Portugal, 1 part Lavender, 1 part Cloves, 1 part Bergamot, 1 part Red Pepper, 1 part Black Pepper, 3 Cinnamon sticks and 2 pints (1 L ) of Spring Water. Begin infusion on Monday, a day which according to the ancients contains an abundance of red energy or on Tuesday. Tuesday is the most cosmically balanced day of the week. Tuesday is officially a Mars day, the third day was forged from the right and left column on the Tree of Life. Tuesday the third day was infused with the cosmic power of restriction which is the central column. The central column energy forges an unification between the right and left columns. Although the left and the right, the positive and the negative are at odds, the left and the right merge with the central column creating purposeful light and brilliance. Tuesday is the best day for any new venture. Allow to infuse for 4 weeks or 28 days. Do not store in direct sunlight or excessive heat.

**Part II Mars Water:** Initiate preparation on a Tuesday. Take a large jar, spring water, and 7 very large Iron Nails. If you can find cut nails this is best, however if you cannot you will need to cut the nails. Place in the refrigerator. For the initial seven days open the jar to assist the oxidization process. Open periodically over the next 3 weeks. Strain the water as needed. You can keep adding water to the original jar with the cut iron n nails, thus providing an infinite supply. Keep this formula refrigerated.

When you are ready to go to war combine 50% of Formula I with 50% of Formula II. For an extra kick you can add Black Salt. This is a very powerful formula so use with care and be certain that your protections – your shield are up!

# CHAPTER FOURTEEN

# MAKING MAGICAL CANDLES

Candles have been used since the beginning of human history. For centuries candles provided light for homes, businesses, churches, and more. In the 1800's paraffin was introduced which replaced tallow as the main ingredient for candle making. Electricity is now the main source of light. However, candles are still widely used for other purposes. Candles create an ambiance for relaxation, meditation, and even romance. Candles are used for festive occasions such as holidays and birthdays. They invoke sanctity which is why they have a rich tradition in religious services in many faiths and cultures.

When making magical candles it is wise to plan in advance. For instance if you are creating candles for abundance and prosperity it is best to utilize the seasons of Spring and Autumn on a Tuesday, Thursday, or Sunday. Only use the month of Taurus or Iyar (lunar Taurus) if you want long term results, for this energy is not about speed but longevity and protection. For love, marriage, and partnerships the best months are April, June, September, and October. I would initiate candle making on the days of Tuesday, Friday, and Sunday with the moon in Libra or Leo. If you are only seeking lust and passion Scorpio or Mar Chesvan (lunar Scorpio) would be best, initiated on a Monday. If you are creating candles for hexing, reversible, uncrossing, or those of a destructive nature the best time would be in August or Menachem Av (lunar Leo) on a Monday or Tuesday. Many practitioners make 6 – 12 candles or more depending on projected use. These are great for resale and gifts. Refer to Chapter 17 on Timing to plan your candle making.

## **Making Container Candles**

## **Supplies**
Presto Kitchen Kettle (Best) or Double Boiler
Stainless Wire Wisk
Wick Trimmer
Hand Held Butane Torch
Glue Gun
Aluminum Wax Pour Pot or LG Pyrex Glass Measuring Cup
Wick Bar Holder
Wick Centering Tool (You may also use a firm straw or a small copper tube.)
Digital Scale
Thermometer with side clip
Aluminum Foil
Paper Towels
Old Newspapers

Inexpensive Plastic Floor Mat

Glass Containers – (I prefer wide mouth Mason jars or jelly jars. You can also utilize clean mayonnaise, jelly, pickle, or relish jars.)

Cookie Sheet

Gardening Gloves (I prefer the ones with the rubber grip dots on the palms.)

## Ingredients

Single Pour Container Wax – IGA 4630

Classic Container Wax – IGA 4786

Fragrance/Magical Oil - (Use only high quality oils. If you do not make your own it is best to purchase from occult, craft or candle making businesses. I highly recommend Sun' Eye oils and incenses.)

Liquid Candle Dye - (Do not use food coloring for it contains water – wax and water do not mix.)

Cotton Core Wicks – have a rigid inner core that will help keep your wick standing straight while burning. Cotton Core Wicks tend to mushroom less than other wicks preventing increased soot production due to carbon build up.

## Step One:  Preparation and Safety

Candle making can be a messy project, so you want to be certain that your work area is clean, safe, with all tools and ingredients organized. For easy cleanup, place foil, paper towels, and old newspapers on your counter tops. Place old newspapers or a plastic mat on the floor. Organize and arrange your tools, supplies and ingredients. Place your mason jars or glass containers on a cookie sheet. Heat up the oven and reduce heat to 150 degrees. Place the glass containers on the cookie sheet into the oven and leave there until you are ready to pour the candle formula into them. This will keep the glass from cracking and will insure a more quality product. I keep a small household fire extinguisher or a large box of baking soda nearby for wax does have a flash point if overheated. This is why we never leave my melting wax unattended.

## Step Two:  Formulating the Wax Mixture

Measure out the wax you will need. For example if you are going to make 3 – 8 oz. (230g) candles you will need 1-3/4 pound (790 g) of wax. I use ½ half, ¾ lb. (395g) Single Pour Container Wax – IGA 4630 and ½ half, ¾ lb. (395g) Classic Container Wax – IGA 4786. Place your wax in the Presto Kitchen Kettle or Double Boiler. Once the wax starts to melt clip the thermometer on the side. Once the temperature reaches 170 degrees add your candle dye to the wax. Mix for 2 -3 minutes with wire wisk. Be certain that the wax is at 170 degrees and now add your candle dye to the wax. Proceed to mix the color in for at least 2-3 minutes with the stainless wire wisk. You can test the color on a white paper towel and add more dye until you reach the desired color. Always mix the color in well (2-3 minutes) when adding more dye so that the color bonds with the wax.

Now we shall add the fragrance or magical oil. You will use 1 oz. (30 ml) of oil per 1 lb. (450 g) of wax. Warm the oil before adding and be certain that your wax is at 170 degrees. Using the wire wisk stir the fragrance in slowly for a minimum of 2 – 3 minutes so that the fragrance bonds with the wax.

## Step Three:  Preparing the Container (s)

Be certain that you candle wax is maintaining a temperature of 170 degrees. Remove your jars or glassware from the oven. I recommend wearing gardening gloves to prevent burns when handling hot glassware. Now you can place your wick centering tool or you can use a firm straw or copper tube. If you are using the latter, slide the wick into the tube. Hold the tube upside down, add a liberal amount of hot glue to the bottom of the wick tab then place the wick in the center of the container. Hold firmly for 30 seconds and when you remove the tube the wick should be centered. Wider containers will require 2 -3 wicks. If this is the case center the wicks ¾ inches (19.1 mm) apart.

You may need to experiment with wick sizes before starting your project. I recommend buying a sampler pack of wicks. 8 – 9 oz. (230 g) generally require a 44-24-18z wick while others prefer a 51-32-18z wick. I prefer Cotton Core wicks, but Zinc Core wicks are acceptable.

## Step Four:  Securing the Wick

Most people prefer to secure the wick after the wax is poured, however I prefer to do so prior to pouring which eliminates the wick from falling over. There are several methods you can use. My favorite is to take some 6 inch (14.4 cm) wooden skewers like you find in the grocery store. Take a rubber band and wrap tightly around sticks. Lay this across the top of your jar and pull the wick up through and between the sticks until it is standing nice and straight. The sticks will hold the wick up while you pour the hot wax mixture into your containers. I recommend preparing this type of wick holder prior to the candle making process.

You can also use a Wick Holder Bar, which can be purchased at a reasonable price. You simply place the wick into the tab and center.

You can make your own wick holder by:
Taking a Popsicle stick (s), drill a hole in the center of each stick, thread the wick through, rest on the lip of the container, and then clip the wick with a miniature clothes pin or an alligator clip at the point where is comes through the stick. Be certain that the wick is centered. I recommend preparing the sticks prior to candle making process.

## Step Five:  Pouring the Wax Formula

Again be certain your wax is at 170 degrees.  You will now need an aluminum pouring pot or a glass Pyrex measuring cup.  I recommend warming either before pouring so the wax does not harden in the process.  If the temperature is 170 degrees, stir the wax with the wire whisk once more for 1-2 minutes to insure bonding.  At this point you can take some 6 inch (14.4 cm) wooden skewers like you find in the grocery store.  Take a rubber band and wrap tightly around sticks.  Lay this across the top of your jar and pull the wick up through and between the sticks until it is standing nice and straight.  The sticks will hold the wick up while you pour the hot wax mixture into your containers.  This will eliminate the wick falling over.  Now dip your pour pot into the wax and proceed to pour the wax very slowly (to prevent bubbles) into your containers.  Be as precise as possible and do not spill wax on the sides and lip of your container or on your counter tops.  Fill your container to the level you desire, however leave enough room for the second pour.  Once all containers are filled, you can remove the remaining wax from the heat.

As the wax hardens you will notice a sink hole in the middle of the candle.  This is normal and, at this time take a wooden skewer and poke several relief holes around the wicks.

## Step Six:  Second Pour

Allow your candles to completely cool (16 – 24 hours) before a second pour.  Reheat the wax mixture to 180 degrees.  This will create a bonding between the first and second pour to eliminate telltale marks of two pours.  Once the temperature is at 180 degrees, stir for 1-2 minutes with a wire whisk to insure bonding.  Now pour just a hair above your first pour.

Allow your candles to cure for 2 weeks before burning them.  Keep the lids tight on the candles while they are curing and keep away from heat and sunlight.  Trim the business end of your wick (the end you light) to within 1/4 - 1/2 inch from the wax.

## Step Seven:  Cleanup

Take a cookie sheet and layer with paper towels.  Lay your utensils and tools upside-down on the paper towels.  Preheat the oven at 350 degrees and once it reaches this temperature lower to 150 degrees or keep warm.  Place the cookie sheet with your tools on it into the oven for 5 – 15 minutes.  The wax will melt onto the paper towels.  Remove from oven and wipe with paper towels.  I recommend using gloves for even item kept on keep warm can become very hot.

If you use a Presto Kitchen Kettle immediately after your final pour, wipe it a few times with a paper towel.  In order to get the fragrance out of the kettle, you can buy a commercial cleaner or use 1c (240 ml) water to 1c (240 ml) white vinegar on a paper towel to ensure the kettle is clean and pure for future candle making.

# Making Soy Candles

You make Soy Container Candles using the same Steps as in Making Container Candles with the following changes.

## In Step Two:  Formulating the Wax Mixture
**Follow the directions in Step Two with the following changes:**
Naturally you will use soy wax in place of paraffin wax. Being as 1-lb (450g) of soy wax yields 18 oz. (240ml) of liquid, you will need to use 2 lbs. (90 g) of soy wax for 3 – 8oz. (230g) candles.  You will heat the wax to a temperature of 185 -190 degrees before you add your fragrance or magical oil and candle dye.  You will add the candle dye first. Being as soy wax can hold a higher percentage of fragrance or magical oil – you will use 1.5 (45 ml) ounces of fragrance or magical oil as opposed to the 1 oz. (30 ml) used in paraffin wax.

## Step Three:  Preparing the Container (s)
**Follow the directions in Step Three with the following change:**
I recommend using The Heinz Stabilo wicks.  These are a German made all natural, core less, non-directional, flat braided wicks with a special paper filament woven around them.  They are formally known as CD wicks.  This configuration is engineered to promote maximum and consistent capillary action while ensuring a self-trimming wick that will hold the posture of the flame.  CD wicks are used with soy and vegetable wax candles.

## Step Five:  Pouring the Wax Formula
**Follow the directions in Step Five with the following changes:**
Before pouring you want to bring the temperature of the soy wax down to 110 -115 degrees.  With soy wax the temperature must initially be high so the candle dye and fragrance or magical oil bonds together.  Bringing it down to a low temperature helps prevent cracking, flaking, and discoloration.

As the temperature drops, for every 10 -15 degrees, stir well with the wire wisk for 2-3 minutes.  Once the temperature reaches 110-115 degrees, you can pour your soy wax mixture into your containers.
**Follow Steps One through Seven with <u>ONLY</u> the following changes listed above.**

# Making Moulded Candles

## Supplies

Presto Kitchen Kettle (Best) or Double Boiler
Stainless Wire Wisk
Wick Trimmer
Hand Held Butane Torch
Glue Gun
Aluminum Wax Pour Pot or LG Pyrex Glass Measuring Cup
Wick Bar Holder ( For certain molds )
Wick Screws ( For certain molds )
Mould Sealer or Masking Tape ( For certain molds )
Wick Tabs ( For candle molds that do not have a wick hole. You will need pre tabbed wicks or you will need to attach the wick tabs on the wick.)
Digital Scale
Thermometer with side clip
Aluminum Foil
Paper Towels
Old Newspapers
Inexpensive Plastic Floor Mat
Candle Mould (s)
Silicone Spray
Cookie Sheet
Gardening Gloves ( I prefer the ones with the rubber grip dots on the palms.)

## Ingredients

Straight Paraffin Wax – IGA 1343A or Pillar Blend – IGA 4625
Fragrance/Magical Oil - ( Use only high quality oils. If you do not make your own it is best to purchase from occult, craft or candle making businesses. I highly recommend Sun' Eye oils and incenses.)
Liquid Candle Dye - ( Do not use food coloring for it contains water – wax and water do not mix.)
Cotton Core Wicks – have a rigid inner core that will help keep your wick standing straight while burning. Cotton Core Wicks tend to mushroom less than other wicks preventing increased soot production due to carbon build up.

## Step One:  Preparation and Safety

Candle making can be a messy project, so you want to be certain that your work area is clean, safe, with all tools and ingredients organized. For easy cleanup, place foil, paper towels, and old newspapers on your counter tops. Place old newspapers or a plastic mat on the floor. Organize and arrange your tools, supplies and ingredients. Place your mason jars or glass containers on a cookie sheet. Heat up the oven and reduce heat to 150 degrees. Place the glass containers on the cookie sheet into the oven and leave there until you are ready to pour the candle formula into them. This will keep the glass from cracking and will insure a more quality product. I keep a small household fire extinguisher or a large box of baking soda nearby for wax does have a flash point if overheated. This is why we never leave my melting wax unattended.

## Step Two:  Formulating the Wax Mixture

Measure out the wax you will need. For example if you are going to make 3 – 8 oz. (230g) candles you will need 1-3/4 pound (790 g) of wax. Place your wax in the Presto Kitchen Kettle or Double Boiler. Once the wax starts to melt clip the thermometer on the side. Once the temperature reaches 180 degrees add your candle dye to the wax. Mix for 2 -3 minutes with wire wisk. Be certain that the wax is at 180 degrees and now add your candle dye to the wax. Proceed to mix the color in for at least 2 - 3 minutes with the stainless wire wisk. You can test the color on a white paper towel and add more dye until you reach the desired color. Always mix the color in well (2 - 3 minutes) when adding more dye so that he color bonds with the wax.

Now we shall add the fragrance or magical oil. You will use 1 oz. (30 ml) of oil per 1 lb. (450 g) of wax. Warm the oil before adding and be certain that your wax is at 180 degrees. Using the wire wisk stir the fragrance in slowly for a minimum of 2 – 3 minutes so that the fragrance bonds with the wax.

## Step Three:  Preparing the Mould

While your wax is melting you can prepare your mould. If you desire, you can prepare your mould before you begin formulating the wax. Many candle moulds have a small hole for the wick and you will simply need to thread it. For these types of moulds your wicks do not need tabs.

If you are using moulds without a wick hole, such as pillar or votive, you will need to use wicks with a wick tab. Now you can place your wick centering tool or you can use a firm straw or copper tube. If you are using the latter, slide the wick into the tube. Hold the tube upside down, add a liberal amount of hot glue to the bottom of the wick tab then place the wick in the center of the container. Hold firmly for 30 seconds and when you remove the tube the wick should be centered. Wider containers will require 2 -3 wicks. If this is the case center the wicks ¾ inches (19.1 mm) apart.

You may need to experiment with wick sizes before starting your project. I recommend buying a sampler pack of wicks 8 – 9 oz. (230 g) generally requires a 44-24-18z wick while others prefer a 51-32-18z wick. I prefer Cotton Core wicks, but Zinc Core wicks are acceptable.

## Step Four:  Securing the Wick

Most people prefer to secure the wick after the wax is poured, however I prefer to do so prior to pouring which eliminates the wick from falling over.  There are several methods you can use.  My favorite is to take some 6 inch (14.4 cm) wooden skewers like you find in the grocery store.  Take a rubber band and wrap tightly around sticks.  Lay this across the top of your jar and pull the wick up through and between the sticks until it is standing nice and straight.  The sticks will hold the wick up while you pour the hot wax mixture into your containers.  I recommend preparing this type of wick holder prior to the candle making process.

You can also use a Wick Holder Bar, which can be purchased at a reasonable price.  You simply place the wick into the tab and center.

You can make your own wick holder by:
Taking a popsicle stick (s), drill a hole in the center of each stick, thread the wick through, rest on the lip of the container, and then clip the wick with a miniature clothes pin or an alligator clip at the point where is comes through the stick.  Be certain that the wick is centered.  I recommend preparing the sticks prior to candle making process.

## Step Five:  Pouring the Wax Formula

Again be certain your wax is at 180 degrees.  You will now need an aluminum pouring pot or a glass Pyrex measuring cup.  I recommend warming either before pouring so the wax does not harden in the process.  If the temperature is 180 degrees, stir the wax with the wire whisk once more for 1-2 minutes to insure bonding.  At this point you can take some 6 inch (14.4 cm) wooden skewers like you find in the grocery store.  Take a rubber band and wrap tightly around sticks.  Lay this across the top of your jar and pull the wick up through and between the sticks until it is standing nice and straight.  The sticks will hold the wick up while you pour the hot wax mixture into your containers.  This will eliminate the wick falling over.  Now dip your pour pot into the wax and proceed to pour the wax very slowly (to prevent bubbles) into your containers.  Be as precise as possible and do not spill wax on the sides and lip of your container or on your counter tops.  Fill your container to the level you desire, however leave enough room for the second pour.  Once all containers are filled, you can remove the remaining wax from the heat.
*As the wax hardens you will notice a sink hole in the middle of the candle.  This is normal and, at this time take a wooden skewer and poke several relief holes around the wicks.

## Step Six:  Second Pour

Allow your candles to completely cool (16 – 24 hours) before a second pour.  Reheat the wax mixture to 190 degrees.  This will create a bonding between the first and second pour to eliminate telltale marks of two pours.  Once the temperature is at 190 degrees, stir for 1-2 minutes with a wire wisk to insure bonding.  Now pour just a hair above your first pour.

Allow your candles to cure for 2 weeks before burning them.  While the candles are curing, keep away from heat and sunlight.  Trim the business end of your wick (the end you light) to within 1/4 - 1/2 inch from the wax.

## Step Seven:  Cleanup

Take a cookie sheet and layer with paper towels.  Lay your utensils and tools upside-down on the paper towels.  Preheat the oven at 350 degrees and once it reaches this temperature lower to 150 degrees or keep warm.  Place the cookie sheet with your tools on it into the oven for 5 – 15 minutes.  The wax will melt onto the paper towels.  Remove from oven and wipe with paper towels.  I recommend using gloves for even item kept on keep warm can become very hot.

If you use a Presto Kitchen Kettle immediately after your pour your final pour, wipe it a few times with a paper towel.  In order to get the fragrance out of the kettle, you can buy a commercial cleaner or use 1c (240 ml) water to 1c (240 ml) white vinegar on a paper towel to ensure the kettle is clean and pure for future candle making.

# Making Layered Candles

In the Art of Magic, layered candles are referred to as double action candles, when there are two layers and when there are three layers, triple action candles. The most popular version is the double action reversible with the red bottom layer and the black top layer. A black topped double action candle could be created for any purpose. The black represents the crossed condition which has to be burned off. The color on the bottom layer metaphysically is saying to the perpetrator, "I will not give you my power and it is my will that will prevail."

When making container candles the other color is the first layer and you could add your zodiac oil or one that resonates with you. The second layer is the black and you can add uncrossing, unhexing, or reversible oil to the wax formula. When making molded candles the black is the first (bottom) layer and the other color is the second (top) layer. When making layered candles of this nature you will need two sets of tools, one for the uncrossing formulas and one for the other colors or fragrance candles. Be certain to keep these tools separated.

You will need to have an extra set of the following supplies: Presto Kitchen Kettle (Best) or Double Boiler, Stainless Wire Wisk, Wick Trimmer, Aluminum Wax Pour Pot or LG Pyrex Glass Measuring Cup, Wick Bar Holder (For certain molds) Wick Screws (For certain molds), Mold Sealer or Masking Tape (For certain molds), Wick Tabs (For candle molds that do not have a wick hole, you will need pre-tabbed wicks or you will need to attach the wick tabs on the wick.), Thermometer with side clip, Candle Mold (s), Cookie Sheet, Gardening Gloves (I prefer the ones with the rubber grip dots on the palms.)

During the ritual of making your candles, visualize what the purpose of the candle is and will be.

## Common Color Correspondences used in Candle Magic:

**Black/Red:** Reverse away blocks or obstacles in love, sex, energy or creativity in order to Attract Inspiration, Passion, Love, Romance, Creativity and Strength.

**Black/Green:** Reverse away blocks or obstacles in health, Money, Employment, and Bad Luck issues or situations. In order to Attract Prosperity, Healthy Habits, Fertility and Positive Attitudes.

**Black/White:** Use for Cleansing, and Spiritual work, Purifying your Space of Negative Energy. This can also be used to Thwart Gossip. Use the appropriate oil to the wax formula.

**Black/Brown:** Remove Obstacles or Jinx's related to Court Case Spells

**White:** Spirit Drawing, Spiritual Blessings, Healing, Paving the way for manifestation

**White/Blue:** Peace, Protection against Malochia (The Evil Eye) Kindness

**White/Yellow:** Psychic Power, Attraction, Money (Gold), Road Opener, Devotion, Mental Stimulation, and Prayer

**White/Green:** Money Spells, Prosperity, Gambling Luck, Business Luck, Fertility

**Pink/Red:** Love Spells, Passion, Lust, Romance

**White/Pink:** Affection, Friendship, Attraction

**White/Purple:** Spiritual Power, Commanding, Control, Mastery, Ambition

**White/Orange:** Dreaming True, Psychic Power, Road Opener

**Gold/Green:** Open Doors and Roads.

**Purple/Gold:** To insure Success and Victory in all your endeavors

# Double Action Layer Container Candles

*You will need the Supplies and Ingredients outlined under Making Container Candles. Be sure to wear latex or food service gloves when handling the black wax.
*Follow Steps One through Five under Making Container Candles. In Step Two you will need to divide your unprepared wax before melting for each of your colors. In Step Five the only change will be that you will fill the container half full with wax as opposed to the top.
*Allow your candles to completely cool (16 – 24 hours) before a second pour.
*Follow Steps One through Five again. Fill your container to the level you desire, however leave enough room for the second pour. Once all containers are filled, you can remove the remaining wax from the heat.
*Allow your candles to completely cool (16 – 24 hours) before a third pour.
*Now follow Steps 6 and 7.


# Double Action Layer Moulded Candles

*You will need the Supplies and Ingredients outlined under Making Molded Candles. Be sure to wear latex or food service gloves when handling the black wax.
*Follow Steps One through Five under Making Molded Candles. In Step Two you will need to divide your unprepared wax before melting for each of your colors. In Step Five the only change will be that you will fill the container half full with wax as opposed to the top.
*Allow your candles to completely cool (16 – 24 hours) before a second pour.
*Follow Steps One through Five again. Fill your mold to the level you desire, however leave enough room for the second pour. Once all containers are filled, you can remove the remaining wax from the heat.
*Allow your candles to completely cool (16 – 24 hours) before a third pour.
*Now follow Steps 6 and 7.

# Preparing Double Action Candles for Burning

## Preparing Container Candles
Take a cured candle and on the black wax at the top write the name of the one coming up against you, your nemesis, with a nail. If you have added the oils to your wax mixtures, you will not need to anoint the candle.

## Preparing Molded Candles
**For Taper Candles:** Cut off the top of the candle (the other color) so it will stand straight when it is turned upside down. On the black end carve a new tip for this will now be the top of the candle. **For Pillar Candles:** Cut the wick off the top of the candle (the other color) for this will now be the bottom of the candle. On the black end carve a new tip for this will now be the top of the candle. This is referred to as butting the candle. During the mold and wick preparation of taper or pillar style candles, some choose to pull a piece of wick through the wick tab before pouring the wax. This will provide some extra wick to utilize when they are carving a new tip on the black color end of the candle. If enough wick is pulled through very little carving will be needed for the length of wick you need is available.

At the boundary between the two colors take a nail writing from the boundary away from you in the black wax to the top, the one who crossed you nine times counterclockwise. Be certain to hold the black end away from you, not towards you for you are burning off the negative energy. Remember to wear gloves when working with black wax. Now at the boundary of the other color write a short phase that is appropriate for your spell and this time write toward you.

While you are preparing your candle, meditate and visualize your desired outcome. You can place reversible s, uncrossing, or banishing candles – these would be the black top candles – on a mirror and burn them. These are usually placed at your back door, however if you live in an apartment you can burn them in your bathroom. For safety, I have a large aluminum kettle that I place my candle in. I have one I use for black top candles and I have one I use for the candles that represent "constructive purposes." When the timing is right burn your candle. If you need advisement on timing refer to Chapter Seventeen. Remember the "Eye of Karma" sees each of us, so be certain that the action you are planning is justified and correct.

# Frequently Asked Questions (FAQ)

**Q: I have difficulty separating the slabs of soft wax?**
A: Stand the case of wax on its end, vertically (tall) not horizontally (bottom). It is also recommended that you store your wax in a cool place. You can also heat a large butcher or chef style knife with a heat gun and slice the slab to your preferred size. Heat the knife again and slide it in between the slabs lifting a little as you go.

**Q: The waxes you recommend are expensive, is there an alternative?**
A: Yes, you can use what is referred to as "straight paraffin wax." This type of paraffin does not have a binder so you will need to add Vybar to the mixture, otherwise your fragrance or magical oil and candle dye will seep from the wax. You could also use IG 4630 One Pour Container Wax.

**Q: Can I use food coloring or crayons as a dye to add color to my wax?**
A: No, this would compromise the quality of your candle. Food coloring contains water, wax and water do not mix. The wax that crayons are made with is not the same type of wax that is used in making candles. The result would be clogged wicks which would not burn properly.

**Q: How much liquid melted wax does a pound (450 g) of solid wax make?**
A: 1 pound (450 g) of Paraffin wax by weight will equal approximately 20oz (595 ml) of liquid melted wax; 1 pound (450 g) of Soy wax by weight will equal approximately 18oz (535 ml) of liquid when melted; 1 pound (450 g) of Beeswax by weight will equal approximately 16oz (475 ml) of liquid when melted.

**Q: I used an ounce of fragrance as directed, but there is very little scent throw?**
A: It is true that some scents and oils are more difficult to mix than others. Be certain that the oil you are using is of high quality. Warm your fragrance or oil well. Add 1 Tbsp. (25 g) of Vybar per pound (450 g) of wax and stir in for 2-3 minutes with a wire wisk. Now add your oil and whisk in well for 2-3 minutes.

**Q:  I do not have an oven, so how can I heat my jars or clean my tools when I am finished?**

**A:**  Take a heating pad and turn it on high.  Place a towel over the heating pan.  You can start this before you begin the candle making process.  If you are making container candles place your jars on the cookie sheet and cover with another towel to hold the heat in.  Once you pour your wax into the containers, layer the cookie sheet with paper towels.  Place your tools on the cookie sheet and allow the wax to melt off and then clean with paper towels.  You can also use a heat lamp to heat your glass containers and use along with the heating pad.  Just place the heat lamp over the cookie sheet with the jars and then the tools.

**Q:  I would like to make designs and write on my candle.  I have used nails and other sharp objects but it is not smooth.  What to do?**

**A:**  You can use a Heat Pen for this task.  It looks like a pen and heats up when plugged in.  I use it to create designs and write on my candles.  I use it to carve/write on my all-purpose fragrance candles, especially those I gift, and on my magical candles as well.

**Q:  When I make molded candles the bottoms are not as smooth as I would like in addition to bubbles and sink holes, what can I do to resolve this?**

**A:**  Use an Electric Frying Pan, Skillet, or Griddle.  Heat up and set the candle on it and slowly move the bottom of the candle around on the pan until it is flat.  You can use a heat gun (these are generally used to strip paint) to fix bubbles and sink holes.  You can also use a heat gun to pre-warm containers and re-melt wax on your tools to make removal easier.

**Q:  I like the idea of making my own candles, but I like the glass encased retail candles which have pictures of the Saints (Santos), Angels, Zodiac signs, etc..., – is there a solution?**

**A:**  Yes, there is a resolution.  You can buy these pictures from occult or curio stores on the internet for a reasonable price.  You can also copy or scan the picture you need, size it to the proper dimensions, cut to fit, and use a glue stick to attach it to your container.

# CHAPTER FIFTEEN

## MAKING TALLOW CANDLES

Tallow was one of the first mediums for making candles and soaps. Candles were essentially made from tallow and beeswax until around 1850. Candle makers would use the fat rendered from cows or sheep which was the primary materials used in candles in Europe. The only negative was that the odor from the process was very pungent due to the glycerin contained in tallow. In 1811 two French chemists patented stearin which is also derived from animals, but had no glycerin content. Around 1850 when paraffin was introduced the manufacture of tallow candles ceased, with the exception of people who lived in remote areas and continued to make their own tallow candles.

A misconception that I saw in one of the oldest books on candle magic stated that the use of tallow candles is evil and satanic. I disagree with this for tallow candles were used for centuries before paraffin and other types of candle wax was introduced. In South America and Africa there are those in the dark arts who do make candles from human tallow and naturally this would be in the category of evil and satanic.

In Brujeria circles tallow candles are made and used for these candles are considered more powerful when using for candle magic. Rather than animal sacrifice using a tallow candle would serve this purpose for fat can be rendered from any animal. I know I may be ridiculed for this because there are those of certain religious practices who still sacrifice animals. I purchase my fat or suet from a butcher or local farmer and believe me they are happy to be rid of it. In this way all the parts of an animal are used, nothing is wasted. I can understand that vegans, vegetarians, and animal activists would be opposed to this. We each have the right to our opinions or beliefs, as long as they are legal. Even if we cannot accept another's opinion or lifestyle we can at the very least tolerate one another.

Candle making can be challenging initially, however after you have made a few batches of candles it will become second nature.

# Making Container Candles using Tallow

## Supplies

Presto Kitchen Kettle (Best) after tallow is made.
Large Pot
Chef's Knife
Stainless Wire Wisk
Wick Trimmer
Fine Mesh Strainer
Glue Gun
Aluminum Wax Pour Pot or LG Pyrex Glass Measuring Cup
Wick Bar Holder
Wick Centering Tool (You may also use a firm straw or a small copper tube.)
Digital Scale
Thermometer with side clip
Aluminum Foil
Paper Towels
Old Newspapers
Inexpensive Plastic Floor Mat
Glass Containers – (I prefer wide mouth Mason jars or jelly jars.  You can also utilize clean mayonnaise, jelly, pickle, or relish jars.)
Cookie Sheet
Gardening Gloves (I prefer the ones with the rubber grip dots on the palms.)
A Fan

## Ingredients

Suet or fat to make the Tallow - 5 – 10 pounds (2250g. - 4500g.)
Beeswax – 1lb (450g) to each 5 (1250g) pounds of suet used to make tallow
Stearic Acid (Stearin)
Fragrance/Magical Oil - ( Use only high quality oils.  If you do not make your own it is best to purchase from occult, craft or candle making businesses.  I highly recommend Sun' Eye oils and incenses.)
Liquid Candle Dye - ( Do not use food coloring for it contains water – wax and water do not mix.)
Cotton Core Wicks – have a rigid inner core that will help keep your wick standing straight while burning.  Cotton Core Wicks tend to mushroom less than other wicks preventing increased soot production due to carbon build up.

## Step One:  Making the Tallow

Melting animal fat is called rendering.  Rendering should be done in a well-ventilated area and I use a fan for this purpose.  Freeze your suet, this will make it easier to chop up.  Once the suet is frozen to the consistency of soft butter or sorbet, you can either chop it up into small pieces or place it in a food processor.  Be certain to cut off any meat that's left on the fat.  Place in a large pot add enough water to cover the fat.  Add 1 Tbsp. (30 ml) salt for every 1 lb. (450 g) of suet or fat.  If the fat is ground well, it should only take around 30 minutes.  If you choose to use a crockpot set on medium or low, this could take 3-5 hours.  Check and stir occasionally.  If you don't cover the kettle it will cook faster, but I prefer to cover.  Your tallow is ready when only solids left in the pot are browned meat and gristle.  Use a fine mesh strainer and pour into a large metal bowl.  Allow to cool at room temperature, then cover and place in the refrigerator.  Allow to set overnight.  Every pound of fat or suet will yield around 2 ¼ c. (535 ml) of oil (grease).  An alternative to this process is using lard rather than making the tallow.  Grocery stores usually carry lard rendered from pigs, but some butcher shops or specialty shops carry lard made from cows or sheep.  In Step Three you would use the lard rather than the tallow along with the other ingredients.  You will need to use 2 lb. (900g.) of Beeswax instead of 1 lb. (450g.) when using 5 lb. (2250g.) lard.

## Step Two / Day Two:  Preparation and Safety

Candle making can be a messy project, so you want to be certain that your work area is clean, safe, with all tools and ingredients organized.  For easy cleanup, place foil, paper towels, and old newspapers on your counter tops.  Place old newspapers or a plastic mat on the floor.  Organize and arrange your tools, supplies and ingredients.  Place your mason jars or glass containers on a cookie sheet.  Heat up the oven and reduce heat to 150 degrees.  Place the glass containers on the cookie sheet into the oven and leave there until you are ready to pour the candle formula into them.  This will keep the glass from cracking and will insure a more quality product.  I keep a small household fire extinguisher or a large box of baking soda nearby for wax does have a flash point if overheated.  This is why we never leave my melting tallow or wax unattended.

## Step Three / Day Two:  Formulating the Tallow Mixture

Remove the bowl of tallow from the refrigerator.  Take a knife cutting along the sides to loosen the hardened tallow.  Remove the tallow and clean the bottom side with paper towels removing as much residue as possible and rinse off the rest with cool water.  Break into small pieces and allow to dry on paper towels.  Do not allow any of this to go down your sink drain for it will clog it up.  The remaining gelatin like substance is to be disposed of, but not down your sink or toilet.  Take a garbage bag and pour into this.  I recommend discarding this outside in a dumpster, for it does have a pungent odor.

Take your dry tallow along with the beeswax and place in a Presto Kettle or Crockpot. Once the tallow and beeswax begin to melt clip the thermometer on the side. Once the temperature reaches 148 degrees add the stearic acid (stearin), 2 Tbsps. (60 ml) per every 1 lb. (450 g) of suet used to make tallow. Mix for 2 -3 minutes with wire wisk. Now add the candle dye. Proceed to mix the color in for at least 2 - 3 minutes with the stainless wire wisk. You can test the color on a white paper towel and add more dye until you reach the desired color. Always mix the color in well (2 - 3 minutes) when adding more dye so that he color bonds with the tallow.

Now we shall add the fragrance or magical oil. You will use 1 oz. (30 ml) of oil per 5 lbs. (1250 g) of suet used to make tallow. Warm the oil before adding and be certain that your wax is at 148 degrees. Using the wire wisk stir the fragrance in slowly for a minimum of 2 – 3 minutes so that the fragrance bonds with the tallow.

## Step Four / Day Two:  Preparing the Container (s)
Be certain that your tallow/wax is maintaining a temperature of 148 degrees. Remove your jars or glassware from the oven. I recommend wearing gardening gloves to prevent burns when handling hot glassware. Now you can place your wick centering tool or you can use a firm straw or copper tube. If you are using the latter, slide the wick into the tube. Hold the tube upside down, add a liberal amount of hot glue to the bottom of the wick tab then place the wick in the center of the container. Hold firmly for 30 seconds and when you remove the tube the wick should be centered. Wider containers will require 2 -3 wicks. If this is the case center the wicks ¾ inches (19.1 mm) apart.

You may need to experiment with wick sizes before starting your project. I recommend buying a sampler pack of wicks. 8 – 9 oz. (230 g) generally require a 44-24-18z wick while others prefer a 51-32-18z wick. I prefer Cotton Core wicks, but Zinc Core wicks are acceptable.

## Step Five / Day Two:  Securing the Wick
Most people prefer to secure the wick after the tallow is poured, however I prefer to do so prior to pouring which eliminates the wick from falling over. There are several methods you can use. My favorite is to take some 6 inch (14.4 cm) wooden skewers like you find in the grocery store. Take a rubber band and wrap tightly around sticks. Lay this across the top of your jar and pull the wick up through and between the sticks until it is standing nice and straight. The sticks will hold the wick up while you pour the hot tallow mixture into your containers. I recommend preparing this type of wick holder prior to the candle making process.

You can also use a Wick Holder Bar, which can be purchased at a reasonable price. You simply place the wick into the tab and center.

You can make your own wick holder by:
Taking a Popsicle stick (s), drill a hole in the center of each stick, thread the wick through, rest on the lip of the container, and then clip the wick with a miniature clothes pin or an alligator clip at the point where is comes through the stick.  Be certain that the wick is centered.  I recommend preparing the sticks prior to candle making process.

## Step Six / Day Two:  Pouring the Tallow Formula

Again be certain your tallow/wax is at 148 degrees.  You will now need an aluminum pouring pot or a glass Pyrex measuring cup.  I recommend warming either before pouring so the tallow/wax does not harden in the process.  If the temperature is 148 degrees, stir the tallow/wax with the wire whisk once more for 1-2 minutes to insure bonding.  At this point you can take some 6 inch (14.4 cm) wooden skewers like you find in the grocery store.  Take a rubber band and wrap tightly around sticks.  Lay this across the top of your jar and pull the wick up through and between the sticks until it is standing nice and straight.  The sticks will hold the wick up while you pour the hot wax mixture into your containers.  This will eliminate the wick falling over.  Now dip your pour pot into the tallow and proceed to pour the tallow/wax very slowly (to prevent bubbles) into your containers.  Be as precise as possible and do not spill tallow on the sides and lip of your container or on your counter tops.  Fill your container to the level you desire, however leave enough room for the second pour.  Once all containers are filled, you can remove the remaining tallow from the heat.  Keep the tallow/wax in the kettle to use for a second pour.

As the tallow/wax hardens you will notice a sink hole in the middle of the candle.  This is normal and at this time take a wooden skewer and poke several relief holes around the wicks.  Allow your candles to completely cool at room temperature (16 – 24 hours) before a second pour.  Once cool you can place in the refrigerator overnight if you desire.

## Step Seven / Day Three:  Second Pour

If you refrigerated your candles overnight, take them out and allow to set at room temperature for at least an hour before your second pour.  Reheat the wax mixture to 150 degrees.  This will create a bonding between the first and second pour to eliminate telltale marks of two pours.  Once the temperature is at 150 degrees, stir for 1-2 minutes with a wire whisk to insure bonding.  Now pour just a hair above your first pour.

Allow your candles to cure for 2 weeks before burning them.  Keep the lids tight on the candles while they are curing and keep away from heat and sunlight.  Trim the business end of your wick (the end you light) to within 1/4 - 1/2 inch from the wax.  I keep my tallow candles refrigerated.

### Step Eight / Day Three:  Cleanup

Take a cookie sheet and layer with paper towels.  Lay your utensils and tools upside down on the paper towels.  Preheat the oven at 350 degrees and once it reaches this temperature lower to 150 degrees or keep warm.  Place the cookie sheet with your tools on it into the oven for 5 – 15 minutes.  The tallow will melt onto the paper towels.  Remove from oven and wipe with paper towels.  I recommend using gloves for even item kept on keep warm can become very hot.

If you use a Presto Kitchen Kettle immediately after your final pour, wipe it a few times with a paper towel.  In order to get the fragrance out of the kettle, you can buy a commercial cleaner or use 1c (240 ml) water to 1c (240 ml) white vinegar on a paper towel to ensure the kettle is clean and pure for future candle making.

## Making Moulded Candles using Tallow

Follow Steps One through Three under Making Container Candles using Tallow.  When making moulded candles the only change would be when you are preparing your candle mould.  While your wax is melting you can prepare your mould.  If you desire, you can prepare your mould before you begin formulating the wax.  Many candle moulds have a small hole for the wick and you will simply need to thread it.  For these types of moulds your wicks do not need tabs.

**If you are using moulds without a wick hole, such as pillar or votive, you will need to use wicks with a wick tab.**  Now you can place your wick centering tool or you can use a firm straw or copper tube.  If you are using the latter, slide the wick into the tube.  Hold the tube upside down, add a liberal amount of hot glue to the bottom of the wick tab then place the wick in the center of the container.  Hold firmly for 30 seconds and when you remove the tube the wick should be centered.  Wider containers will require 2 -3 wicks.  If this is the case center the wicks ¾ inches (19.1 mm) apart.  **Spray your mould lightly and evenly with cooking spray or silicone spray.**

You may need to experiment with wick sizes before starting your project.  I recommend buying a sampler pack of wicks.  8 – 9 oz. (230 g) generally require a 44-24-18z wick while others prefer a 51-32-18z wick.  I prefer Cotton Core wicks, but Zinc Core wicks are acceptable.

Most people prefer to secure the wick after the wax is poured, however I prefer to do so prior to pouring which eliminates the wick from falling over.  There are several methods you can use.  My favorite is to take some 6 inch (14.4 cm) wooden skewers like you find in the grocery store.  Take a rubber band and wrap tightly around sticks.  Lay this across the top of your jar and pull the wick up through and between the sticks until it is standing nice and straight.  The sticks will hold the wick up while you pour the hot wax mixture into your containers. I recommend preparing this type of wick holder prior to the candle making process.

You can also use a Wick Holder Bar, which can be purchased at a reasonable price. You simply place the wick into the tab and center.

You can make your own wick holder by:
Taking a popsicle stick (s), drill a hole in the center of each stick, thread the wick through, rest on the lip of the container, and then clip the wick with a miniature clothes pin or an alligator clip at the point where is comes through the stick. Be certain that the wick is centered. I recommend preparing the sticks prior to candle making process. **Now follow Steps Six, Seven, and Eight under Making Container Candles using tallow.**

## Making Layered Candles using Tallow
### (Double Action)

In the Art of Magic, layered candles are referred to as double action candles, when there are two layers and when there are three layers, triple action candles. The most popular version is the double action reversible with the red bottom layer and the black top layer. A black topped double action candle could be created for any purpose. The black represents the crossed condition which has to be burned off. The color on the bottom layer metaphysically is saying to the perpetrator, "I will not give you my power and it is my will that will prevail."

When making container candles the other color is the first layer and you could add your zodiac oil or one that resonates with you. The second layer is the black and you can add uncrossing, unhexing, or reversible oil to the wax formula. When making molded candles the black is the first (bottom) layer and the other color is the second (top) layer. When making layered candles of this nature you will need two sets of tools, one for the uncrossing formulas and one for the other colors or fragrance candles. Be certain to keep these tools separated.

You will need to have an extra set of the following supplies: Presto Kitchen Kettle (Best ) or Double Boiler, Stainless Wire Wisk, Wick Trimmer, Aluminum Wax Pour Pot or LG Pyrex Glass Measuring Cup, Wick Bar Holder (For certain molds)Wick Screws (For certain molds), Mold Sealer or Masking Tape (For certain molds), Wick Tabs (For candle molds that do not have a wick hole. You will need pre-tabbed wicks or you will need to attach the wick tabs on the wick.), Thermometer with side clip, Candle Mold (s), Cookie Sheet, Gardening Gloves (I prefer the ones with the rubber grip dots on the palms.). During the ritual of making your candles, visualize what the purpose of the candle is and will be.

## Common Color Correspondences used in Candle Magic:

**Black/Red**: Reverse away blocks or obstacles in love, sex, energy or creativity in order to Attract Inspiration, Passion, Love, Romance, Creativity and Strength.

**Black/Green:** Reverse away blocks or obstacles in health, Money, Employment, and Bad Luck issues or situations. In order to Attract Prosperity, Healthy Habits, Fertility, and Positive Attitudes.

**Black/White:** Use for Cleansing, and Spiritual work, Purifying your Space of Negative Energy. This can also be used to Thwart Gossip. Use the appropriate oil to the wax formula.

**Black/Brown:** Remove Obstacles or Jinx's related to Court Case Spells

**White:** Spirit Drawing, Spiritual Blessings, Healing, Paving the way for manifestation

**White/Blue:** Peace, Protection against Malochia (The Evil Eye) Kindness

**White/Yellow:** Psychic Power, Attraction, Money (Gold), Road Opener, Devotion, Mental Stimulation, and Prayer

**White/Green:** Money Spells, Prosperity, Gambling Luck, Business Luck, Fertility

**Pink/Red:** Love Spells, Passion, Lust, Romance

**White/Pink:** Affection, Friendship, Attraction

**White/Purple:** Spiritual Power, Commanding, Control, Mastery, Ambition

**White/Orange:** Dreaming True, Psychic Power, Road Opener

**Gold/Green:** Open Doors and Roads.

**Purple/Gold**: To insure Success and Victory in all your endeavors.

# Double Action Layer Container Candles

*You will need the Supplies and Ingredients at the beginning of this chapter. Be sure to wear latex or food service gloves when handling the black wax. *Follow Step One Making the Tallow. Then proceed to Steps Two on Day Two through Step Six on Day Two. Under making Container Candles for Tallow in Step Three / Day Two: Formulating the Tallow Mixture, divide the tallow and the beeswax in equal halves. Allow your candles to completely cool (16-24 hours) before a second pour.
Follow Steps Two on Day Two through Step Six on Day Two again. Fill the second layer to the correct level and be sure to leave room for a third pour. Once all containers are filled, you can remove the remaining tallow/wax from the heat. *Allow your candles to completely cool (16 – 24 hours) before a third pour.
Now follow Steps Seven / Day Three and Step Eight / Day Three.

# Double Action Layer Moulded Candles

*You will need the Supplies and Ingredients outlined at the beginning of this chapter. Be sure to wear latex or food service gloves when handling the black wax.

First follow Step One Making the Tallow. Now you can follow the steps outlined for preparing the candle mould under Making Moulded Candles out of Tallow. Then proceed to Steps Two on Day Two through Step Six on Day Two. Under making Container Candles for Tallow in Step Three / Day Two: Formulating the Tallow Mixture, divide the tallow and the beeswax in equal halves. Allow your candles to completely cool (16-24 hours) before a second pour. Follow Steps Two on Day Two through Step Three on Day Two again. Fill the second layer to the correct level and be sure to leave room for a third pour. Once all containers are filled, you can remove the remaining tallow/wax from the heat. *Allow your candles to completely cool (16 – 24 hours) before a third pour. Now follow Steps Seven / Day Three and Step Eight / Day Three.

# Preparing Double Action Candles for Burning

## Preparing Container Candles

Take a cured candle and on the black wax at the top write the name of the one coming up against you, your nemesis, with a nail. If you have added the oils to your wax mixtures, you will not need to anoint the candle.

## Preparing Molded Candles

**For Taper Candles:** Cut off the top of the candle (the other color) so it will stand straight when it is turned upside down. On the black end carve a new tip for this will now be the top of the candle. **For Pillar Candles:** Cut the wick off the top of the candle (the other color) for this will now be the bottom of the candle. On the black end carve a new tip for this will now be the top of the candle. This is referred to as butting the candle. During the mold and wick preparation of taper or pillar style candles, some choose to pull a piece of wick through the wick tab before pouring the wax. This will provide some extra wick to utilize when they are carving a new tip on the black color end of the candle. If enough wick is pulled through very little carving will be needed for the length of wick you need is available.

At the boundary between the two colors take a nail writing from the boundary away from you in the black wax to the top, the one who crossed you nine times counterclockwise. Be certain to hold the black end away from you, not towards you for you are burning off the negative energy. Remember to wear gloves when working with black wax. Now at the boundary of the other color write a short phase that is appropriate for your spell and this time write toward you.

While you are preparing your candle, meditate and visualize your desired outcome. You can place reversible s, uncrossing, or banishing candles – these would be the black top candles – on a mirror and burn them. These are usually placed at your back door, however if you live in an apartment you can burn them in your bathroom. For safety, I have a large aluminum kettle that I place my candle in. I have one I use for black top candles and I have one I use for the candles that represent "constructive purposes." When the timing is right burn your candle. If you need advisement on timing refer to Chapter Seventeen. Remember the "Eye of Karma" sees each of us, so be certain that the action you are planning is justified and correct.

# CHAPTER SIXTEEN

# CEROMANCY:
# THE ART OF READING CANDLE AND THE FLAME

Ceromancy (Ancient Greek (keros / wax ) is one of the world's most ancient forms of divination. Starring at a flame and viewing wax drippings is a great method of determining if your magic is working effectively. Additionally the way a candle unfolds or deconstructs as it melts can be very significant. I will provide information on how to read glass encased candles, free standing candles, how to read the flame, how to read the smoke, and how to dispose of candle wax. It is important to note that candles poorly made will burn badly no matter how you dress them, pray over them, etcetera... Also, the environment such as the temperature in the area, the presence of wind or a draft, and other factors can play a large part in how a candle will burn.

## How to Read the Signs in Glass Encased Candles

Novena or glass encased candles are commonly used in the Voodoo, Hoodoo and Santerian tradition. However many who practice candle magic who create their own candles use mason or other glass jars to pour their homemade formulas into. I prefer the use of glass encased candles over freestanding candles.

**A clean even burn from the top to the bottom:** This is an indication that all will go well with your spell and that you will get what you are petitioning for. Please be certain to choose the correct spell, the correct novena, and use the correct timing. For if not, even though your candle may burn clean, the expected results will not manifest. On a positive note, a clean burning candle does imply all will be well although desired wishes do not manifest speedily.

**Black smoke on the glass, a dirty sooty burn:** If the **soot does not travel all the way down the glass**, and is only at the top or perhaps stops in the middle, the negative influence or obstacle has been unblocked.

If the **black goes down the entire length of the candle** it means your working has been blocked and there are still forces preventing you for attaining your desired result. It could also indicate someone has casted a spell against you or has significant spiritual protection. If this is the case burn another candle to break through their defenses.

If the **soot is at the bottom of the candle** it is a warning that negative influences are being sent to you. There are many challenges facing you and there is a tough road ahead. Someone(s) may be working against you. At the top of the glass on the inside, take a sharp object and inscribe the symbol of your spiritual comfort – such as a cross – all the way around or in front and back. I recommend accelerating your protections and start a series of uncrossing rituals.

**White smoke on the glass:** White soot is another matter all together. This can indicate spiritual communication, purity, and exorcism. It could indicate that the spirits have heard your prayers and removed the negativity from the working. This is especially true in unhexing or uncrossing rituals. Look to the amount of soot to tell you if it is completed or not.

If the **soot only goes half way down or less**, the cleansing was successful.

If the **soot is carried through the length of the candle** you may need further cleansing and spiritual work.

If the **soot is at the bottom of the candle**, it signifies the presence of outside aid or help either spiritually or physically.

If the candle **burned half black and half white** this means that one aspect is overriding the other. Look to which is on top to see what was undone. If **black is on top**, your spirits cleared it. If **white is on top** the spirits of another have combated your attempts.

If the **soot is on only one side of the candle,** this is a sign that what you are doing is incorrect. Either the candle fixing wasn't appropriate or the spirits aren't happy with the candle itself.

**When the glass breaks or explodes:** If the **glass cracks but does not break** it means there was some opposition that was broken. It may have been sent to the spell to try to deflect it or it may have been encountered along the way. If it **does not break or shatter** then the spell is protected and was successfully defended.

However, if the **glass breaks or shatters** it means you are up against something larger than yourself. Malicious forces have either protected your target or have been attracted to your working and are trying to interfere. It can also indicate someone is casting against you and you are not spiritually protected or strong enough as what was thrown at you was larger than what you were sending out. Either way, do a stronger working and light another candle to try to combat it.

Blockages could be the result of someone coming up against you, however you could be creating the blockage yourself thus sabotaging your spell. Examine all possibilities.

**When a candle leaves wax residue:** If there is around 1/2" (1.27 cm) or more in the bottom, the spell needs to be repeated. Wax on the sides of the glass indicates where there are personal hindrances to the progress of the spell.

**Accelerated Burn:** This is considered a good sign, however the rewards may be short lived and the spell will need to be repeated.

**Signs on the glass:** It is good to look for signs on the glass, particularly those left in soot or wax residue. For instance, if there is heavy black soot and a skull is imprinted in the soot – naturally this is not a good sign. If it is white soot and there is a dove – this is a good sign.

Use your own intuition to come to a conclusion regarding the significance of your desired outcome.

## Reading Freestanding Candles

The way a candle unfolds or deconstructs as it melts can be very significant. It is wonderful when the candle seems to collapse outward or unfold like a flower. I consider that to be a sign that your wish will be granted. It represents possibilities and paths opening for you. A candle that is too lopsided in one direction or another universally means that you are dealing with a situation that is way out of balance. If the flame is buried by the wax, to me that is often a sign that the wish will not be granted.

If they do burn cleanly and leave no trace other than a circle and a bit of charred wick, then the spell worked very well indeed. Flat smooth wax puddles means the spell worked well.

**A free-standing candle runs and melts a lot while burning:** This gives you an opportunity to observe the flow of wax for signs. For instance, if you are burning a bride-and-groom type candle for love, and the man's wax runs all over the woman's, then the man desires the woman more than she desires him. If you are burning an abundance or prosperity candle and the wax melts and runs down onto the monetary offering, the spell is working well and the candle is blessing the money. Some people try to intentionally influence the way melting wax runs with the intention of increasing the likelihood that things will go favorably for them. Most practitioners allow nature to take its course and watch running wax for signs, without interfering in its movements.

**A free-standing candle burns down to a puddle of wax:** When this happens, examine the shape of the wax for a sign. You may see something of significance there, for the shape may suggest an outcome regarding present or future matters. Wax puddles come in all kinds of shapes; most candle-workers treat them like tea-leaves when they interpret them.

There is much lore in the Mexican tradition regarding the wax remains - they leave messages such as: long serpent-like strings indicating evil intent being neutralized and probably a repeat spell is required.

Heart shaped wax puddles of positive when working love spells.

A Coffin shaped puddle indicates success when burning a candle against a nemesis.

Flat wavy papery remains usually with two claw-like projections are read as scorpions which mean malicious gossip and back biting that is being neutralized. Repeat the spell until wax burns clean.

Twisted pillars of wax, bizarre shapes or monsters is read as turbulence and further healing is required.

Wax remains in the shape of sex organs usually means some sort of infidelity or a venereal disease.

A hooded figure means the "Santa Muerte" Holy Death has been invoked and requires a further ritual to neutralize this.

Shapes of animals, cats, goats, domestic animals and fowls can mean that an animal sacrifice took place to strengthen a spell against you. A further ritual is called for to neutralize the spell (the source, usually Santería or Palo Mayombe). Many make or buy tallow candles for uncrossing and unhexing spells. On a positive note, it could be an animal spirit that is close to you.

**A free-standing candle lets out a lot of smoke but burns clean at the end**: Signifies hidden trouble or someone working against your wishes. Things will not go well at first, but with repeated work you will overcome.

## Reading the Flame
### ( Pyromancy )

The flame represents the source of our creation, your inner light. It speaks to us of the soul spark that is above and below, within and without, that which links us all together originating from the same source of thought consciousness. Each flickering candle flame contains 'millions of tiny diamonds, roughly 1.5 million gems are created every second, however they disappear in the blink of an eye. The flame is powerful indeed!

**If the candle lights and splits into two or more flames:** this indicates the presence of others, either spirits, deities, or human, getting involved. Look to the rest of the candle to interpret whether this person is good or bad. If you are **trying to split up a couple** and both flames stay lit, the couple will stay together. If you are **doing a working for attract a lover** and the second flame seems to rise out of the wax your working will be successful especially if both flames grow into one large flame.

**If the candle does not light:** this means that this type of working will not work for what you need and another type of spell should be used.

**If the candle flame is high:** it means there is a lot of power behind the spell and little resistance. If the candle burns low it means there is a strong opposing spiritual force and a cleansing and or banishing may be needed.

**If the flame makes a crackling or popping sound:** it indicates conversation. Either the spirits are trying to talk to you or the target is talking about you. Look to the purpose of the candle and the other actions of the flame to determine which is which.

**If the flame flickers:** there is a spirit around. If the flame pops while flickering, it is the spirit trying to communicate to you. Open yourself up to it. If it is a devotional candle and it is flickering it means you are in contact with your deity and any prayers or petitions will be heard.

**If you attempt to blow out the flame and it does not go out:** this means the spirit does not want you to extinguish it. The same can be said if you blow it out and it flicks back on. Let the spirit complete its work, something important may be in the works that you do not want to interrupt. If you are uncomfortable ask the spirit to protect the candle or ask for permission and try to extinguish it again.

**If the entire top of the prepared candle catches fire:** it means all the resources of the prepared candle are being used due to spiritual influences creating obstacles. Look to the other signs to see if the candle was successful. If the preparations do not collect along the glass as the candle burns, but remain pooled together, it means all the resources are needed and will burn at the end of the candle. The soot, flame, and glass should be read for the outcome.

**If the flame burns high and calm and produces no soot:** you are in the presence of a larger entity or guardian spirit, most likely benevolent. The same can be said for high aggressive flames that flicker in large strokes. These tend to be darker spirits and deities, both are there to listen or aid you.

**If the flame goes out while burning:** this means the spirits cannot help you and the answer you seek is already determined. This can also happen if you unexpectedly get the result before the candle is finished.

**Burn marks on the glass:** Where the flame burns the label with the Saint (Santo) can indicate that there is a nemesis or frienemies that are stabbing you in the back and/or casting you the evil eye.

**A healthy flame:** has a bright red core, surrounded by a blue halo and then a yellow color. A blazing red center tells you that spirits are getting to the heart of the matter. A red center that is dim or just a pinpoint reveals a situation that may not be motivated by the heart. If the wick of the candle starts building a little bulb at its tip, chances are that you have opposition or a third party working against you. If there is a lot of blue in the flame, I take that as a sign that angels and spirits are protecting you from a possibly unhappy outcome.

**Extinguishing a flame:** Use your thumb and index finger to put out the wick, or use a candle snuffer, a plate, -- magical or spiritual candles are never blown out.

## Reading the Smoke of the Flame
### ( Capromancy )

The candle smoke wafts towards you it means that your prayer is more than likely to be answered. If it wafts away from you, then it means that you will need a great deal of perseverance in order to have your prayer answered.

If the smoke blows to your left "you are getting too emotionally involved with the situation and are in danger of subconsciously sabotaging your own prayer so that it will not be answered. If it blows to the right you will need to use your head rather than your emotions to pursue the situation."

## Disposal of Candle Wax

If the formula you are using dictates the proper disposal of wax remains, follow the instructions. If not, when the spell is of a positive nature, discreetly bury the remains in your yard. If you don't have a yard wrap in a white paper towel or napkin and place in the trash receptacle. If the spell is of a negative nature take the remains away from where you or people you love reside in addition to your place of employment and bury or throw into a dumpster and do not look back.

# CHAPTER SEVENTEEN
# TIMING

Timing is an essential component regarding the success of magical undertakings. There are instances regarding emergencies where timing cannot be calculated to perfection and the Universe does make exceptions for such cases. Planetary days and hours, even the month is important in spell casting. The Moon is very important when using witchcraft. Meticulous calculations can bring you one step closer to success especially when forces may be working against you. Proper calculations add a boost of power to your spells. Even when you are ill and a spell must be performed regardless, the proper timing will ensure success.

Spells for gain, increase, attraction, bringing things, and those of a more constructive nature would be performed during a Waxing Moon which is from New Moon to Full Moon. Spells for decrease, thwarting, freezing, and those of a destructive nature are performed during a Waning Moon which is from Full Moon to New Moon. The highest energy is during the Full Moon and the next highest lunar energy is during the New Moon.

It is advisable to work with the Seasons for nature shows us there is a time for planting (Spring), a time for growing and maturation (Summer), a time for reaping and harvest (Autumn), and a time for rest and planning (Winter).

Midday and Midnight will always be exactly halfway between sunrise and sunset. Sunrise of each day inaugurates the first hour of the day which is characteristic of that particular planetary day and named likewise. Such as Friday is a Venus day so the first hour of sunset until the second hour is Venus. The dividing line between the planetary hours of each day is referred to as a cusp.

Use your ephemeris to check on Retrograde Planets, especially Mercury. This is not a good time to begin any new projects or ventures, signing contracts of any type, buying electronic or electrical items, and yada, yada. This aspect is great for reviewing, catching up on, or finishing old projects and fixing issues of a personal or business nature. If you are born during a Mercury retrograde you will generally thrive. Another example is when Venus is in retrograde do not start any love spells and on a personal note do not decide to change your hair style or color during this time.

I recommend creating and maintaining your own Book of Shadows. You can refer back to spells that have been beautifully executed and successful in addition to those that were not. On the following pages is information on the Planetary days and hours, their significance, Moon phases and their significance, and the significance of Cosmic Danger Zones.

# Table of Planetary Days and Hours
## Traditional Method

Refer to instructions under Calculating Planetary Hours.

| Day | Sunday | Monday | Tuesday | Wed. | Thursday | Friday | Saturday |
|---|---|---|---|---|---|---|---|
| Ruler | Sun | Moon | Mars | Mercury | Jupiter | Venus | Saturn |
| Sunrise-1st Hour | Sun | Moon | Mars | Mercury | Jupiter | Venus | Saturn |
| 2nd Hour | Venus | Saturn | Sun | Moon | Mars | Mercury | Jupiter |
| 3rd Hour | Mercury | Jupiter | Venus | Saturn | Sun | Moon | Mars |
| 4th Hour | Moon | Mars | Mercury | Jupiter | Venus | Saturn | Sun |
| 5th Hour | Saturn | Sun | Moon | Mars | Mercury | Jupiter | Venus |
| 6th Hour | Jupiter | Venus | Saturn | Sun | Moon | Mars | Mercury |
| 7th Hour | Mars | Mercury | Jupiter | Venus | Saturn | Sun | Moon |

(Repeat for remaining hours till sunset.)

| Day | Sunday | Monday | Tuesday | Wed. | Thursday | Friday | Saturday |
|---|---|---|---|---|---|---|---|
| Sunset-1st Hour | Jupiter | Venus | Saturn | Sun | Moon | Mars | Mercury |
| 2nd Hour | Mars | Mercury | Jupiter | Venus | Saturn | Sun | Moon |
| 3rd Hour | Sun | Moon | Mars | Mercury | Jupiter | Venus | Saturn |
| 4th Hour | Venus | Saturn | Sun | Moon | Mars | Mercury | Jupiter |
| 5th Hour | Mercury | Jupiter | Venus | Saturn | Sun | Moon | Mars |
| 6th Hour | Moon | Mars | Mercury | Jupiter | Venus | Saturn | Sun |
| 7th Hour | Saturn | Sun | Moon | Mars | Mercury | Jupiter | Venus |

(Repeat for remaining hours till sunrise.)

# Table of Planetary Days and Hours
## Modern Method

In this method simply look up the time in the left column and find the ruler of that hour under the day of the week.

| Starts at | Sunday | Monday | Tuesday | Wed. | Thursday | Friday | Saturday |
|---|---|---|---|---|---|---|---|
| Midnight | Sun | Moon | Mars | Mercury | Jupiter | Venus | Saturn |
| 1:00am | Venus | Saturn | Sun | Moon | Mars | Mercury | Jupiter |
| 2:00am | Mercury | Jupiter | Venus | Saturn | Sun | Moon | Mars |
| 3:00am | Moon | Mars | Mercury | Jupiter | Venus | Saturn | Sun |
| 4:00am | Saturn | Sun | Moon | Mars | Mercury | Jupiter | Venus |
| 5:00am | Jupiter | Venus | Saturn | Sun | Moon | Mars | Mercury |
| 6:00am | Mars | Mercury | Jupiter | Venus | Saturn | Sun | Moon |
| 7:00am | Sun | Moon | Mars | Mercury | Jupiter | Venus | Saturn |
| 8:00am | Venus | Saturn | Sun | Moon | Mars | Mercury | Jupiter |
| 9:00am | Mercury | Jupiter | Venus | Saturn | Sun | Moon | Mars |
| 10:00am | Moon | Mars | Mercury | Jupiter | Venus | Saturn | Sun |
| 11:00am | Saturn | Sun | Moon | Mars | Mercury | Jupiter | Venus |
| Noon | Jupiter | Venus | Saturn | Sun | Moon | Mars | Mercury |
| 1:00pm | Mars | Mercury | Jupiter | Venus | Saturn | Sun | Moon |
| 2:00pm | Sun | Moon | Mars | Mercury | Jupiter | Venus | Saturn |
| 3:00pm | Venus | Saturn | Sun | Moon | Mars | Mercury | Jupiter |
| 4:00pm | Mercury | Jupiter | Venus | Saturn | Sun | Moon | Mars |
| 5:00pm | Moon | Mars | Mercury | Jupiter | Venus | Saturn | Sun |
| 6:00pm | Saturn | Sun | Moon | Mars | Mercury | Jupiter | Venus |
| 7:00pm | Jupiter | Venus | Saturn | Sun | Moon | Mars | Mercury |
| 8:00pm | Mars | Mercury | Jupiter | Venus | Saturn | Sun | Moon |
| 9:00pm | Sun | Moon | Mars | Mercury | Jupiter | Venus | Saturn |
| 10:00pm | Venus | Saturn | Sun | Moon | Mars | Mercury | Jupiter |
| 11:00pm | Mercury | Jupiter | Venus | Saturn | Sun | Moon | Mars |

# Calculating Planetary Hours

To calculate the hours accurately all you need do is look up the hours of sunrise and sunset for any particular day and then divide the hours between sunrise and sunset by 12 for the day needed. This will determine the length of the planetary hour. You can find the time of sunrise and sunset by consulting a Farmer's Almanac or an Ephemeris. The following table will then show you which planet rules each of these hours

Example: If the sun rises at 7:00 a.m. and sets at 6:00 p.m. there are 11 hours of daylight. 11 hours multiplied by 12 = 55. Each daylight hour will last 55 minutes. The first hour would be from 7:00 a.m. through 7:55 a.m. and the 2nd hour would be 7:55 a.m. through 8:50 a.m., etcetera.

After sunset, example: If the sun sets at 6:00 p.m. and rises the next day at 7:00 a.m. there are 13 hours of darkness. 13 hours of darkness multiplied by 60 is 780 minutes. 780 minutes divided by 12 is 65, so each hour of darkness would last 65 minutes.

# Significance in Spell Casting

The planetary hours have traditionally been used in electing favorable times to initiate activities, and also to time prayers, spells, and magical rituals. The following table shows the sorts of activities traditionally favored by each planet:

**Sun Hours:** General success and recognition; spiritual illumination; decisiveness, vitality; activities requiring courage or a mood of self-certainty – making big decisions, scheduling meetings for reaching decisions, giving speeches, launching new projects; seeking favors from father, husband, boss, authorities. Cast spells during the days of hours of the Sun to expedite success, new money, luck, and instant action. However, do not undertake spells during solar eclipse.

**Venus Hours:** Love; friendship; artistic and social success; enjoyable, sociable and aesthetic activities such as parties, social gatherings, recitals / exhibitions, weddings, visits, dating and seeking romance; planting ornamentals; buying gifts, clothing, luxuries; beauty treatments; seeking favors from women.

Venus guards well the natural order of things, so it is best not to use this energy to attract someone who is married. Venus does not smile favorably on home wreakers. Venus is a good time for spells of female virility and fertility for both humans and animals.

**Mercury Hours:** Success in studies, communications; children; making a good impression; routine activities and activities needing clear communications; teaching / learning; important business letters / phone calls; meetings to develop or communicate ideas; buying / selling; routine shopping, errands, travel; job applications / interviews; seeking favors from neighbors, co-workers.

Mercury hours can bring about rapid changes of all types. To change bad luck to good cast your spell in a Mercury hour on a day of Venus. Do not use this for repeated money spells for it will backfire on avarice. Mercury is a manipulator and can be used to accomplish mental feats of all types.

**Moon Hours:** Health; home (buying home, moving); journeys / vacationing (time of leaving home or takeoff); activities remote in time or space – meditation, making reservations, finding lost objects or people; planting food crops; hiring employees; seeking favors from mother, wife, employees. Cast spells for romantic pursuits of a lustful nature. Also spells for attack and control can be initiated due to the Moon's hypnotic influence those who are weak will be vulnerable at this time.

**Saturn Hours:** Discipline and patience; giving up bad habits; overcoming obstacles; success with difficult tasks or difficult people; projects of long duration – breaking ground, laying foundations; planting perennials; treating chronic illness; making repairs; seeking favors from older people (not relatives) or difficult people.

Saturn's energy is not evil, it is best used to thwart, freeze or slow down matters. It could be constructively used to freeze a progressive disease placing it in an arrested state and then reinforce it in a Sun Venus influence.

**Jupiter Hours:** Wisdom, optimism; money (borrowing / lending/ investing / earning / winning); activities necessitating enthusiasm; buying lottery tickets; seeking advice / consultation; settling disputes; seeking favors from grandparents, aunts and uncles, advisers (doctors, lawyers, accountants, astrologers).

Jupiter's influence is one of expansion, it brings more, abundance. However it brings more of what already exists. When casting a money spell in this energy be sure to include a dollar bill, Euro, GBP, etcetera. Jupiter's energy tends to make the rich richer and the poor poorer. When using in a money spell use a dollar bill as a seed and the Moon must be in waxing in Virgo or Capricorn.

A spell cast during a Jupiter Mars cusp can increase male virility and fertility in humans and animals. Jupiter is generally used from the Autumn Equinox to the Vernal Equinox when the Sun's power is weaker. Naturally this would depend on the area of the world in which you live.

**Mars Hours:** Courage, adventure; enforcing your will; success with drastic action (lawsuits, conflicts, going to war, surgery); sports, exercises; risk-taking; making complaints; firing employees; seeking favors of husband or boyfriend.

For example, A man should ask a woman out on a date during a Venus hour; a woman should ask a man out on a date during a Mars hour; one should ask one's boss for a favor during a sun hour; money should be invested during a Jupiter hour; medical treatments should commence under a moon hour (except surgery should commence under a Mars hour); and so on.

Mars does not care about right or wrong.  Mars is a Gladiator, it is motivated to conquer and win at any cost.  Remember the karmic consequences associated with the Martian energy, retribution must be equal, no over drought.  If you are the victim of injustice, for a favorable outcome perform your spell on a day of Mercury or Venus in a Mars hour with the Moon in an Air sign, New Moon – first quarter.  To obtain freedom or liberation perform your ritual exactly on a Mars Sun Cusp.  For psycho-kinetic magic use a Jupiter Mars Cusp.

## MOON PHASES

The Moon spends a day or two each month in each of the twelve signs of the Zodiac.  These timings can be used to good advantage to boost your spell work.

**New Moon:**  The magic of the New Moon begins on the day of the New Moon to three and a half days after.  The energy of the New Moon should be used for new ventures, projects, quests, new beginnings etcetera.  The New Moon is also successful when used for healing, forgiveness, and love spells.

**Waxing Moon:**  The Waxing Moon or First Quarter Moon begins seven days after the new moon and is effective for seven days.  The energy of the Waxing Moon can successfully be used for abundance, artistic creations, career advancement, divinations, energy raising, fertility rituals, friendship, goals, good luck, growth, harmony, happiness, healings for increasing health, love magic, to increase wealth, increase power, buying real estate, sex spells, increase strength, travel, teaching, weight gain, wisdom, bringing forth – weather workings, unions -- business or personal/marriage, and wish magic.

**Gibbous Moon:**  The Gibbous Moon in Waxing begins ten through thirteen days after the New Moon.  A Gibbous Moon is when more than half, but not all, of the Moon is illuminated.

**Full Moon:**  The Full Moon begins fourteen days after the New Moon and is effective for three and a half days.  The Full Moon exhibits the most power and energy.  This energy is great for any divination, prophecy, protection, love, legal matters, financial, and attraction spells.  Any spell that you feel needs an energy boost the Full Moon can successfully be done at this time.  Great for house blessings, beauty, health, developing or strengthening intuition, love magic, omens, developing or strengthening psychic powers, conjuring spirits, shape-shifting, transformations.

**Gibbous Moon:** The Gibbous Moon in Waning is when more than half, but not all, of the Moon is illuminated.

**Waning Moon:** The Waning Moon begins three and a half days after the Full Moon and is effective for ten and a half days. Spells for banishing, exorcism, binding, thwarting, freezing, destruction, slowing illness and addiction can be done at this time. This energy is productive for ending addictions, breaking bad habits, reversing bad luck, bindings, breaking curses/hexes, exorcisms, overcoming fear, curing illness, reverse love spells, banishing negativity, banishing nightmares, overcoming difficulties, selling real estate, and weight loss.

**Disseminating Moon:** The Disseminating Moon is in Waning and begins three through seven days after the Full Moon. Spells initiated at this time are usually done during The Time of the Souls or what is also referred to as the Dead Time.

**Last Quarter Moon:** The Last Quarter Moon is in Waning and begins seven through ten days after the Full Moon.

**Dark Moon:** The Dark Moon begins eleven through fourteen days after the Full Moon.

**Dark Moon:** The Dark Moon begins ten and a half days after the Full Moon and lasts for there and a half days. The energy of the Dark Moon is great for eliminating bad habits, banishing, binding, and justice can be done at this time.

**Moon Void of Course:** This is the time that the Moon spends between Astrological signs. The term Void refers to empty and Course refers to the path the Moon travels. A Void can be anywhere between a few minutes to almost two days. Spells requiring Lunar energy cannot be performed at this time for Lunar energy is not available.

**Lunar Eclipses:** Lunar Eclipses represent the perfect union of the Sun and the Moon. Eclipses are partial or Penumbral.

**Blue Moon:** A Blue Moon is when there are two Full Moons in a single calendar month. This occurs every 2-3 years.

**Dead Time:** More appropriately referred to as The Time of the Souls, Dead Time is usually between 3:00 a.m. and 4:00 a.m. This time is generally used for Spells from the Dark Side. Spells of control and dominance are particularly effective during this time for while a person of interest is sleeping they are vulnerable. It is also said the darkest hour is just before dawn.

# SIGNIFICANCE OF THE MOON IN EACH SIGN

**Moon in Aries:** This is a great time to perform spells relating to employment ventures, all new projects relating to money, strength, courage, and passion spells. Aries is a Cardinal Fire sign, which is extremely energetic and innovative. Aries in a Waning Moon is great for banishing rituals and exorcisms. Aries, naturally with the ruler being Mars is a great energy for welding tools or weapons as well.

**Moon in Taurus:** Moon in Taurus is a fabulous time for spells relating to love, creativity, banishing, and uncrossing spells. Fruition for spells performed at this time requires patience, but the results will be long lasting and stable. Taurus is a Fixed Earth sign, which creates stability and is protective. Taurus is not a good time for money spells if you need immediate financial flow, but Taurus being the sign of the Banker if you are seeing a long term investment this would be the time to perform such a workshop or spell.

**Moon in Gemini:** This is one of the best signs for healing and uncrossing spells. The Moon in Gemini can be unpredictable and unstable. Gemini is a Mutable Air sign which makes it a great energy for communications, multi-tasking, and for works demanding tremendous mental energy.

**Moon in Cancer:** This is an excellent Moon for any spell work involving children, family, home, divination, and fertility. Cancer is a Cardinal Water sign making it energetic and emotional. Spells for domination and control can be cast at this time for the power during the energy of the Moon can influence those who are easily swayed.

**Moon in Leo:** Any spells involving career, fame leadership, prosperity, and abundance can be successful at this time. Leo is a Fixed Fire sign making it aggressive, creative, stable, and unchangeable. This is a great time to cast spells for money particularly if the money is coming from someone else. Love and spells for romantic pursuit work well at this time.

**Moon in Virgo:** This Moon ensures success for any spell involving education, healing, and stability. Virgo is a Mutable Earth sign making it protective and materialistic. This is wonderful for healing spells or works for humans and animals. Spells for money to be used for homework well and spells of romantic conquest are great if the Moon is in Waxing.

**Moon in Libra:** This is an excellent for working a spell in partnerships. A suitable time for spells involving couples, balance, fairness, marriage, and peace. Libra is a Cardinal Air sign making it inventive and intelligent. If the Moon is Waning the energy can be used to derail a relationship or union. The Moon in Waxing is the perfect time to create a relationship or union.

**Moon in Scorpio:** This Moon is good for divination and sex magic. Scorpio is a Fixed Water sign making it unchangeable and emotional. This is a grand energy for devising secret plans to be used at a more appropriate time. Unless you are a Scorpio or have many Scorpio aspects in your natal chart, do not launch an attack at this time for it will backfire. Also it the odds are favoring your opponent it is best to "let sleeping dogs lie."

**Moon in Sagittarius:** This is an excellent time for experimenting with new magical spells, but it is not a good time for psychic work or divination. Sagittarius is a Mutable Fire sign making it creative, intellectual, and aggressive. If the Moon is in Waxing you can cast spells for expansion. This is a very favorable time for Educational pursuits of a higher nature.

**Moon in Capricorn:** This Moon's energy is good for spells to bring about life's basic needs and for stability. Capricorn is a Cardinal Earth sign making it the most materialistic of all of the signs. Money spells and those for material necessities are generally successful at this time.

**Moon in Aquarius:** This is the best Moon time to work on humanitarian efforts. These efforts must be done with a pure agenda and not based on a selfish agenda. Aquarius is a Fixed Air sign making it intellectual yet unchangeable. This is one of the best energy s for psychic development and telekinesis.

**Moon in Pisces:** This is a good energy for divination, past life regression, psychic work, and spirit communications. Pisces is a Mutable Water sign meaning it is unpredictable, deceptive, and extremely emotional. You can cast spells to confuse or elude your nemesis at this time. If you are a Psychic reader you will notice an increase of "psychic vampires" at this time with their tales of woe and self-pity. This is also a fabulous time to enjoy entertainment and attend amusement parks, in other words if you can escape at this time for leisure do so.

# COSMIC DANGER ZONES

Kabbalah teaches us that the course of history transpires as a result of the cyclical energy processes of the year rather than because of physical events. Therefore, by looking at the time at which each moment in history occurs, we can better understand why it happened.

There are seven planets that the Kabbalistic Astrology is based upon: the Sun, the Moon, Mercury, Venus, Jupiter, Saturn, and Mars. Each planet controls two signs, except for the Sun, which controls only Leo (Av) and the moon, which controls only Cancer (Tammuz).

Mars controls Aries (fire) and Scorpio (water)
Venus controls Taurus (earth) and Libra (air)
Mercury controls Gemini (air) and Virgo (earth)
Jupiter controls Sagittarius (fire) and Pisces (water)
Saturn controls Capricorn (earth) and Aquarius (air)
Moon controls Cancer (water)
Sun controls Leo (fire)

Because the sun and the moon control one sign each, an unbalanced situation is created in each of these months. For example, this imbalance causes the crab, the symbol for the month of Tammuz, to walk sideways rather than forward and backward. This also gives the month of Tammuz the opening for Cancer to begin, and it is the only month that is named after a disease.

Certain times and places speak strongly of an underlying force responsible for a world of order and beauty. Yet we cannot close our eyes to the pain, violence and chaos that make their presence so cruelly felt. The problem rests with Di-nim (ungovernable energy). Also in the Eastern philosophies during these particular 3 months the Yang energies prevail creating much unbalance.

During the months of Tammuz, Av, and Tevet, the energy of the Force is such that there is no revelation of the Shekinah, the feminine force of God, and the appropriate cosmic vessel which insures the manifestation and stability of the force. At such times the dynamic intensity of the force is so severe that no vessel is capable of making contact with, or handling the energy of the force, which thereby manifests as Di-nim (ungovernable energy) in the universe.

The misfortune which takes place during these three months is the result of negative cosmic forces. The hazards and pitfalls that many of us encounter can be traced to our having come under the influence of these periods of negative energy. Hence it is wise to be cognizant of the danger zones and careful to avoid them.

The Force might be aptly compared to the energy which enters our homes through the electric wires. Controlled it is of immense value, uncontrolled it can be destructive and downright dangerous. Switch on a light, for example, and you receive a wonderful blessing, but stick your finger in a socket and the same energy provides you with a horrible curse.

Metaphysicians understand that Celestial forces are governed by the activity of man. Thus instead of being pawns in the cosmic scheme as other ancients had believed, metaphysicians understand man to be the prime interface between the terrestrial and the celestial forces of the metaphysical domain. Only when the forces are in balance do the heavens declare their majesty and influence.

During Tammuz, Av, and Tevet in the absence of the Temple, the energy vessel of the God the Mother, the violence that threatens our planet cannot be halted. Within the framework of Tammuz, Av, and Tevet, there is very little that the average person can do to influence the cosmic forces. Certain individuals of extraordinary spiritual ability can channel these forces and Kabbalists as well as other belief systems have specific meditations designed to reduce the intensity of the Force during such times and thus make it beneficial. Having accomplished these meditations, the Shekinah transforms the immense power of the force, thus permitting the Kabbalist to function even in an environment of violence and chaos.

The Force must undergo a reduction in order to operate as a viable circuit of energy here on earth. Variations in the revealed energy of the Force influence the beginning of new ventures, inasmuch as the lifeblood of a new venture and its potential success depends on the ability of the force to make itself manifest. During Tammuz, Av, and Tevet, the Force is in a state of Kat nut, a decreased level of activity, hence the increased chance that a new venture will have a negative outcome. However there are always exceptions. Spells of a dark nature will thrive in these energies and this is the time frame when many plans of destruction are initiated and/or implemented.

Those born within such time zones are those who have been chosen with the challenge of helping generate and share tremendous light force within this plane of physicality… and this is accomplished by a proactive lifestyle via not only by words, but by deeds as well… so one must walk the talk.

Again the roots of most misfortunes can be traced to the cosmic danger zones. Armed with the knowledge of these zones, we can transcend the realm of chance, luck, and indetermination, and bring order, fulfillment and supreme tranquility to our lives.

# DAYS OF POWER

## Days of Positive Influence for Constructive Projects

**January:** 1, 2, 15, 26, 27, 28
**February:** 11, 21, 25, 26
**March:** 10, 24
**April:** 6, 15, 16, 20, 28
**May:** 3, 13, 18, 31
**June:** 10, 11, 15, 22, 25
**July:** 9, 14, 15, 20
**August:** 6, 7, 10, 11, 16, 20, 25
**September:** 4, 8, 9, 17, 18, 23
**October:** 3, 7, 16, 21, 22
**November:** 5, 14, 20
**December:** 14, 15, 19, 20, 22, 23, 25

The following are Days of Power according to the Lunar Calendar. You will need to purchase a Hebrew Calendar / Ephemeris to calculate these days.

**Rosh Hodesh:** The first day of a Lunar Month. The first day of the New Moon is the first day of a Lunar Month. Rosh Hodesh of Mars Heshvan (Scorpio) is the most supremely powerful and positive day of the year.

**Fifteenth Day of a Lunar Month:** With the exception of Tebeth (Capricorn) and Tammuz (Cancer) the fifteenth day of a Lunar Month is of immense cosmic power. Although Av is a cosmic danger zone the fifteenth of Av is the most perfect day of the Lunar year. This is a day when the focus on new love is the most beneficial.

**Eighteenth Day of Iyar** (Taurus) is a day when new ventures have the highest probability of success.

**Tuesdays** are the most powerfully balanced day of the week. A perfect day for spell casting.

**Sundays, Thursdays, and Fridays** are cosmically balanced days.

# Days of Negative Influence and Misfortune

**January:** 1, 2, 4, 5, 10, 15, 17, 19
**February:** 7, 10, 17, 27, 28
**March:** 15, 16, 28
**April:** 7, 10, 16, 20, 21
**May:** 7, 15, 20
**June:** 4, 10, 22
**July:** 15, 20
**August:** 1, 19, 20, 29, 30
**September:** 3, 4, 6, 7, 21, 22
**October:** 4, 16, 24
**November:** 5, 6, 28, 29
**December:** 6, 7, 9, 15, 17, 22

**Good Friday through sunrise Resurrection morning;** It is said during this time a majority of the Angelic forces are far from the earth.

You will need to purchase a Hebrew Calendar / Ephemeris to calculate the following days. When using the Lunar Calendar the days are calculated from sunset to sunset.

**The months of Tebeth, Tammuz, and Av** are negative months of influence for constructive projects as mentioned under "Cosmic Danger Zones."

**Mondays** are considered a cosmic danger zone because the energy of purgatory was created on this day.

**Wednesdays** are a day of diminished lunar activity which prevails over all earthly activity.

You will notice that some days of positive influence share some of the same days with negative influences. This simply means that these days are a balance of both energies.

During days and months of negative influence, there are always exceptions. Spells of a dark nature will thrive in these energies and this is the time frame when many plans of destruction are initiated and/or implemented. This is also a good time for crossing, reversibles, and spells of this nature.

# SECTION II

# Occult Mémoires

## PREFACE

In the beginning I chose to incarnate in the feminine form for this was and is definitely a time when the feminine form would be more appreciated in this world as it is known. My interest in the occult was innate at birth, before I drew my first breath! When all other little girls wanted to be ballerinas, ice skaters, nurses, and such ordinary things, I dreamed of being a vampire, Merlin, fairy folk, and all those things that the big people labeled as forbidden. Also I was not afraid of the things that go bump in the night, monsters under the bed or in the closet and such. Being an adult child of a narcissistic parent, during my youth due to the fact that friends were limited or prohibited, my friends were the invisible beings that adults condemned. During the moments when I could escape from the tyranny of my homelife, I enjoyed the time and conversations I spent with the angels, fairy folk, those on the other side, and now I realize my personal spirit guides. Of course even at this tender age under the advisement of my guides I was per spacious enough to understand that such communications would not be considered normal so I shared this secret with no one.

My paternal grandfather was very involved with the Masonic Temple and I didn't realize the magnitude of this until much later in life. I am not aware of what his level of initiation was for naturally he was very secretive concerning the Lodges activities. He always referred to me as the "odd one," which he meant no disrespect. He simply knew that I was not like the others. He considered me an enlightened child and the memories of him and "Grandy" are the best. At times even though they are both in spirit now, they visit me if they are at a place where they may, particularly during times of difficulty and duress.

During my childhood and adolescent years I was forced to succumb to the teachings of a staunch traditional organized religion and temporarily purged of any true spirituality. My step mom found within her some desire to affiliate herself with this path of religiosity which in my opinion was and is an oppressive religion, definitely the most sexually repressed people on this planet and with my experience regarding cults, this belief system brain washed individuals and did meet Litton's eight criteria defining mind control. My major issue with this group is that they believe they are the only belief system that is correct and this simply is contrary to the Creator's plan. I choose not to mention the name of this particular group. But I will add that it was not the Catholicism, Judaism, or even Baptist. Being an ordained minister myself I do believe that there are many paths to God and all of them are right if they do not create harm for none...

individually or collectively. I am so happy that the One Living and True God is the ultimate judge and I do appreciate the gift of freewill that the Creator has given each of us incarnated realizing the human experience!

It was not until my early twenties that I ventured back into the world of the occult and just like The Fool in the Tarot my journey of spirit toward initiation began. I was a neophyte arising from discontent and soul searching being guided through the initiation of the elements unfolding a spiral of knowledge and experience. The risks were many and I certainly was perceived as a fool and mentally unstable by many. To this day I am not uncomfortable with change for it is the only thing in this world that is constant. I must confess my life has been far from drab, but my feeling is that it is not that we regret that which we have done in life, but what we don't do--the challenges missed for true soul evolution. When taking a risk it may not work out as planned and many may perceive it as a failure, but this is not the case for you will have learned from the experience. I recall greeting this change with immeasurable excitement and anxiety; it was a leap into the dark.

It is with great respect and seriousness that I set myself to the task of recording these events and information. To disclose enough to be sufficient without disclosing enough to be dangerous is a challenge in itself.

This is a task I have been procrastinating on for some time now, but the time has come to do so and I only hope that I will discharge it with the honor and the dignity it deserves. There is a fine line between madness and genius and God knows that with that which I have witnessed I have questioned my own sanity at times. This information that I have come to know in the course of many years is knowledge that is shared by the mystic and the demented. This knowledge was gained at great cost by myself and others. The information and events I am sharing is from personal experience and from cases that have come within my scope in which I and others personally analyzed.

I know from personal experience the horror of a psychic assault, its insidious nature, its power and its pernicious effects on the psyche and the physical body. It is very difficult to get people to come forward and bear their souls concerning psychic assaults. Firstly due to the fact that they feel they will not be believed and that they will receive a reputation of being mentally unstable. Secondly because people prefer to repress that which has created such horror that becomes unspeakable. It is my personal opinion that psychic intrusions are more common than is realized, even by people involved in the occult.

Because of my knowledge and experience many people have approached me when an occult attack is suspected, and their experience reintegrates my own. Being a process awareness and astrological counseling psychologist I have learned to interpret occultism in the light of psychology and psychology in the light of occultism, the one explaining and counterchecking the other. There is vast information on the subject from the beginning of history on this planet and it is interesting to note that most of the literature was written by those who had no interest in psychic phenomena, even denying it, yet the materials are laced with and confirm statements made by those who experienced a psychic intrusion.

It is true however, that we must be careful to distinguish between psychic experience and subjective hallucination. The differential diagnosis between insanity, obsession, and psychic intrusion is a very delicate process. I not only wish to share methods of psychic protection but also show methods of differential diagnosis.

I suspect that the authenticity of the text will be questioned by some… however truth is truth regardless and I am but the messenger. My truth may not be your truth as your truth may not be mine… but it is our truth as we know it.

This guide is a serious contribution in an effort to provide those who choose invaluable information which could possibly save their very life or that of a loved one if the need arises. Although I am bearing my soul, there are memories that are best left in my archives. I will be speaking candidly about the forces that exist and are working below the surface of everyday activities. It is my intention within these pages to share comprehensive information and tools which provide protection and defense measures. Being a Lightworker, I believe all inhabitants upon the Earth are entitled to protection affording them the opportunity to stand strong and there truly are no secrets for as one of my favorite proverbs states, "There is nothing new under the Sun!"

# CHAPTER EIGHTEEN

## SIGNS OF PSYCHIC & MENTAL ASSUALT

We live in the midst of unseen forces whose effects alone we perceive. We move among invisible forms whose actions for the most part we do not perceive at all, though we may be affected by them. Not all unseen forces are necessarily evil, there are different classes and orders of spirits just as there are different classes and orders of humans. The real challenge is identifying spirits of truth verses imposters.

An example is, for instance if one is involved in a psychic reading whether it be tarot or other forms of seeking messages or information, a highly evolved being will answer the question in a direct precise manner using few words whereas a low vibrational being will babble on endlessly. It is my opinion that the invisible forces are only a threat to humanity when corrupted and manipulated by the rituals of unscrupulous men and women, whom are referred to as the adepts of the Left-Hand Path or the Reactive Mind.

It is imperative that diagnosis must precede the treatment of psychic assault. We must take into consideration the visible signs of the psychic assault before we can make a determination indicating the source of its origin. The most common form of psychic assault is human ignorance and a malignant mind. All intrusions are not deliberately orchestrated. The injury may be as accidental as going into a ditch or slipping on ice. The very person from whom it emanates may not have initiated the attack that is why we never react to attack by attack. I know this is truth for many Dark Adepts utilize what is referred to as back door magic. It is best not to lower ourselves to the level of our attackers, but rather transmute reactivity into proactivity.

It is to our advantage to be aware of our dreams, for if there is a definite psychic attack of sufficient force, characteristic dreams will appear. Usually a feeling of heaviness or weight is experienced upon the chest as if someone is kneeling or laying on the person sleeping. This sense of weight indicates strongly and for a certainty that the attack emanates locally for this heaviness is associated with the concentration of etheric substance or ectoplasm, and is sufficiently tangible to press down on a scale of measurement when it is possible to record this energy.

A sense of fear, apprehension, paranoia, confusion, and oppression is very characteristic of an assault. Usually the senses are more exaggerated but it usually is always apparent in those that are targeted. Assaults just don't materialize out of the "blue" or from out of "nowhere". We are not at one moment in a balanced state and then just all of a sudden find ourselves in the midst of an invisible battle. The non-sensitive will have a shadow cast on the conscious level during the onset of an assault, however we always perceive subconsciously before we realize consciously.

During the progress of an assault nervous exhaustion becomes more apparent and increasingly marked and in certain cases particularly those who are under the influence of The Death Prayer will begin to waste away to a lifeless, bloodless shell unable to move and yet there is no diagnosis of disease or medical explanation to provide a logical collaboration of the condition. This is a horrible experience, for the person under attack is afraid to sleep for fear they will never wake up, yet they cannot stay awake indefinitely. Of course after a period of time this lack of sleep associated with fear results in a nervous and mental breakdown.

Nervous exhaustion and mental breakdown are the common indicators of an astral attack among white people for many times the assailant is not able to cause the actual death of the person they have targeted. Various cultures into belief systems such as voodoo, kimbanda, macumba, palo, etcetera… believe that Caucasians are vulnerable. At present the reason being is that except for those familiar with various alternative belief systems the white race is merely ignorant concerning the practices of various cultures. I wish to add that not all persons of the various backgrounds or cultures that I previously mentioned are involved in such practices but the majority are usually knowledgeable of it whether they actively practice it or not.

Bruising created during sleep is another form of evidence of an astral skirmish. This is known as the phenomenon of repercussion wherein that which befalls the subtle body is reflected in the dense body. At times the bruises have a definite pattern and at other times not, but they pass from blue to yellow and die away in time as bruises will do. I will share a personal experience which actually involves many aspects of an attack. This was around the Spring Equinox, one night around three o'clock in the morning I perceived wax melting over the headboard of my bed, a feeling of apprehension came over me and I felt a being laying on top of me, a male being, I began to struggle even fight and felt an icy grip around my throat so I had to mentally project words for this being definitely meant to strangle me. I commanded this being to leave by using the name of God that created the most fear for low level entities of this nature. In the morning the area under my left eye was bruised and slightly swollen, in addition to some markings on my throat. I knew the source of the attack and knowing this person what I found perplexing was that they were adroit, possessed an abundance of knowledge, power, financial means, charisma, and yet they perceived me as a threat. At this point in my journey I was intrepid to the point of being a danger to myself. I sent via carrier a dozen black roses to my alleged assailant with a note simply stating, "Thank you for showing me my strength!"

Evil odors are another manifestation of an astral attack. These are characterized by the smell of decomposing flesh. The odors will come and go but during manifestation there is no doubt as to what it is and whether a person is sensitive or not they can smell this stench. I have also experienced this stench coming from drains when a ritual belonging to the element of Earth is performed improperly. I had an acquaintance who did this very thing and not only did the odor emanating from the drains smell foul but when the plumber came to the home all the plumbing had to be replaced for the pipes were full of tree roots, and on the north side of his home the roots had even slightly lifted the home and pushed the flooring up in the bathroom and two bedrooms.

Another phenomenon is the precipitation of slime. Sometimes the marks appear like those of army worms crawling in an ordered formation, it can be a broad smear of slime or may appear as footprints. I assisted a friend in a case where a young woman accumulated a pool of slime under her bed. We discovered during the investigation that her live in boyfriend was heavily involved in the practice of Necronomicon, Sumerian charms used to invoke the assistance of the Ancient Ones of Darkness. I have also seen slime on fountains, not the usual precipitation that occurs but massive oozing and dripping. This was in areas where there were heavy concentrations of the impure tenth class spirits where activities of the most carnal nature were taking place.

Another interesting phenomenon known to occultists is the astral bell. The sound varies from a clear, bell like note to a faint click resembling a knife used to tap on a wine glass. This is usually announcing the possible arrival of an entity who is having difficulty manifesting who may not be maleficent at all, but regardless may not be capable of making an appearance. It could also be something as simple as a knock on the door simply to attract the attention of the inhabitants.

Unexplainable outbreaks of fire can also be seen in this connection. This indicates that elemental forces are at work. Poltergeist, which belongs to the sixth class of noisy and boisterous spirits, is another phenomena that occurs. Of course it is likely that more than one form of phenomena is at work in the same case. I myself have experienced this on more than one occasion.

In all investigations we cannot ignore any possibility so it is wise to examine the natural and material explanations as well, even in the case where it is obvious that a supernatural element exists. It is also advisable to rule out the possibility of fraud which can enter into the most unexpected places. I have identified addicts of substance abuse who take advantage of the occult by claiming to be a victim of attack for the purpose of prolonging and justifying the means. In accepting an explanation our decision should rest upon the weight of the evidence in its favor and not upon the dislikes of the alternatives. With all of our vast scientific studies and hypothesis it is my opinion that there is indeed more to man than just the mind and body. Duality is part of being human, we are neither purely a material being nor a spiritual being and it is our responsibility to harmonize these aspects within and without.

# CHAPTER NINETEEN

# METHODS OF PSYCHIC AND MENTAL ASSAULT

Methods of psychic assault are quite diverse for not only are there the traditional methods that various alternative belief systems employ but there are the personal creations of the practitioner to consider. The very essence of psychic assault is found in the principles and operations of telepathic suggestion. As I mentioned previously we perceive unconsciously before we realize consciously. Left-Hand Adepts or I prefer referring to these ones as low vibrational beings, utilize the hours from Midnight through the hour before dawn to work their manipulations for it is during this time that they feel the soul is most vulnerable. Additionally there are alternative religions who believe the soul is open during the hour of 6:00 p.m. through 7:00 p.m. According to Kabbalistic belief during the time when the sun is setting the energy of judgment is reaching its highest peak and it is at this time that the Minchah prayer is recited for this is the best time to quiet the judgments when they appear in their greatest number and intensity.

If you look on the bookshelves you cannot help but notice the numerous writings on mind control focused on getting what you want. This confirms that for the most part humans do have a desire to control circumstances so that they achieve their personal needs disregarding the true repercussions. Whether it is the magician or the person seeking personal need disregarding the laws of balance and karma, there are many humans on this planet cluttering our ionosphere of negativity all in the name of success or just pure greed and vindictiveness.

One very popular method of psychic assault is hypnosis which I will cover in a chapter of its own. I am not referring to the benevolent use of hypnosis, but rather those who use it for their own selfish motives. Again, there are documented cases where those in the medical field are irresponsible as well, for we are speaking of humans and depending on their level of evolution the professional could abuse the technique just as the black magician would.

Then you have well-meaning individuals who employ the use of prayer which is another topic I will discuss in its own context. How many times has someone come up to you and said, "I'll pray for you." This may appear very benevolent by many but in further exploration you will discover why adding the affirmation, "Protect me from the prayers of others," on a daily basis can provide tremendous protection from these "prayer givers" who actually mean I will pray to see things the right way, my way.
Now that I have shared techniques that could actually be therapeutic in nature, I am prepared to share with you some of the techniques of those who desire to receive for the self alone. Those who work in this realm especially those who are adroit adepts always work insidiously. Again the methods of initiating assaults are found in the realm of

telepathic suggestion. We cannot see the invisible seeds sown in our minds by another, but eventually germination takes place and the shoot makes its appearance above the threshold of consciousness. The adroit adept always aims at making their suggestions harmonize with the bias of personality otherwise the subconscious complexes will expel them before they can take root. An alien seed cannot be planted; the adept must reinforce and stimulate the ideas and impulses that are already there, though latent. In order for these suggestive thought seeds to take hold they must find congenial soil. Herein lies the strength of the defense. We may not be able to stop the minds of others sending us suggestions but we can purify our own natures so that the harmful seeds can find no soil. The mandatory tool to protection is knowledge and I do intend to share this with the intent to create the necessary awareness to promote informed choices.

The primary goal of suggestion is to create a mental atmosphere surrounding the soul of the person being suppressed or healed, until a sympathetic response is elicited within the soul itself. Once this is done the battle is half over for the gate has been opened from within and there is free access and now the suggestion can proceed rapidly. However we are at a critical point in an occult assault for up to this point the defender has the advantage. The person being set up for assault can retain that advantage indefinitely and wear his assailant down even if unable to meet them on equal grounds of occult knowledge. There is absolutely nothing in this world that such an assailant can do with a person who stands their ground, hones their will, maintains harmony, and simply won't pay attention to their machinations.

Until the aura is penetrated there can be no entrance to the soul and the aura is always penetrated from within by the reaction of fear, anger, or desire going out towards the attacking entity. If we can transmute that instinctive emotional reactivity into proactivity, the edge of the aura will remain impenetrable, and will be a sure defense against psychic intrusion.

Another technique is magnetism where an object such as a picture, a candle, a coin, or actually just about anything is decreed upon. This is very popular among people involved in most types of witchcraft. Some may use it in a beneficent manner in charging a talisman or forms of healing services, but it is my experience that most do not. I must make a comment concerning talismans at this time and that being the photon energy entering our earth from outer space at present appears to neutralize the effectiveness of many of these objects.

Businesses called "*botanicas*" who service those into witchcraft and occult energy work, often perform rituals to decree upon all objects in their stores. Not all do, but those that do are easy to identify for unusually dark and heavy energies are present. Have you ever entered such a place with the intention of simply browsing but you found yourself compelled to buy something and when you get into your car and are driving away you are baffled especially when the item is something you didn't need or you could have purchased for a third of the cost at a grocery store? Also once this object is in your home, if the persons owning that business are involved in low vibrational energy you have just given them a formal invitation. In like manner as Dracula, once the invitation is extended the entity may enter at will. Also if you do purchase from such establishments pay with cash, for using a check or credit cards will be giving them too much information which they will use when they do rituals geared toward attracting business and abundance. Also this is not a pleasant piece of information but these types of practitioners will even lower themselves to performing rituals which will create complications in your life so that you will return to them for assistance. Additionally do not divulge personal information concerning yourself or those you love for it is their device to appear friendly so as to elicit as much information as possible from a promising target. It is my experience, that if such ones cannot get to you they will go after those you love. Not all new age stores are a supermarket for the manipulative, however if you enter a metaphysical store of any type that carries large amounts of objects, whether it be oils, candles, incense, baths, books, tools, etcetera…, geared almost exclusively toward control of a destructive nature, this is a red flag to remove yourself from the premises. The first rule of psychic self-defense is to avoid communications and contact with those who practice darkness, after all is it wise to tread were angels would not dare?

However, many will choose to patronize such businesses, simply as they say in Star Trek, "shields up", and remember the rule of "Too Much Information" ("TMI"), which is avoid disclosing too much information about yourself and your matters so that if the persons associated with the business are negatively inclined -- a magnetic link or rapport cannot be formulated. Now I do realize that there are those who did contract to experience the reactive side fully during this incarnation, so with this, view this guide as "keys to survival" during your journey into the underworld.

It is not only those involved in the darker elements who use magnetism, and I'll share an example shared with me by a dear and trusted friend, "I was involved with group who was sharing the Edgar Cayce Studies. One evening I noticed one of the members, -- who was a promising and eager student but who obviously took matters into the shadow, -- was no longer in the general area. Instinctively I went outdoors to find him going from car to car laying his hands on each car and decreeing in Latin. I gracefully walked up to him and inquired of his activities which he shamelessly stated that he simply desired everyone to continue participation in the group in addition to providing continued funding. I did not choose to embarrass him by having him called down at that point however I returned later that week to speak personally with the leader of our group concerning the issue which he later managed quite eloquently."

What I consider one of the most, sneaky ploys of Adepts of Darkness is using others as pawns in their game. For instance when they know your aura is impenetrable due to the number of attempted assaults on your soul they will send people to befriend you. These people will appear out of the blue and they will be so kind and seemingly helpful to the point of almost being nauseating, the behavior is beyond co- dependency. They will do their utmost to elicit personal information from you and they won't stop there they will even question others about you. At times they even go as far as sending the person to gain employment within your workplace so as to be a coworker. They will send these pawns to places you frequent, even churches and organizations. It is extremely important to be cautious with those who appear in this manner for if they cannot get to you personally if you have children they will attack them or those who are most dear to you. Usually I can identify these individuals readily for they actually make inquiries that are absolutely suspicious, they are overly helpful, and at times they even slip up by presenting information that had to have been fed to them by the would be attacker. I am not suggesting one to be paranoid, or hyper-vigilant. Simply, be congenial and be ever aware of the power of silence. There is great wisdom in knowing when not to speak-or not to respond. When you enfold yourself in the creative silence of meditation, the stillness before action is quite profound indeed.

# CHAPTER TWENTY

## MOTIVATING FACTORS

One of my most respected mentors and teachers, a wise elderly first decan Piscean, shared that the three greatest sins are, intentional cruelty, unintentional cruelty, and superstition. I have discovered the truth in his words, which are nothing new under the sun and being as it is I will be sharing motives that create harm which are intentional, those that are thoughtless and those motivated by fear.

Intentional Cruelty is purposely to create pain to another living being and this is the greatest of all sins -- the devices of the Satan energy. Becoming involved in an initiatory fraternity can set you up for intense challenges particularly if you reach a place where you wish to detach from the group. Depending on your level of initiation, secrets have been revealed and oaths have been taken. Some groups take this far more seriously than others with some still believing as many ancient groups did that the only way to detach is through death.

Speaking from experience, it behooves anyone who is considering a commitment in an initiatory fraternity/sorority to investigate the groups' history. Once involved it is very difficult to remove yourself, safely. When I detached by choice of flight from the occult group I was involved with during my youth I found myself hounded on the astrals for years until my vibrations elevated to a level were my pursuers could no longer find me. At this present place in time, many of those I was affiliated with, are literally dead, diseased, or very few, like myself, detached.

Climbing the stairs of purification was more difficult than imagined but I steadily made progress. I admit that I stumbled here and there but I embrace the words of an anonymous writer, "All athletes occasionally stumble. What sets the champion apart is that she immediately rises and shakes off the dust to race on, undisturbed and more aware of the road."

Other forms of intentional intrusion could result from the desire of a certain group to obtain you as a member and if you resist or don't accept the invitation they may come up against you and create harm to coerce you into joining or to teach you a lesson. You must remember that those groups who are on the left hand path or what is labeled as the dark side do not consider any repercussions for their actions for they are riding so high on negative energy that they believe they are invincible and the laws of the Universe do not pertain to them particularly the law of cause and effect.

As I have previously mentioned another intrusion that those of low vibrational energies employ and have no remorse in utilizing is randomly selecting an individual or individuals to experiment on. So it is possible that by being in the wrong place at the wrong time becoming a target of experimental entertainment is quite probable.

On a completely human level we have all encountered persons who have been jealous or envious, gossipers, backstabbers, facilitators of chaos, vessels of gloom and despair, -- and such. It is only sensible to protect ourselves from the thoughts and actions of these un-evolved reactionary selfish beings as well. These are people we encounter in our everyday activities -- at work, at play, within social circles, and there is that saying, "Who needs enemies when you have family."

Unintentional cruelty despite that it stems from sheer thoughtlessness is just as harmful and bears the same consequences as intentional cruelty. These are persons who are motivated by the desire to receive for the self alone and are ignorant of the harm they create due to their selfish natures but as it is said, "ignorance of the law is no excuse!"

Examples of such thoughtlessness are, for instance, if an employer does not pay his employees on the scheduled day, thinking nothing of the difficulties he could be creating for them and their families -- so much suffering may be created by such inconsideration. Another would be if a person makes a promise to call someone, meet someone, or pick someone up within a specific time frame and they fail to do so -- again much suffering can be created by acts of thoughtlessness. Careless words and speech are just as harmful as those that are malicious. Acts of this nature can leave a person physically and psychologically exhausted hence classifying it as an intrusion. It is wise to be aware of unintentional cruelty for it bears the same Tikkun or karmic consequences, -- karma never forgets and it does not take into account that man or woman forgets.

Cruelty resulting from fear, superstition, motivates such persons to come up against any who do not share their convictions or beliefs. Throughout history the majority of humankind has acted out according to their fear based analogies and beliefs. The inquisitors did it, many religious people did it in the name of God, the government did it in the name of freedom and technology, cultures did it and all try to excuse or justify their cruelty by saying that it is the custom -- it is progress. Again karma does not excuse fear based cruelty, "superstition,"-- the time always comes for the bill to be paid and it usually presents itself when the human least expects it.

By sharing this information I am not encouraging hyper-vigilance but rather utilizing my experienced experiences and knowledge by creating awareness for informed choices so that a person can make an educated decision in order to be "one step ahead." The three greatest sins, -- intentional cruelty, unintentional cruelty, and superstition -- are fatal for they sin against love. Will, Wisdom, and Love are the three aspects of the Logos; if we wish to be one with the Source of Creation we must share these aspects within our world extending these to all beings, -- great and small.

# CHAPTER TWENTY-ONE

# VAMPIRISM

Do vampires exist in our modern day society? Vampires are part history, part religion, part philosophy, and part poetic imagery so yes, absolutely, vampires do exist! Whether such a creature exists as a myth, a story form, or legend, believing in vampires from a psychological perspective is a way of viewing the world as we know it or the lessons we have thus learned. In other words our very thoughts and beliefs of what we take in from our five senses in this world of physicality can give us reason enough to see vampires everywhere and even realize that each of us could become a vampire ourselves. The types of vampires that I am going to address are "psychic/energy vampires", not the Dracula of Bram Stokers novel or the vampires of Ann Rice's creation. In the days of old pathogenic conditions as pemphigus vulgarus (gives rise to bite like lesions), morphea (causes violet colored lesions around the lower lip) and hypohidrotic ectodermal dysplasia could have been associated with believing such afflicted individuals to literally be vampires. I must comment however that there are individuals in this world who do feed literally on human blood but for the most part it is done consensually among their own familiars. Psychic or Energy vampires are individuals who drain others of their vital energy and are of two types, those who are conscious of their actions and those who are unconscious of their vampirism. The latter are the most common group for most people do not intentionally wish to deliberately deplete others of their life force, but there are those who do.

Conscious psychic/energy vampires deliberately machinate methods to take energy from others and many can orchestrate this so eloquently that much time will pass before the victim is aware of the intrusion, if ever. Some employ the use of magic. While others, have an instinctive ability whether it is natural or developed to directly drain their victims vital energy either from their aura or on the astral plane. I am certain that most of us must confess that during sometime in our life we have been in contact with a person(s) who has left us emotionally and/or physically depleted after being in their presence whether in the flesh or via telephone. As on the physical level when someone forces themselves on you without your consent it is rape, likewise when these conscious psychic/energy vampires attempt to attach and take your energy this is a form of "psychic rape."

During my youth when I was involved in the dark light due to my unbridled egomania and catlike curiosity, myself and others would go out "energy hunting" under the direction of our leader. Many of the members preferred clubs for gathering energy however I preferred more upscale victims so I would frequent theater, museums, and such. This is going to sound morbid but I preferred "fine dining", not one night stands but rather higher quality subjects that afforded me long term usage. Of course what I am

An American Witch's Book of Spells 191
Alex G. Bennington מלה הזי כהת אלד סאל אום

referring to is obtaining energy from sex. Sexual activity produces tremendous energy which is readily available to feed upon. Once the victim is entangled in the web, sex is an inevitable consequence. It is advisable to restrain the victim by means of straps, scarves, cuffs, etcetera for this gives you control over the ritual. The victim is sexually aroused to the point of frustration but orgasm is not permitted. Many times drugs are administered to make orgasm difficult or impossible. It is best to be in the dominant position in order to have almost total control over the session. The more frustrated the victim becomes, the more sexual energy that is building in the root chakra, the heat generated can be felt, and for those of us who are clairvoyant a brilliant red glow can be seen around the genitalia at which the adept vampire can siphon off this energy and when the victim does reach orgasm the adept vampire visualizes all this energy being released into them, stored and used for later proceedings or as needed to sustain them energetically.

At this point I wish to say, now that I am energetically correct due to practicing Kabbalistic principles, I understand that sex provokes heightened consciousness when we tune into the spiritual purpose of sex which ignites true passion without stealing the energy of my partner. In Kabbalah the cosmic and the erotic are intimately intertwined. Sex is not a mere mechanical sport, but a sacred dance of the two souls becoming one. When we use sex for ego that is when we drain our relationships. I have come to appreciate the male energy and know with certainty that sexual energy is used for "Light-making"… Love, if you will, into the world by creating circular energy.

Another form of a psychic/energy vampire are incorporeal beings referred to as incubus and succubus. They are related to beings such a Mara and the Night Hags, presenting only minor differences in their nature and preferences. Many of my acquaintances of the Black culture would refer to visitations by "The Hag" and what was interesting is that these visitations occurred when the person was not "living right" as they would refer to it. The appearance of these beings, often reflect the creation of the victims' mind. But may also, be nightmarish in appearance feeding on fear rather than lust. Some mortal vampires will create a servitor or employ the services of an incorporeal being to visit the victim with specific orders to drain the victim of their life force and return this energy to them upon completion of the task. I personally have experienced visitations from incubi during my young adulthood. And, I must confess, at one point in my life when I was particularly lonely I created an invisible lover which required the assistance of others to de-animate him. Usually, when an incorporeal being decides that they like you they will return for multiple visitations and they come at will, their will, not your beckoning.

If one wishes to remove these beings I recommend substances such as salt and gold, dream catchers, the Lesser banishing Ritual of the Pentagram, and the use of mirrors which I will discuss in more detail later on under "Methods of Defense".

From my own experience, once I changed my life from being a reactive person, full of fear and anger, to being a proactive being with certainty, continuously seeking truths and sharing, the visitations of incorporeal negative beings ceased. By raising our vibrations to a higher level such low vibrational beings are not inclined to reach us.

As a process awareness psychologist it is my opinion that vampirism probably accounts for certain mental disturbances and conditions including deteriorating physical health. I and others of my profession have encountered many cases where a morbid relationship existing between two persons resulted in one party, usually the one considered the negative one of the pair experiencing lethargy, pallor complexion, depression, and appearing highly suggestible. In these cases the person suffering once detached from the dominator usually always improves quite remarkably once this unhealthy codependent relationship is severed with the suppressive person and the duo is no more. The truly needy person, the dominator commonly protests to the extreme offering one of their passive/aggressive "I win you lose" ultimatums. Freud calls this an Oedipus complex where the soul of the parent (dominator) is drawing upon the psychic vitality of the child (victim).

When vampirism is suspected particularly that deriving from possible magical means or incorporeal beings it is wise to go over the victim's body with a magnifying glass with detailed precision in order to possibly locate minute punctures which cannot be identified with the naked eye. These are bites that could easily be mistaken for insect bites, however they are not. Examine the neck, particularly behind, under the ears and the lobes, the inner surface of the forearms, the tips of the toes, upon the breasts, the inner thighs, and the pubis. This type of examination usually pays off when many punctures are discovered that otherwise would have gone unnoticed or simply suspected as insect bites.

I realize that in the world in which we live the majority of us must function among many fellow humans as opposed to cloistering ourselves away as hermits, so in view of this I offer the following recommendations. If you find yourself in the presence of another that you suspect drains your vitality if at all possible keep this person to your right side, if you are left-handed keep them to your left. If you have any knowledge of metaphysics keep the individual to the side of your projective hand, not the receiving hand. Many times the projective hand is the hand you write with. When sitting cross your legs at the ankles. Also you can cross your arms at the wrists or hold your thumbs and index fingers of each hand together. If you feel a pull or tugging in your abdominal area (the solar plexus region, our center of power) place a napkin or some object over this area if you cannot fold your hands over it. Usually this sensation is detected when sitting directly across from another. These simple measures have proven themselves successful for it closes your energy loop keeping your aura and personal energy re-circulating within your being.

One of the rules of survival is self-preservation, and as we can come to realize some take this to the extreme. Along with this drive comes the need to protect ourselves which is our obligation. Self-defense in any form is not a substitute for common sense. It is advisable to avoid unnecessary risks, particularly dangerous situations, and questionable associations. Do not invite the vampire in for once you do they perceive that an open door policy has been engaged!

# CHAPTER TWENTY-TWO

# PRAYER

Pray, Prayer, Praying, this is a form of wireless communication that all of us have employed at on at least one occasion if not regularly. We may have even requested others to "pray" for us during times of special need and we have all certainly had zealous beings willing to give prayers for us.

I would like to share an analogy of one of my old masters who compared prayer to painting. When considering a painting project there are not only a multitude of colors to choose from but textures and techniques as well. If one is not wise and does not take into consideration all factors revolving around and within the project the end result would not only be dissatisfying but possibly disastrous. So when we pray for ourselves or others it is wise to know "how to paint" by using a sharp sense of discrimination. Shun our own desires, determine using our higher intellect and power what is truly best, "<u>**let Thy will be done**</u>," and <u>**not**</u>, "<u>**my will be done**</u>."

I have learned from experience, as many of you have to "**be careful what you pray for … you just might get it!**" Usually I do get what I request but it doesn't manifest in the way I expect. I am especially particular who I ask to pray for me or someone I hold dear for I do want genuine "painters." People who have "Kah" are at a level where when such a request is made the thoughts they project through prayer and the power of the spoken word will strictly be in the best interest of the person or being prayed for. In understanding "thought" just as it says in the ancient writings, "**Thought is the beginning of all Creation and it emanates from the Mind and The Mind is The All.**"

I knew an old priest of the white cloth who always proclaimed that as long as you have your head, your mind, you have what it takes to fulfill desire. In dissecting the word desire, it means to create so indeed all creation begins with thought.

We understand the benevolent aspect of prayer. What I wish to present is knowledge concerning prayer's potential for harm, which does not annul its power for good, which remains immense. Refusing to contemplate the negative side of life constitutes what depth psychologists call "repressing the shadow"--- banishing our nasty, undesirable qualities to the unconscious corners of the mind. To grow psychologically and spiritually we must engage the dark side of the self. As Carl Jung put it," a whole person is one who has both walked with God and wrestled with the devil."

Are prayers and curses related? I will say this and I make this statement from experience, that there is no difference between sticking pins into a wax image of an enemy and burning candles in front of an image of one of the Saints. Like a magnet prayer has both negative and positive poles and like fire it can either destroy or provide light.

In a recent survey one in twenty Americans admit they have deliberately prayed for harm for others. Most negative prayers are unintentional and are offered so casually that most people do not realize they are engaging in them. The intention projected using forms of prayers can be compared to "spells". We all use little spells, possibly on a daily basis which arise from the continual flow of intentions going on between all of us. Then there are bigger spells, which are deliberate intentions, which will render enough power to produce major changes and those who play in this arena are playing with a loaded gun.

I am going to share what is an example of engaging in reckless prayer. John had just been promoted to General Manager of a store in another region. While familiarizing himself with his new unit and responsibility he soon discovered that there were those who felt the promotion should have been theirs. Anyhow, rather than fighting among themselves any longer, they decided to make Johns' appointment difficult even to the point of creating sabotage. After a short time John become annoyed with the petty behavior and remembered a seminar he attended several years back using the power of your mind through affirmations by projecting your intentions using various techniques to manifest the desired result. He began working with the techniques in the morning and at night and remembered that the teacher said to be diligent for thirty days. John simply wanted these individuals to just disappear, mind their own business and focus on issues of their own. After thirty days passed, things began to occur in succession. Two assistant managers were terminated by upper management, several employees were terminated for theft, two employees were involved in automobile accidents both within the same day in different areas of the city both sustaining bodily injury. John felt bad for he believed his intentions manifested and he now was confronted with the ethics of power.

There are many who take curses and spells lightly and dabble in them for sheer amusement. Then there are those adepts who either, receive a new recipe of another's creation, or their own, and randomly choose a subject to experiment. Most spells do contain prayers; nevertheless there are many irresponsible beings out there who entertain themselves by using negative prayers as a playtime tool. However the adepts I knew were unconscionable and maliciously went after their subjects with no mercy. These are movies of the past I review at times and only when necessary for purposes such as this and it is simply a confirmation for myself that my present mission is in harmony with Divine Guidance and Timing. Many of these types of people believe that they escape retribution for their crimes and perhaps they may in this lifetime. But, the Law of Cause and Effect is one of the Seven Inescapable Laws of the Universe and eventually the time to pay the bill arrives.

When praying I have discovered it is best to give it to God, the Universe, or the Source depending on your title of preference, completely avoiding adding instructions as to what we anticipate or expect. If we surrender our issues to the Creator, when we let go, everything turns out perfectly.

# CHAPTER TWENTY-THREE

## HAUNTINGS

Most parapsychologists consider Hauntings to be "recordings" of past events that are repetitiously "replayed and "decoded" by those sensitive enough to perceive them. Actually there are two forms of Hauntings, one is due to a discarnate soul who interferes with a particular person or persons and there are those Hauntings due to the conditions prevailing in a particular place.

First I will address Hauntings due to the interference of a discarnate soul. Many times these are souls who do not realize they have crossed over. These souls are in distress on the Inner Planes. Non-acceptance of the reality of death may cause a person to become earthbound after death. Many of these may have been labeled as good people on this earth however due to the probability of not understanding the afterlife and its progressions these souls will linger close to the earth refusing to accept post mortem conditions.

An example of the well-meaning or unknowing dead would be the death of a spouse with the one who crossed over being confused and clinging to the surviving partner for various reasons. Usually it is more prevalent when the one who died did so as the result of an accident, a terminal illness, or in other words not by natural means.

Incidents of this nature can be resolved for the most part quite easily for the one who has crossed over can be communicated with by person(s) who are sensitive.

One may best pray for these discarnate souls at the 11th hour on Saturday mornings for this works with the rhythm of the souls of the dead and such prayers enlist heavenly helps namely those of the first heaven where dwell the Saints and the Men in White Apparel. Additionally prayers by the living enable the angels to come closer to these souls who are unaware of their angels but are made more aware of the angels by these prayers.

The evil earthbound dead are interested only in the world of the living and after death their emotions become a raging torment for they are unable to die to their emotions which are of the lowest octave. These discarnate beings vested with all their rage and anger seek out former environments and persons with whom they have a vendetta against or dominated. These beings can be seen by the living as an apparitional body and are often what people refer to as ghosts. They can devitalize and cause harm to the living. They do have the ability to use audible sound and use the latent kinetic force in objects. The evil earthbound dead were parasitical while living and this need to prey on others continues after death. The forces of the Satan energy work through the evil earthbound dead and prey upon those who like themselves while incarnate were filled with malice, avarice, covetousness, or lust.

I wish to share an experience concerning an incident where a woman was referred to me for assistance involving the imprisonment of her daughter for the murder of the woman's' son-in-law. This woman was very insistent and I was reluctant to agree to a session due to my "gut feeling" that something just wasn't right. However after careful consideration I agreed. I am not going to use any names for this was a significant case and highly publicized trial. The woman desired to record the session which I did not object to, however the deceased son-in-law evidently did for when she arrived home the tape was void of any sound. During my session with her she showed me pictures and I was already aware of the images for the son-in-law was present during this session communicating with me stating, "this woman's daughter my former wife, did murder me, in fact she planned that my death appear to be the result of a robbery. I hate her, I was not ready to die, I was cheated, I miss my daughters, I miss my life! She took it upon herself to play God and for what greed, sheer greed!" Of course the woman was not aware of his communication with me, although I did advise her of his presence. She told me of the terrifying phenomena that he was creating although he was on the other side within the household and at the prison. The woman was completely in denial concerning any guilt on her daughters part and proceeded to ramble on concerning the amount of money spent on attorneys thus far and although a great deal of money was left due to his death the majority was in trust for the dead mans' daughters. I proceeded diplomatically never lying to her and I did agree to correspond with her imprisoned daughter on one occasion. I knew that the daughter was definitely guilty and probably would never be released from a life in prison, so the only comfort I could provide was advice on coping and viewing this situation as a challenge in addition to realizing that she did have some form of freedom, and that being "her thoughts."

I did recommend a man who had a reputation of being a very powerful exorcist to assist with helping the angry discarnate son-in-law find peace and I can only hope that the woman did contact him. In this case I do not label the departed son-in-law as evil, vindictive yes, but not evil. In this case he was refusing to accept his post-mortem state initially to assure that his former wife was convicted of his murder however after this was accomplished rather than moving on he chose to remain in order to create further chaos and be ever vigilant in maintaining his former wife's imprisonment.

Before I proceed any further, I feel compelled to interject my interpretation of "evil". As an old master of mine once said, "evil is confused with negativity, take the word evil and spell it backwards and you get live, so how a person lives as an incarnate being determines the true meaning of the word evil and if they themselves are indeed evil… they are negative." It is worth mentioning for the record that when this Earth was created the energies were both positive and negative for one does not exist without the other. The real accomplishment is utilizing both forces to create balance, harmony.

Wickedness in high places or in religious atmospheres is indicative of the earthbound bigots and many of the priests of magic who lived in Persia, China, Chaldea, Babylon, Egypt, or Atlantis who are still in an earthbound state. As astral gurus they seek to impose their wills upon the unknowing in our world of physicality. When an astral guru or a spectral entity takes possession of a living person, it may truly be said that the person can no longer call his soul his own for this being has "walked in".

Those discarnate beings who haunt certain places and make racket, are amusing themselves at the expense of credulity and cowardice. Some of these beings pretend to be the devil or give themselves infernal names. Bear in mind that there are spirits everywhere, and wherever you may be they are ever present at your side. Many of the earthbound dead do not intrude upon the lives of the living but are referred to as observing entities and simply wander from place to place unaware of their state of consciousness. In regards to those mischievous beings simply laugh at them, they will grow weary if they see that they cannot terrify or annoy you. Show them that you are not their dupes and they will not return.

Death does not produce magic, transforming persons instantly good and pure. The emotions and the mentality are the same after death as they were in the world of physicality. It is wise at all times to armor ourselves with the "OR", "The Light", by binding our natural inclination to receive for the self alone and transmute this reactivity into acts of sharing with humanity thus becoming proactive beings for only in this way can we be insulated and protected from the subterranean, astral dot and dash, psychical and inverted communication.

Now regarding Hauntings due to the conditions prevailing in a particular place; these are events somehow recorded and stored in a manner similar to a video tape, which is admittedly not yet understood. At times certain conditions prevail and trigger the start button on the tape and these stored events begin to replay and playback. Since hauntings appear to be the repeating performance of recorded past events the characters involved are part of the recording and their actions are replayed over and over. The scene and the action do not usually change from showing to showing. It remains the same as watching a video over and over. The characters in a haunting are called "haunting apparitions" and unlike a ghost these apparitions cannot be communicated with for they are simply part of a movie, a recording, so interaction is not possible. A true haunting of this nature is a fragment or portion of an actual event and those hauntings that are reported are predominantly of events that involved tragedy, death or emotional trauma.

Witnesses of Hauntings frequently experience fear, anxiety, and long term stress. Because Hauntings and haunting apparitions are recordings there is no connection or interaction possible between the living and any aspect of the haunting. Simply understanding the innocuous nature of this type of haunting creates a removal of the haunting in the same manner as living next to a high traffic area, after a while the noise fades into the background. Additionally there are some psychic practitioners who have been noted for affecting a haunting by in the sense taping over the event transforming the haunting location into a sort of some positive emotionally charged event, a "good vibes" situation.

# CHAPTER TWENTY-FOUR

# PSYCHIC VOYEURISM

Psychic voyeurism is a term I use to describe the morbid curiosities of occultists. I personally classify it as visual rape for these people dabble into the affairs of others without their permission and knowledge for the most part, always seeking to "view" others affairs by means of various forms of divination, astral intrusion, and a multitude of techniques acquired by adepts. I personally have enough to consider concerning my own spiritual evolution without meddling in other people's affairs particularly using magical tools to do so, but there are those who seem to expend much energy on being just plain noisy. I have had people come to me on a number of occasions requesting that I look into another person for them and I politely decline for unless I have that person's permission to go into their space, I will not. I would not appreciate another doing this to me so it basically is taking into practice and consideration the golden rule, "Do unto others as you would have others do unto you."

It is very common among those on the reactive path to invade others privacy especially if they have been working a spell or the juju on them. Those on the reactive side often underestimate the protective powers of others. They somehow feel that they are invincible and that nothing they conjure up could possibly fail. I am a person who respects the beliefs of others, for those who stand firm in their convictions concerning their belief system are as strong as any others who stand firmly in their own. Those on the left-hand path however do not feel that any other path is more powerful than their own.

During the course of working their conjurations on others they will constantly, sometimes on a daily basis, utilize various forms of divination to determine the progress of their psychic dictatorship. If they are not getting the desired results they will at the appropriate moon phase, day, and planetary hour increase the intensity of the existing spell or add one more horrific to the present operation. It is very important to use caution regarding items containing DNA, such as hair, nail clippings, worn clothing, blood, linens, towels, etcetera… for times such as these are a very powerful tool in the hand of an Adept Occultist. I additionally advise being particularly cautious as to who you permit to take or have in their possession a photo of you or someone you love. Those who work the left-hand path are unconscionable and will and can use any item containing personal concentrated energy to work their machinations.

Again I am going to reintegrate the use of "pawns." These persons are used as voyeurs, for they have been ordered to view and gather as much information as possible on a target or an experiment. These persons are ordered to particularly focus on any vulnerabilities. In one case a young girl who was ignorant of these ways divulged too much information to actually several pawns and her life became chaotic to the point where she literally felt she was having a nervous breakdown.

They would leave mementos of their nightly visits on her doorstep or windowsill, call her home continuously hanging up, leave objects on her car, she would receive suspicious chain letters, and they would create tension at her place of employment.  It is unfortunate that all of these occurrences had no grounds for legal measures for those who work the reactive left-hand path do know how to cover their actions so that the so called system of manmade justice cannot be employed.  When she lost her employment due to her deteriorating mental, emotional, and physical state I knew that her best refuge was flight and sometimes this is not easy to achieve but evidentially her Guardian angels and Guides agreed with this measure and everything fell into place.  At present after receiving assistance from traditional medicine and counseling balanced with spiritual counseling and knowledge she is healing and has discovered her true strength.

As I have mentioned before it is my opinion that that information shared in these pages can provide protection, for the knowledge concerning these insidious forces will expose the intentions of those who I consider disciples of the anti-Christ energy.  In Qabalistic Numerology "Christ" means "knowledge of love and light," so anti-Christ would denote those who are against the knowledge of love and light.

# CHAPTER TWENTY-FIVE

# PSYCHIC ADDICTION

Along with those who abuse hypnosis I place psychics who abuse their power at the top of the list of the most heinous crimes committed against humanity. Such people in my opinion are an axis of evil. Perhaps, desperation or greed is responsible for such behavior. But, regardless, it is a choice. Ultimately, fear is the real culprit. Such choices are not without consequences. Often these types of mediums receive their information from low vibrational beings which lead them further down the road of destruction for themselves and those they victimize. Also, as I have mentioned previously these types of people ride so high on negative energy that they believe that even kryptonite (metaphorically speaking) cannot bring them down. However, no one in the human experience can escape Tikun or Karma for cause and effect is one of the seven laws of the Universe.

Naturally, such psychics prey on vulnerable or desperate people, often people of goodwill. They generally bait people with free readings or often I see them advertise cheap readings. It is always good to remember that there is really no such thing a free lunch, if you will. I am not saying that most of these people are not psychic for often they truly are mediums who have chosen to use their gifts in a non-benevolent manner. I do not have an issue with mediums or psychics who use their gifts secularly for they are entitled to this choice of a vocation, it is when they cross the boundaries and abuse these gifts by employing extortion. In my opinion such people as murderers falling within the realm of the angel of death. I say this because by their actions they are tapping into this principality and by doing so their actions bear like results. Death is not limited to the physical body. The end of a friendship, the failure of a business, the destruction of finances, the dissolution of a marriage, the loss of dignity, destruction of trust, are all expressions of death. I am clair-sentience and clair-cognizant myself, however there is a code of ethics and professionalism that does exist for those who choose to interact with humankind as we do. Being a spiritual doctor, if you will, I adhere to the oath, "***Primum Non Nocere***", "**First Do No Harm**." Also as a teacher I encourage students to stand on their own legs as opposed to creating a dependency on me for I choose not to encourage "cling-ons", which has earned me the title, "the reluctant guru".

Once these mediums lure you in with a free or cheap reading, they can tell you things that will convince you that they are truly clairvoyant, they will try to establish a good rapport with you in order to gain your trust and check you out to be certain that they can play you, once they have accomplished this the real deception begins for they know that they have fertile soil in which to nourish the seed they have planted. Most often they will tell you that you are experiencing hardships or whatever issue you are facing because someone has placed a curse on you or I have even heard that they will claim that a person is suffering from a curse placed on an individual's family in another generation. Now granted in some cultures people do strongly believe in generational curses and I am not attempting to invalidate or minimize this, for to them it is very real. Once these seeds of fear are planted, these charlatans will water and feed these seeds in order to accomplish their goal which is to extract as much of your finances as possible and some have been known to drain people completely. I am not saying that people can never fall under the influence of a curse, for they can, but generally when people of this nature come to me seeking the situation is examined thoroughly so as to provide the person with the tools they need to preferably remedy the issue for themselves. At times more is needed and in these cases either I work with another individual to perform deliverance or I refer them to another person with high ethical standards who can help them effectively and proactively. The fees of real advisors and facilitators with ethics reflect an average hourly professional rate, never inflated to satisfy greed or a hypertrophied ego. Never is a person told that in order to break the evil curse they must hand over their life savings because money is the root of all evil… this is ludicrous and again a heinous crime against humanity. More often than not many who contact persons such as myself, have in fact exhausted most if not all of their resources, financially, emotionally, and mentally. In these cases human kindness is extended.

I do believe that people can be influenced by psychic intrusion and this can be resolved with the application of proper knowledge and technology. In Kabbalah we believe that when we behave reactively we nourish the Klipot. The Klipot are shells of negativity and they are called shells because they confine and conceal sparks of light just as a shell confines and conceals a nut. Klipot steal sparks of light from us to sustain them and when we act badly the light we draw from such behavior goes directly to the Klipot. So often times due to bad behavior, a person will be surrounded with many negative energy shells, because for every reactive action we attract 100 negative angels. These particles of energy are exemplified by our selfishness and intolerance. So often times we create our own so called curse and the beautiful thing is that we truly do have the power to correct this ourselves without paying another person an over inflated fee. The initial step is that our actions and words embody tolerance, compassion, and self-control over our ego self and its constant stream of judgments for this ignites positive forces.

Another avenue of psychic abuse can be via telephone and Internet services. Again the offer of free readings or the promise of making everything beautiful with a rendition of the Cowsills, I love the flower girl playing in the background. Again just sharing a little of my sarcastic humor, but in all honesty the Internet has opened a new mode of communications for those of us in the psychic sciences. I personally love the net for it has afforded me the incredible opportunity of helping others on a global scale and I do thank those in the scientific community who created this avenue of communications. As with all forces though, there is a negative and a positive for one does not exist without the other.

There are some basic red flags that are very obvious, for identifying those who prey on others in the psychic sciences. However, often when a person is needy they do not see the forest for the trees.

These predators tell you that you are experiencing misfortune because you are under the influence of a curse. Even if this were true if they start eliciting large sums of money or demanding other precious items such as jewelry and such… this is a scam. One common tactic is that they tell you that you must surrender your money for it is evil. They usually ask you to wrap the money in a white or red cloth. They will want you to hand the money wrapped in the cloth to them personally and they will perform a ceremony with you which seemingly is to remove this so called evil. Regardless a bait and switch takes place… counterfeit money wrapped in a cloth will be destroyed while the real money will be in the charlatan's pocket.

Another methodology of these people is to basically keep you active either cleansing yourself or performing some ritual that they have deemed necessary… for you… Not! … for their pocketbook... Yes. Once they know that they can control you in this manner they will sell you baths, candles, oils, crystals, statues, etcetera at very absorbent prices. Often many of these products can be purchased at a fraction of the cost elsewhere.

Many people I speak with have fallen under the influence of those who basically sell love spells, so to speak. I had one young lady by the name of Cathy who came to me and has granted me permission to share her story, told me that she was online performing a do it yourself tarot reading on an Oracle website and noticed an advertisement for a free reading by a medium who claimed to be able to create love between you and the person of your desire. Anyhow, Cathy promptly contacted her and the first few sessions were all right, or so she thought. An early red flag for Cathy was when the medium insisted that she telephone her at specific times. This was a tactic employed by the medium to determine Cathy's vulnerability and obedience. Cathy said she paid her a small fee for some so called spiritual work designed to bring the person she desired to her. Well, a week passed and then a HUGE RED FLAG manifested, the medium tells Cathy that there is so much negativity surrounding her and this man she desires that the work she has done thus far was not powerful enough and in order to break this she needs to do some really powerful work and the materials for this work is very expensive… with the corrupt medium slyly adding, "Isn't being with the man of your dreams worth it?" Anyhow, Cathy paid this medium very significant sum of money and the end result? Cathy never did unite with this man she desired and in reality all she was merely experiencing was lust and the relationship was not meant to be. If she would have come together with this man all the result would have been is what I refer to as a "genital relationship". This was a costly lesson for Cathy financially and emotionally, however what was more interesting is that Cathy came to know that this man she thought she wanted is an alcoholic and has tremendous anger issues, not only through her own personal observations after the fact but via the grapevine as well. I did encourage Cathy to report this crime to the proper authorities as another step in an attempt to discourage these predators. The bottom line is, if someone says that they are all powerful and can accomplish certain feats, don't buy it… walk away… sleep on it as our elders often say, ask for guidance from you higher self or others you trust, and in the morning what you think you want and what you truly need will be in prospective and you can use your hard earned cash in a more productive manner.

Now I wish to address all you seekers. If you have a reading more than once a month, you may be psychic dependent. If you are consulting several advisors or psychics regularly, then you may be psychic dependent. If you cannot make a decision without first consulting a psychic or advisor, then you ARE suffering from psychic addiction. You need to make a check and balance sheet. Honestly write down that which has proven helpful and has manifested into reality in a positive sense and then write down that which was, just words placating your ego, entertainment, or simply what you wanted to hear but bore no fruit. Now calculate how much money you have invested in these communications. Now visualize how you could have used that money more productively and visualize the future with you no longer wasting those dollars and create a movie visualizing yourself achieving a tangible goal that truly benefits you or those you love. If you choose to continue to seek advice on occasion (no more than once a month), choose an advisor who is REAL, not dysfunctional, manipulative, or egotistical, and charges a reasonable professional fee for their services.

Last but not least, utilize **_Discrimination_**. I am not using this word in the context that you might suppose but rather in dissecting the word using **Qabbalistic Numerology** we can possibly discover its true meaning.

D (4) + I (1) + S (6) + C (3) + R (2) + I (1) + M (4) + I (1) + N (5) + A (1) + T (9) + I (1) + O (7) + N (5)

**ADD** these numbers together.

$(4 + 1 + 6 + 3 + 2 + 1 + 4 + 1 + 5 + 1 + 9 + 1 + 7 + 5 = 50)$

We get the number 50. Then 50 reduces to 5 $(50 = 5 + 0 = 5)$. **Five** is a number which correlates with the energy of Mercury. So if we use our minds we can achieve balance where our choices are concerned and discriminate in a proactive manner.
"Dis"…removes "Crimi"…energy associated with matters **not** conducive to global responsibility and **not** acceptable to or in society. A…higher intelligence T…power ion…shun, not be involved in. So discrimination is using our own personal power and choice to remove ourselves from that which is not for the good of our selves or humanity by using our higher intelligence and not involving ourselves with such persons or in such matters.

If you or someone you know has been a victim of a psychic, or astrology scam, please report this crime of fraud to one or all of the following agencies.

**United States of America**
• Federal Trade Commission - The Federal Trade Commission provides information to help consumers spot and avoid fraudulent practices in the marketplace, and can be contacted at the following:

FEDERAL TRADE COMMISSION
600 PENNSYLVANIA AVENUE NW
WASHINGTON DC 20580-0001
1-877-FTC-HELP

• FBI Internet Fraud Complaint Center
• National Fraud Information Center
• US Postal Service - The U.S. Postal Inspection Service should be contacted if you think you may have been victimized by a fraudulent promotional offer.  You can contact them at the following address, or check the government pages of your telephone book:

US POSTAL INSPECTION SERVICE
OPERATIONS SUPPORT GROUP
222 S RIVERSIDE PLAZA SUITE 1250
CHICAGO IL 60606-6100

**1.800.372.8347**

• State Attorneys General.

Your state Attorney General or local office of consumer protection is also listed in the government pages of your telephone book.

## Other Countries:

### Australia
• Australian Securities and Investment Commission
• Australia Scamwatch
• Consumers online (Australian Government)
• The Australian Communications Authority monitors the compliance of the legislation in Australia.  Visit their website, if you would like to report/complain about spam, or obtain more information on spam laws, spam reduction, and Internet security.
• South Australia Office of Consumer and Business Affairs
• Western Australia Department of Consumer and Employment Protection - Scamnet

### Canada
• Better Business Bureau
• Industry Canada Consumer Connection (Scams)
• Phone Busters (Telemarketing Complaints)

### New Zealand
• Commerce Commission
• NZ Securities Commission
• NZ Serious Fraud Office
• For more information about lotteries and gaming laws in New Zealand visit the Department of Internal Affairs website (www.dia.govt.nz).

### United Kingdom
• www.ripofftipoff.net

# CHAPTER TWENTY-SIX

## NON-OCCULT DANGERS INCIDENT
## TO INVOLVEMENT WITH THE DARK SIDE

As with most groups ours began with good intentions which over the course of time became corrupt due to the arrogance and imperfections of the leaders. Practically all the members, fraters and so ores, were riding high on negative energy and believed themselves invincible. The majority were women. This is common in esoteric groups and many of these women are very naïve concerning the underworld activities revolving around groups involved in the dark side.

One of our male leaders, Gary, due to his avarice became involved in drug trafficking linked with a Cartel in a foreign country. Also he became addicted to cocaine in addition to his alcoholism as was the case with many members of our group. I personally never used or needed illegal substances or narcotics, for I had the capability of going into an altered state naturally and my gig was power. The women of the group were not permitted to witness or be involved in any of the illegal business transactions, so I suppose the only confirmation for my suspicions is based on observations and eavesdropping in addition to intuition. Gary was a psychological bully and progressively became more narcissistic. But, in his own sick way he was always very protective of certain members, particularly the women -- however this was strictly for selfish reasons. The male members of the group did proclaim to respect the female energy however their attitudes were passive/aggressive thereby reflecting something entirely different. Many of the females were submissive, subjective, – zombies! They suffered many abuses inflicted by the predatory males within our group and those ones that they were lent out to. I and a few others on the other hand were not so compliant in many ways and did question motives and actions. Those like myself were tolerated for our strengths and gifts were considered valuable. Additionally Gary and I shared an unhealthy adoration for one another.

It is common knowledge within esoteric circles that most occult groups are not infrequently used for carnal, mundane exploits whether it is drugs, politics, sexual perversions, or other unethical and unlawful practices. Many people would be surprised as to the membership of many occult groups, very surprised!

As I mentioned previously our leader would encourage us to go out -- hunt for victims to vampirism -- not only for the energy, for our actions enabled him to live vicariously through this type of sexual predatory behavior due to his physical impotence.

Any female that became involved with Gary as a girlfriend or mistress set herself up to endure much pain physically, emotionally, and mentally. Shimon was a sadist and addict. When he was in a drug induced state these women would receive beatings and abuses that no being should be subjected to. Some of us would interfere at times whereas the others out of fear or simply being in a zombie like state did absolutely nothing. I must comment that every female Gary became involved with committed suicide.

There was one incident that was particularly suspicious and supposedly there were no witnesses, but on one occasion there was this particular woman that he considered his wife and with Gary this meant chattel… exclusive property -- anyhow from what was disclosed he went home one day and she had her belongings packed, loaded in the car and she was going to leave him. Again it was claimed that she committed suicide. However, what made it suspicious was that the gunshot wound was to the head particularly the face and women are not known to commit suicide in this manner. I honestly do not believe that Gary intentionally killed her. But, what I do believe is that he walked in while she was leaving. They had an altercation. He pulled a gun threatening to kill her if she tried to leave. They struggled and the gun accidentally fired.

Additionally all involved were expected to recruit new members according to Gary and the council's prerequisites. Most of the members used promises to seduce new members while others deceived them into believing that the group was beneficent and was concerned about humanity particularly those less fortunate. I and a few others used more sophisticated and pervasive techniques. Hidden manipulation governed every step of our recruiting process. We would push psychological and emotional buttons using an "admiration bomb" which is an emotional overflow of admiration and attention. We would sell certainty and confidence. Our subjectives did not know that they were being systematically deceived and rendered suggestible by use of counseling processes that are no more than covert hypnosis.

At one point during my involvement with this dark "House" as we called it, I became interested in an Irish born man by the name of Jim. I truly felt passion and love for this man, which was a reality I had not experienced until that point in time. A meeting was called in which this specific matter was addressed and I was informed that I was to discontinue this relationship or suffer the consequences. Evidently my fraters had decided that we must only consummate with our own, with the exception being business transactions. The others were instructed to shun me and my rights to office space on the property site were relinquished. I simply made the adjustments necessary and this was the beginning of my realization that it would be best to cut my losses and move away from this entanglement. Of course when they saw that their attempts to thwart the relationship failed they stepped up the harassment. I had a will of iron and was still not breaking, so they went to a place that was totally wicked. One day Jim simply vanished, he was no more -- I can't prove it, but I know in my heart that Gary and select others were responsible for his disappearance… it is with certainty that they gave him an ultimatum that he could not refuse.

I became involved with the group again but only for a short time.  I made my final decision to detach when I overheard the men's group discussing the sacrifices that would require preparation for one of our major annual events.  The group had reached a new level of darkness after Gary engaged in intermingling with some undesirables from South America who practiced Kimbanda.  Evidently these so called businessmen put on a benevolent front posing as ambassadors of good will by supporting a number of orphanages exclusively habitated with male children.  What shocked me was that their conversation was laced with innuendos that these boys in these foreign orphanages were being cultivated as a crop of so called perfect offerings used in ritual sacrifice.  Evidently if someone in a country such as ours required one of these boys, -- and only members affiliated with this cult could make such a purchase, -- they were brought in through Canada or a private carrier… human trafficking.  Even though at this point I could consider myself nothing less than a low vibrational being, there was a spark of light within my soul that encouraged me to discontinue my membership in this club.  I knew I had to disassociate and plan my escape carefully.

I kept all my plans within my mind, my thoughts were exclusively mine.  Not once did I use the spoken or written word to disclose any intentions and I certainly didn't trust anyone that I was presently affiliated with.  I soon discovered that I was not the only one planning a departure.  Rosemary, one of my so ores, approached me and said, "Karm I don't know why I'm trusting you but I am.  I have to get me and my kids out of here.  Did you read that literature that's being passed around?"  I replied that I was familiar with it and she proceeded, "I am not going to be sold to some idiot in a foreign country as a wife, concubine or whatever!  I need some good advice and I am so emotionally distraught right now that I am afraid I will make a mistake."  I calmly advised her first of all not to speak of anything to another soul expect her immediate family.  I continued with, "Rosemary go to a payphone, call your parents be honest and explain to them what you have become involved in, remain calm.  I would suggest telling Shimon that you are sending the children to visit your family for the summer, believe me he will be all right with this.  It would be good if your family could make arrangements to have the children flown into another city and state rather than that in which they actually reside… pick them up there and then drive them to their actual residence.  If I were you I would go ahead and sell my car.  But, don't part with it until the very day of your departure.  Get the children to the airport and then take a cab to a bus station where you will have already made arrangements and will be in route to reunite with your family.  As the hours pass and you have not returned Gary will believe that you left with the children.  He will check with the airlines, they will tell him that only the children boarded and all of this will give you the edge for he knows you hate buses and would never suspect that you left via bus."

Rosemary further replied, "Al that is good, but I still feel I need to tell the police or something, just in case something happens to me, do you know what I mean?" I answered by saying, "Rosemary, if you do choose to go to the police simply state that the reason you want to make a report is that you have been involved in an occult group that you are leaving and that you are afraid if you are caught that they will harm you and you simply want to make this public record just in case something of this nature were to occur. Do not go into tales of the supernatural or unlawful activities otherwise they may not take you seriously and may choose to Baker Act you. Also, I reminded her of Gary's connections within the police force."

I suppose Rosemary took my advice for within a week she was gone. Fortunately Rosemary and I were never really close so I was never suspected of assisting her. Although Rosemary opened up to me I never uttered one word that I was planning to leave for I simply could not trust anyone regarding my intentions. My plans were carefully laid. I am not going to disclose the exact details of my flight path. However, I will share the following. Fortunately I never disclosed all information concerning my family, clients, or other pertinent personal matters to my fraters and so ores. My gig had always been power and control so I was not susceptible to suggestibility which is what entangled the majority of the group. I discreetly gathered many sources of info, data, and pictures -- along with notarized individualized letters. I sent numerous certified packets with this vital information by overnight mail to trusted persons I knew throughout the United States and I did not prepare or mail these until the very day I left. I telephoned each person informing them of the packet, not to open it, put it in a safe place, and if were to mysteriously disappear or be discovered dead, to immediately take the packet to the authorities, preferably the FBI, and the press. I have listed resources in the back of this book for those who wish to detach themselves from cult situations or for those who know of others tangled in the web of cult affiliations.

I had put my foot down to the Universe and had adamantly decided to improve my life. I was hounded on the astrals for a time, but as I grew spiritually and my vibrations elevated those negative ones were not able to reach me any longer, I became invisible so to speak. My catharsis was lengthy and even though I do not wish to have that much fun again, the experience did bring me to a point where I listen to love rather than fear and I know I am receiving guidance and instruction from my true self… my Higher Consciousness… which is one with Divine Universal Love and Wisdom.

# CHAPTER TWENTY SEVEN

# RISKS CONSEQUENT TO THE PRACTICE OF MAGIC

In order to successfully counter psychic intrusions in my opinion it is necessary to understand the nature and intelligence of organized unethical practitioners who by society's definition would be classified as evil. In all things, there is positive and negative for one does not exist without the other. In Kabbalah the right, left, and central columns refer to three forces of energy that are the spiritual and physical building blocks of our universe. Physically they are the positive (right), negative (left) and neutral (central) forces found in everything from the light bulb to the atom. The Satan energy is the principle of negativity, the cosmic thrust block, the scavenger and I prefer to refer to this left column energy as "the challenger." Also Satan is not pronounced "say-tin" as many are accustomed to, but rather the a's are pronounced as they are in the word Saturn.

Refusing to contemplate the negative side of life constitutes what depth psychologists call repressing the shadow, banishing our nasty, undesirable qualities to the unconscious corners of the mind. Those who are considered true adepts know that a whole person has walked with God and wrestled with the Satan.

Exactly what is Magic? Magic is the Art and Science of creating changes in consciousness to occur by the projection of our thoughts and will -- it is the ultimate Divine Knowledge of Natural Philosophy. In our present time science is the accepted magic of choice, science is the logical outcome of magic. Magic as an art form remains as unpredictable and powerful as the weather unless your skills are well honed along with balance and focus, otherwise your magic will take on the "butterfly effect." This principle of contemporary science, "The Chaos Theory", is so widely accepted that it hardly needs repeating, "The flapping of a butterfly's wings in China can amplify into a tornado in Kansas." Every action we take whether by use of magic or on the mundane, carnal level is subject to consequences that spread out forming like ripples on a pond. The corrupt action of one person can create a tornado of negativity that can affect millions, in the same manner our positive actions result in positive global effects. All events that transpire, both personal and global, are the sum total of our positive and negative interactions.

Working magic requires a responsible attitude and if one does not employ this it is best to abstain from the practice or otherwise you may find yourself playing with a loaded gun. Before working magic it is wise to consider the consequences and ask yourself, "If this working backfires on me, and affects me instead of the intended target, can I live with the results?" One of the seven laws of the Universe is cause and effect, karma or in Hebrew it is called Tikkun. As the Kybaloin states, "Every Cause has its Effect; every

Effect has its Cause; everything happens according to Law; Chance is but a name for Law not recognized; there are many planes of causation, but nothing escapes the Law. *"*

I can share with you that those who are involved on the reactive side are riding so high on negative energy that they actually believe that the laws of the Universe do not apply to them. I must reiterate that I know this from experience for during my youth when my ego was unbridled I too was one of these unethical purveyors of energy. It was during this time that my life was like a roller coaster ride and as far as I was concerned during that phase, the more dangerous the better. It is my hope that the information within these pages will create an awareness that will be considered in making choices concerning issues and matters resulting in proactive formulations.

When I started on my journey into the occult I developed my powers quickly for I had recovered my former memories of my previous incarnations and the capabilities acquired during these experiences. I fearlessly experimented frequently and I did experience some curious results on numerous occasions. Usually such mishaps occurred when I was overly tired, ill, angry, or had been consuming alcohol. I have always consumed alcohol in moderation, however when working with the invisible forces even a moderate amount is too much. People who know me are amazed that I am still standing on my two legs especially former occult associates -- actually I can honestly say cult associates -- for very rarely is it that a person walks away from such a fraternity/sorority. I came into this world with imperceptible psi. Low-level luck is invisible, whereas big luck isn't -- and invisibility is a valuable quality in natural selection where deception counts. In Larry Niven's Sci-Fi book Ringworld, a young woman named Teela Brown is sought by an alien forming a crew for a hazardous space expedition. There is nothing exceptional about Teela except that she has imperceptible psi, which the alien discovers is only indigenous to the human species and this invisible luck would insure the success of the mission. Astrologically, persons who have Libra in Jupiter possess this psi factor particularly if it is located in the twelfth house.

Although this may appear to be off the topic I am going to take the liberty of elaborating on the Libra in Jupiter aspect. Former 42nd President of the United States, William J. Clinton, is a perfect example of the lucky Libra in Jupiter aspect. For a time it appeared that Bill Clinton was facing serious allegations of both financial and sexual scandal. Although public reaction to the scandal was mixed, Clinton survived his trial in the Senate and, ever responsive to changing public moods, remained popular. Despite apparent defeat Mr. Clinton regardless of appearances, as they say, he pretty much came out smelling like a rose. The Libra in Jupiter aspect often gives the Illusion of a lamb being led to slaughter. However, many times at the very last second during the eleventh hour the troops come in and an almost miraculous turnaround occurs.

One of the major issues and risks consequent to the use of the art of magic is the misuse of "power." Once you reach a point where you perceive yourself a master, if egomania dominates your being, the danger of the corruption of power becomes inevitable. When studying the history of various cults it is discovered that the leaders initially had the best intentions however with time their minds became jaded resulting in corruption. Do the names Jim Jones, Sun Myung Moon and David Koresh ring a bell! On a positive note, "Power" can be very constructive if it is expressed with love, for we all have the power of the Creator within us! Power stemming from Divine Love can radiate out to the world in miraculous ways.

When one chooses to develop psychically and/or is coming into their power they will be challenged by the other side which can also be referred to as levels of initiation. If the one studying and developing in the manic arts yields themselves to persistent intrusion from earthbound entities -- or when one by wrong sentiment regarding their thoughts inadvertently extends an invitation to the earthbound dead -- they make themselves a vessel in which this discarnate being may dwell. The entity sets up a series of barrages against the left side of the body and if the person has inappropriate or insufficient means of protection the entity will gain entry. The earthbound entity will literally crawl into the body and set aside vital thread connecting the ego and the soul of the host. The entity then takes possession of the brain and begins to think and act through the hosts' nervous system. From that moment forward the person living is possessed or what the scriptures refer to as "being beside himself." (Mark 3:21)

When one consistently uses their psychical power rather than spiritual power they become a vehicle for entity possession. One characteristic of earthbound entity possession is a condition called astral jaundice. The skin of the subject develops a waxy, yellow pallor, and the flesh beneath the eyes, are flecked with purple and brown, appearing bruised. These subjects are either, listless and depressive, or experience states of delusions of grandeur, egotism, and vanity. Once the entity has taken full possession the subjective person will not be capable of looking anyone in the eyes. Additionally spasmodic jerking of the body is indicative of low vibrational entity possession.

Earthbound entities love disorder and chaos. These entities can only penetrate a mind and thought similar to that of their own. They are repelled by pure love, by prayers, by clean and orderly atmospheres. It is impossible for them to interfere with the ethical industry of the living, nor can they penetrate persons with unfamiliar routines and habits. Earthbound entities are attracted only to that which they were familiar to while they were living in the physical world. The person who truly wishes to live the spiritual life would be wise to make themselves pure of heart, so that he/she may rise above these subterranean forces. However, if one chooses to explore the dark path, as I did, my only advice is to proceed with caution.

In the future the advanced Psychiatrist will understand humankind by placing an emphasis upon the soul, rather than upon the mind and subconscious mind. They will come to recognize the difference between the obsessed person and the possessed person. Obsession usually occurs when one is in a weakened or depressed state in which one takes upon himself the characteristics of former lives resulting in a decided personality change.

Selfish magic always produces negative consequences and that from Divine Love positive ones. It is said, as you will, that "The needs of the many always outweigh the needs of the few, -- or the one." In Kabbalah we strive to use our freewill to restrict our reactive behavior which is completely selfish -- the desire to receive for the self alone-- and transmute it into proactive behavior -- which is the desire to receive with the intention of sharing. The Satan energy (challenger) tempts us with momentary pleasure --which long term results in chaos, whereas proactivity may deliver momentary struggle and challenge as we discontinue our reaction, but its effects outweigh the obstacles-- that being, long lasting fulfillment and Light!

# CONCLUSION

In this game of life the Creator has afforded each of us the gift of freewill. The choices we personally make determine for the most part whether we will experience fulfillment or chaos. Each one of us is born into this world with enormous talent, but for most, this talent remains untapped because we have been playing the game without really understanding how it is to be played. We make up our own games, our own rules and change the rules as it behooves us. If we are to come to know the rules of the game of life we must first remove the blindfold we came into this world wearing.

In the Endless World each of us struck a deal to incarnate in order to change our nature, however before actual incarnation we drank from the cup of forgetfulness which created the blindfold. The Creator has provided many tools to recover that which was lost and to assist us in resolving our Tikkun or Karma thus transforming our nature.

According to a Kabbalistic tale during the nine months we spend in our mother's womb, an angel holds a candle for us, teaching us the wisdom of the universe. We behold everything, from the beginning of the world to the end of the world. When we are born, the angel gives us a sharp blow on the upper lip and it makes up forget everything we have learned. Yet memory traces remain in our souls, the idea of God resonates with us, and it is on this resonance, on these residual memories, that we build our consciousness.

As in any game there is an objective and an opponent. Any athlete realizes that they must be focused regarding training not only physically, but mentally and emotionally as well. The game of life is the most challenging game experienced for obstacles are continuously presented, therefore we must prepare tenaciously for this game can be a win /win for all.

Each of us are great souls, we all contribute to the collective. Not all come here to seek riches, fame or fortune. Some have painted me as a Saint, while others have painted me a Monster. However, most consider me one of the many "real angels that fly under the radar." I appreciate all people and the energy they contribute. Society as a whole tends to judge adversely those who perform what the 2% in this world considers menial or servants work, but these people are actually the glue holding humanity together, they are the "real angels" working under the radar. Real Angels are people who help others without the need for notoriety or reward;

their acts for the most part are anonymous. Time and time again we hear it said that you can be anything you want to be, but this is not true for we each perform according to our gifts. It is wise to remember that all of the fame and fortune made on this planet stays on this planet. In the game of life it is not the strongest, the fastest, the prettiest, or the wealthiest who have the true advantage, but rather the one armed with true wisdom who makes good choices. I believe if the will is honed that no one can stop you from realizing your purpose for being.

**To New Heights,**
**Alex G. Bennington**

# ABOUT THE AUTHOR

Dr. Alex G. Bennington is an ordained minister of interfaith and metaphysical beliefs, with a Doctorate in Philosophy. Alex has been clairvoyant and clairaudient since youth. Doc has conducted workshops and lessons in truth over the past 33 years and is the founder of The Angels of Light Network. Doc continues to courageously share controversial insight regarding religion and spirituality based on experiences and education, including but not limited to numerology, with a poignant style that is admired and respected.

American Witch
http://www.anamericanwitch.wordpress.com

The Angels of Light Network
http://www.dralexstarr.wordpress.com

# Recommended Reading and/or Biographies

The Zohar, (*Splendor or Radiance)* is considered the most important work of Kabbalah. The Zohar is not one book, but a group of books. These books include scriptural interpretations as well as material on theosophic theology, mythical cosmogony, mystical psychology, and what some would call anthropology.

Alcyone. *"At The Feet of the Master"*. The Theosophical Publishing House., 1910.

Berenson – Perkins, Janet. *"The Kabbalah Decoder, Revealing the Messages of the Ancient Mystics."*. Barrons., 2000.

Berg, Rav P.S. *Days of Power, Part One.* Published by The Kabbalah Centre., 2005.

Brendle, Thomas R. and Unger, Claude W. *"Folk Medicine of the Pennsylvania Germans."*

Brown, Deni. *"The Herb Society of America Encyclopedia of Herbs and their Uses".* Dorling Kindersley., 1995.

Cavandish Richard. *"The Black Arts: A Concise History of Witchcraft, Demonology, Astrology, and Other Mystical Practices Throughout the Ages."* The Berkley Publishing Group., 1967; Periger Books., 1983.

Chestnut, Charles. *"The Conjure Woman."* Houghton, Mifflin and Co., 1899.

Colton, Ann Ree. *"Men in White Apparel."* Published by the Ann Ree Colton Foundation., 1989.

Crowley, McGregor, and Liddell. *"The Goetia: The Lesser Key of Solomon the King: Lemegeton - Clavicula Salomonis Regis, Book 1."* Red Wheel/Weiser., 1995.

Crowley, Aleister. *"777 And Other Qabalistic Writings of Aleister Crowley: Including Gematria & Sepher"* Red Wheel/Weiser., 1973.

Day, Christian. *"The Witch's Book of the Dead."* Published by Red Wheel/Weiser LLC., 2011.

Fitzgerald, Dr. B.J. *"A New Text of Spritual Philosophy and Religion."* DeVorss and Company., 1982.

Filmore, Charles. *"The Metaphysical Bible Dictionary."* Unity Books., 1994.

Fortune, Dion. *"The Mystical Qabalah." Society of Inner Light, 1935.,* Published by Red

Gabriel, Ingrid. *"Herb Identifier and Handbook.".* Sterling Publishing Co., Inc. 1980.

Gamache, Henri. *"The Magic of Herbs Throughout the Ages".* Sheldon Publications., 1942.

Gonzalez – Wippler, Migene. *" Santeria; African Magic in Latin America."* Original Publications., 1981.

Haskins, Jim. *"Voodoo and Hoodoo."* Scarborough House Publishers, 1978., Stein and Day., 1978.

Hassen, Steven. *"Combatting Cult Mind Control"*

Kardec, Allan. *"The Spirits Book."* International Spiritualists Council., 2006; *Originally published as "Le Livie Des Esprets." Paris., 1857*

*Kardec, Allan. "The Book on Mediums."* Published by Samuel Weiser, Inc., 1970;

MacNutt, Francis. *" Deliverance from Evil Spirits. "* Published by Chosen Books., 2000.

Mickaharic, Draja. *A Century of Spells.* Samuel Weiser., 1988.

Regaud, Milo. *"Secrets of Voodoo."* City Lights Books., 1985., *First Published in 1914.*

Rose, Donna. *The Magic of Herbs.* Mi-World Publishing Co., 1985.

Sicafus, James A. *Papa Jim Magical Herb Book.* Papa Jim II., 1985.

Thomas,George A. *Black and White Magic by Marie Laveau.* International Imports., 1991.

Three Initiates. *The KYBALION, Hermetic Philosophy.* The Yogi Publication Society., 1940.

Turner, Elizabeth Sand. *"Let There Be Light."* Unity School of Missouri., 1965.

Yronwode, Catherine. *Hoodoo Herb and Root Magic.* Lucky Mojo Curio Co., 2002.

*I have a library of nearly 3,000 books. These books I have recommended are in context with the subject matter within the pages of this book.

# Numerology for "WITCH"

6   W    A Spiritual
1    I     Seer
9   T    with the power
3   C    and creativity
5   H    to attract and deliver positively with intellect real actions and advice

$2 + 4 = 6$: The Divine Soul at home creating and building relationships on a multitude of levels and in turn sharing knowledge and information.

Զ Զ Զ Զ Զ Զ Զ Զ Զ Զ Զ Զ Զ Զ Զ Զ Զ Զ Զ Զ Զ Զ Զ Զ Զ Զ Զ Զ Զ Զ Զ Զ Զ Զ Զ Զ Զ Զ Զ Զ Զ Զ Զ Զ Զ

As a gesture of appreciation for the purchase of my book I would like to offer you the following:

A set of Talismanic Seals from the 6th and 7th Books of Moses

A set of The Pentacles of Solomon

OR

An Astrological Natal Chart/A Solar Return Chart

If you desire any of these complimentary offers please contact me at
AmericanWitch9@aol.com

## Best Wishes,

Alex G. Bennington

---

CPSIA information can be obtained
at www.ICGtesting.com
Printed in the USA
LVOW03s2158090816

499736LV0002SB/511/P